Hypnosis

Related Titles
of Interest

Rational-Emotive Therapy with Alcoholics and Substance Abusers
Albert Ellis, John F. McInerney, Raymond DiGiuseppe & Raymond J. Yeager
ISBN: 0-205-14434-9

Hypnotherapy: A Modern Approach
William L. Golden, E. Thomas Dowd, & Fred Friedberg
ISBN: 0-205-14334-2 Paper   0-205-14335-0 Cloth

Handbook of Alcoholism Treatment Approaches: Effective Alternatives
Reid K. Hester & William R. Miller (Editors)
ISBN: 0-205-14390-3

Helping People Change: A Textbook of Methods, Fourth Edition
Frederick H. Kanfer & Arnold P. Goldstein (Editors)
ISBN: 0-205-14382-2 Paper   0-205-14383-0 Cloth

Behavioral Medicine: Concepts and Procedures
Eldon Tunks & Anthony Bellissimo
ISBN: 0-205-14484-5 Paper   0-205-14485-3 Cloth

Dream Analysis in Psychotherapy
Lillie Weiss
ISBN: 0-205-14499-3 Paper   0-205-14500-0 Cloth

Hypnosis

The application of ideomotor techniques

David B. Cheek, M.D.

Allyn and Bacon

Boston • London • Toronto • Sydney • Tokyo • Singapore

Copyright © 1994 by Allyn and Bacon
A Division of Paramount Publishing.
160 Gould Street
Needham Heights, Massachusetts 02194

Library of Congress Cataloging-in-Publication Data

Cheek, David B.
    Hypnosis : the application of ideomotor techniques / David B.
Cheek.—Rev. and enlarged ed.
        p.   cm.
    Previously published in 1968 under the title: Clinical
hypnotherapy.
    Includes bibliographical references and index.
    ISBN 0-205-15595-2
    1. Hypnotism—Therapeutic use.   I. Cheek, David B. Clinical
hypnotherapy. II. Title.
    RC497′C5 1994   93-29853
615.8.512—dc20   CIP

Printed in the United States of America
10 9 8 7 6 5 4 3 2   97 96 95 94

To the memory of Leslie M. LeCron
1892–1972

The Author

David B. Cheek, M.D., is a Diplomate of the American Board of Obstetrics and Gynecology and a Fellow of the American College of Surgeons, the American College of Obstetricians and Gynecologists, and the American Society of Clinical Hypnosis, of which he is a past president. He is the author of 42 professional papers on uses of hypnosis in medicine and surgery, has contributed chapters to six books about hypnosis, and is co-author with Ernest Rossi of *Mind-Body Therapy.*

Contents

Foreword

When I first learned about hypnosis in the early 1960s, David Cheek and Leslie LeCron were doing their Hypnosis Symposiums. I heard Cheek talk about regression to birth. My first reaction to this was more than disbelief; it was a judgment that I might be associating with kooks! I "knew" that I couldn't recall my own birth, and concluded that no one else could either, and simply pigeonholed it as the idiosyncrasy of an enthusiast. The rest of the information made sense. The credentials were there, and I pressed on with my education.

Then one day I suggested to an asthmatic patient that she regress to the first time that breathing became too important. She began to gasp for breath, appeared desperate. Her face turned blue. During this abreaction, she did not answer questions about what was happening. I gave her suggestions that there was plenty of air and she could breathe all right. I asked her to remember everything and to return to today. She relaxed, breathing became slower, and color returned to her cheeks.

Then she told me she had experienced being born at home with the cord around her neck, her nose full of secretions, and no doctor to help. I was still dubious about what had happened, but could not ignore the change that had occurred at this turning point in her history. After more than 50 years of orthodox treatment, she discontinued all medication and had no more episodes of asthma.

Then I learned about the Babinski reflex and found I could reproduce it in a naive somnambulist who had regressed to two months of age. This is a normal reflex for the first six months of life. It consists of lifting the big toe and flaring up and out of the other toes when we run a fingernail or a key from toe to heel on the outside of the infant's foot. This reflex is superceded by a grasping, downward reflex of the toes as the infant begins the process of learning to walk. Gidro-Frank and Bowersbuch[1] had reported the reappearance of the Babinski reflex when adults were age-regressed in hypnosis to the first six months of life. The Babinski reflex is a sign of pyramidal tract dysfunction when it is found in an adult. Like a blush, this is objective evidence of a thought causing a physiological change, but more astonishing.

Then I was personally regressed to my own neonatal life, and quite clearly pictured a personal trauma that not even my mother knew about. This was something I could check, because I was born in the hospital where I practice. For the first time, I retrieved the microfilm record of my first days, and there it was. As with the case of the asthma patient, my symptoms disappeared after this regression. In trance, I had recovered a memory imprint that affected me under stress and could not assuaged until brought up to consciousness and rational reprocessing.

The imprints of the preverbal years are much more powerful than ever thought possible, and classical listening therapy by its very nature omits them. This is a reasonable explanation of why so many neuroses and psychosomatic disorders remain unresolved even after years of therapy. Hypnotic regression with the help of ideomotor signaling opens the door to exploration of the emotional imprints formed before language skills are learned.

Leslie LeCron and David Cheek were talking about birth imprints 30 years ago, and also about subconscious hearing under anesthesia. Cheek was talking about emotional causes of spontaneous abortion, toxemia of pregnancy, and subconscious pain perception.

When we started the course on clinical hypnosis at Tulane Medical School in 1970, I chose the first edition of *Clinical Hypnotherapy* as the textbook. The new revised and renamed edition is a welcome update.

Dabney Ewin, M.D.

---

[1]Gidro-Frank, L., and Bowersbuch, M. K. (1948). A study of the plantar response in hypnotic age regression. *Journal of Nervous and Mental Disease, 107,* 443–458.

Introduction

This book contains my understandings and philosophy about hypnosis derived from 50 years of clinical use as an obstetrician and gynecologist and instructor in seminars for professionals interested in hypnosis. I have drawn many of my ideas from the writings and from my personal association with Leslie M. LeCron and Milton H. Erickson, but I take full responsibility for what is expressed in these chapters.

Between 1943 and 1956 I was reading about and using authoritative techniques aimed at helping my patients to stop pain, have an easy labor, reverse surgical shock and hemorrhaging, or get over unpleasant symptoms. Sometimes my commands worked successfully, but problems often remained unchanged or got worse.

Some of my patients who seemed honest and who expressed desires to get relief from allergic symptoms, habits, persistent pain, or to end years of infertility were unconsciously blocking results, and I had insufficient tools to find the reasons. Conversational hypnosis, as I was using it, did not reach the levels of memory storage and physiological reactions to stimuli where sources of resistance occurred. The reasons for abandonment of hypnosis by the hypnotists of the nineteenth century became clear and discouraging.

A dramatic change occurred when I met Leslie M. LeCron and joined the faculty of his "Hypnosis Symposiums". I learned about the combination of unconscious muscle action-ideomotor techniques with hypnosis. The tools for breaking amnesia and removing resistance to therapy were available.

I am dedicating this book, *Hypnosis: The Application of Ideomotor Techniques* to Leslie M. LeCron because of his great contribution to our knowledge of hypnosis. LeCron wanted to introduce the word "Ideomotor" in the title of *Clinical Hypnotherapy* which we co-authored in 1968 but the editorial staff at Grune & Stratton did not think the word was adequately recognized in the literature on hypnosis. I am grateful to Mylan Jaixen, Editor at the Allyn and Bacon division of Paramount Publishing for permitting this addition now.

LeCron deserves credit for forming a panel of a physician, a dentist, and a psychologist teaching uses of hypnosis after World War II when such training was not available to members of the healing arts in their teaching institutions. He deserves credit for developing simple, easily learned techniques for accessing cause-and-effect relationships in psychology and psychosomatic medicine.

There have been extensive changes in thought about hypnosis since 1956. Its values have been recognized by the British Medical Association and the American Medical Association. Instruction is available in many medical schools. There are excellent workshops being given by the International Society of Clinical and Experimental Hypnosis, by the American Society of Clinical Hypnosis and by the Milton H. Erickson Foundation in Phoenix, Arizona. A number of professional papers published by journals of hypnosis have contained the word "ideomotor" as have several books.

During interviews with people who have suffered from maladaptive physical and emotional patterns of behavior we can use symbol muscular answers to questions as reflected by the swings of a pendulum or movements of designated fingers to locate the start of that behavior and help patients reassess the causal experience in the light of mature understandings and judgment.

The significance of human imprinting and its correction by exposure to adult reasoning capabilities cannot be overstated. In this renamed, rewritten, and expanded version of *Clinical Hypnotherapy* I have stressed the fact that pessimistic or threatening imprints take priority and will override the effects of love and nurturing but that reassessing the causal experience has great therapeutic value for removing the results of trauma.

William James (1950) credited W. B. Carpenter for the initial use of the word ideomotor, meaning a muscular response to a thought. Around 1929 Milton Erickson experimented with using symbol movements of opposing hands to represent "yes" and "no" answers to questions when hypnotised subjects were unable to talk. He gave up this method, he told me, because there were too many variations in the ideomotor answers he obtained.

LeCron told me that his first understanding of ideomotor action came from reading the works of Beaudoin (1920). He knew that Bernheim (1895) had written about ideomotor action. LeCron said that around 1929 he also recognized that body action would respond repeatedly to various thoughts. If he held a small weight attached to an eight-inch string and repeatedly thought "yes-yes-yes," the pendulum would pick up the action and maintain a direction of swing such as a circle or a straight side-to-side movement.

The direction would change when he thought "no." Finger signals proved to be more rapid and more reliable as his work continued. Once the symbol movements are selected for "yes," "no," "I don't know," and "I don't want to answer," the pendulum or finger signals will reflect information that is often unknown consciously. This is the underlying principle of ideomotor techniques.

I want to express my thanks to those who have contributed their knowledge and advice in the preparation of this book. First would come Mylan Jaixen, my kindly and stimulating Editor at Allyn and Bacon. I am grateful to my wife Dolores, who has guided my enthusiasm and wisely advised me as she studied each page of my writing. Susanna Hassan-Galle, Ph.D., and James S. Gordon, M.D., of Washington, D.C. have helped me with their emotional support and their vast knowledge of alternative resources for healing. William C. Harrison, formerly a science writer for the Associated Press, has guided me through the first part of the work. My reviewers, E. Thomas Dowd of Kent State University and Lynn Holland, M.S.W., in private practice in Metuchen, New Jersey, have been very helpful with their critique and suggestions. I am grateful also to Pat Brumm of Santa Barbara, a journalist, lecturer and editor of several trade journals, for her proofreading of the finished product. She suggests that this might be a "people book" rather than one for specialists only.

I owe additional thanks to those who may not know how much I have drawn from their experience and humanity. These include, first of all, the late Milton H. Erickson, pioneer in the field of hypnosis and First Editor of the American Journal of Clinical Hypnosis. Erickson was always a thoughtful, gentle, yet an encouraging critic of my work. William S. Kroger in 1942, drew my attention to the uses of hypnosis in gynecology and obstetrics. He has remained a friend and advisor through the years. Robert N. Rutherford, Founder and Editor of the *Western Journal of Surgery, Gynecology and Obstetrics,* has been most helpful in his advice and his willingness to publish some of my efforts.

David B. Cheek, M.D.

Hypnosis

1

Hypnosis: Values and Misconceptions

Hypnosis in 1993 is well established as a useful tool in many areas of living. We no longer have to teach diverse, often confusing, methods of inducing hypnosis. The ones we find useful and easily explained to patients are outlined in Chapter 5.

Values of Hypnosis

It is now generally recognized that people enter hypnosis spontaneously when they are sick, endangered or frightened. Milton Erickson (1961) pointed out that people enter hypnosis as they mentally review sequential events. An hypnoidal state is entered when recalling a tune, remembering the visual images of waves breaking on a beach, the movements of a candle flame, and the words of a poem. As Erickson reported (1961):
This is Erickson's report in his 1961 paper:

A sixteen-year-old boy, who regularly drove a milk wagon, had never before been hypnotized. He was asked to sit quietly in a chair and silently review in his own mind every feeling throughout his body as he systematically recalled the events of the twenty-mile milk route over which he regularly drove a team of horses.

The further explanation was given that, even as one can remember names, places, things, and events, so could one remember body feelings of all sorts and kinds. This he was to do by sitting quietly in the chair with his eyes closed and to imagine himself driving along the highway, feeling the reins in his hands and the motions of the wagon and the wagon seat.

Shortly it was noticed that he was shifting his hands and body in a manner suggestive of the actual experience of driving a team of horses. Suddenly he braced his feet, leaned backward, and presented the appearance of pulling hard on the reins. Immediately he was asked, "What are you doing now?" His reply was, as he opened his eyes, "Going down Colemen hill."

. . . At one particular stretch of the road where there were no farm houses, the boy went through the motions of pulling on the reins and calling "Whoa!." He was told to "drive on" and replied, "Can't." He was asked why he couldn't. The laconic reply of "Geese" was given. The writer immediately recalled that on infrequent occasions in his own experience, a certain flock of geese happened to choose the moment of the milk wagon's arrival to cross the highway in single file on their way to another pond, thus stopping traffic.

This observation led to Erickson's recognition that review of any sequential sensory impressions was a basic process in inducing hypnotic trances. Practically every induction of hypnosis, with the exception of a sudden shock, will involve a request for the subject to remember sequential sensory events.

People enter hypnosis spontaneously as they close their eyes and imagine a weight pulling an outstretched arm down toward the floor during a test of postural suggestion. They can also go into hypnosis wondering which way a pendulum might swing or which finger will lift unconsciously to represent the repeated "yes," "no," and "I don't want to answer" thoughts as they select ideomotor signals for these thoughts (LeCron 1954, Rossi and Cheek 1988). Each of these inductions involves the recalling of sequential events.

Since publication of *Clinical Hypnotherapy* in 1968, it has become generally recognized that hypnosis can be of great value in educational fields, for improving self-respect, for relieving pain, for diminishing the effects of a stressful world, for augmenting immune capabilities, for diminishing the cardinal signs of inflammation, and for improving the memory of witnesses and victims of crime.

We have learned with the help of ideomotor review methods that the amnesia of general anesthesia can be broken and that anesthetized patients are aware throughout the operation (Cheek 1959a, 1981). With this knowledge we can talk in constructive ways about what we expect of a patient during the recovery period. We can give hope to the cancer patient who has concluded that cancer equates with death. We are aware now that operating room conversation should be no different from what it would be with the patient awake and under local anesthesia.

Unconscious review methods have revealed that some complications of surgery and pregnancy are caused by repeated troubled thought sequences that are not consciously remembered on awakening. Recognition permits the patient to regain normal physiological behavior (see Chapters 16, 20, 21). We can teach surgical and obstetrical patients to sleep deeply and restfully at night. We can prepare their unconscious mind to immediately awaken them and permit them to realize that the trouble was only a dream and not a reality as it otherwise might seem to be. By using techniques to be considered at length in Chapter 11, it is now possible to break through the amnesia that prevented Breuer, Freud, Jung, and others from recognizing the causal trauma responsible for neurotic behavior. Removal of secondary, satellite traumatic experiences is not enough.

Ideomotor search and reframing techniques now permit patients to become co-therapists and colleagues with us in the therapeutic process. They learn the mechanics of search and reframing. They then are prepared to search for a troublesome causal thought that can otherwise lead to a "flashback" recurrence of symptoms after a period free of distress. Flashbacks can occur during any treatment and can make a patient feel that hypnosis is no better than any other previous therapy. Flashbacks may unconsciously occur when a patient has begun to feel that freedom from a problem is perhaps "too good to be true."

Another value of ideomotor techniques combined with light hypnosis is that they allow recognition of resistance factors at the start of therapy rather than after continuing costly and frustrating failures. Resistances usually relate to assumed guilt, negative identifications of self with unfortunate friends or relatives, or an unconscious need for illness as an escape modality. Illness can be a powerful negative force if a troubled patient is involved for example in litigation of some sort. The illness and pain take on an unconscious weight of justification for the litigation.

Conscious discovery of previously unrecognized resistance factors strengthens patients' self-respect and allows them to make the corrections themselves. Often this is done without need for conscious recognition or discussion with a therapist.

Misconceptions

Despite the increased acceptance of the value of hypnosis, there are still some widely held misconceptions about the technique. Four such false ideas are:

1. Some people cannot be hypnotized.
2. Hypnosis weakens the mind and creates an addiction.
3. Hypnosis can be used to make a subject tell the truth.
4. Hypnotized people are zombies

Understanding why these ideas are incorrect will aid the professional in the effective use of the valuable tool of hypnosis.

The idea that some people are unhypnotizable is incorrect. Physicians, attorneys, and business executives may initially have problems with feeling they may lose control in some way. Their intellectual evaluation of what is going on may interfere only as long as it takes for them to feel that using hypnosis gives them even more control and power than they previously had.

Motivation is a major consideration here (Cheek 1957). There has to be a meaning to the use of hypnosis. I have reported people who seemed unable to enter hypnosis at one time but were excellent subjects at another time when they really needed hypnosis. It is up to the therapist to make clear what that personal need is. At critical moments of danger, shock, hemorrhage or loss of consciousness, the hypnotic state is already in place and ready to be used.

Hypnosis does not weaken the mind or create an addiction. The state of hypnosis has survival value. Hypnotized subjects will protect themselves from harm as long as each request for action is given permissively. The danger of misguided coercion through persuasion is ever present regardless of whether hypnosis is knowingly used.

Hypnosis cannot be used to make a subject tell the truth. People in a hypnotic state can withhold the truth or lie, as Brunn (1968) found in the case of a man who murdered his wife and had a genuine amnesia for the crime. Evidence offered verbally by a hypnotized witness may be as inaccurate and misleading as that extracted from an eyewitness to crime when hypnosis has not knowingly been used. Leading questions are a source of error in forensic uses of hypnosis. The danger of misleading verbal communication (leading questions) during conversational hypnosis is diminished when ideomotor methods are used to check the subconscious validity of the verbal level evidence (see Chapter 29).

Hypnotized people are definitely not zombies. They are totally aware of their surroundings. Some of them demonstrate sensitivity to telepathic communication. You can occasionally find a hypnotized person giving an appropriate finger signal to a question *before* you have formed the question into words. Your hypnotized subject pretty much knows your thoughts. We must hold and project our thoughts of confidence, respect, and healing at all times when working with a sick, injured, anesthetized, or normally hypnotized subject. Lightly hypnotized subjects can come out of hypnosis at any time; those in a deep trance may be so lethargic that they cannot put out the energy to come out, but they can register ideas and can be subsequently angry with a therapist who has given suggestions that were not acceptable.

Be attentive at all times to the appearance of your patient or client. Find out what is the matter if you see signs of distress, or simply ask for a gradual return to consciousness with whatever feeling needed to be reported to you. Failure to recognize your subject's distress may lead you into trouble with that client.

2

What Does Hypnosis Seem to Be?

There have been almost as many theories about what the theorist believes explains the phenomena of hypnosis as there have been people willing to commit their thoughts in printed form. All are descriptions of hypnosis rather than inclusive statements that might qualify as a satisfactory theory.

Historical Views of Hypnosis

One of the earlier ideas was that hypnosis is a form of sleep. Encephalographic tracings during a hypnotic state are identical with those in the waking state. At times, however, a hypnotized subject may fall asleep and confuse the recording.

Ferenczi (1926) thought of hypnosis as a relationship of a child to a parent. This probably reflects the role of a hypnotized subject accepting without critical assessment the coercive commands of a stage hypnotist. In nature the survival of young birds and mammals in a time of danger depends on absolute obedience to the commands of the attending parent. At verbal levels of communication, a few hypnotized subjects will respond to commands in this way. They may have positive and negative hallucinations. I have found, however, that most people continue to maintain critical judgment in deciding whether or not to accept suggestions.

R. W. White (1941) thought of hypnosis as an artificially induced state during which the subject acts the way he or she thinks a hypnotized subject would behave. This view neglects recognition of spontaneous trance states that occur with children and adults at times of stress. As Milton Erickson demonstrated many years ago, a person trying to perform in any designated way would probably go into hypnosis spontaneously with the effort of remembering sequences of action.

White's view does not take into account the hypnotic state that occurs with loss of consciousness or confrontation with a great real or imagined threat. It does not explain why people go into hypnosis when disoriented in time or space. It does not explain the trance that occurs when people are attempting to recall sequential events.

Sarbin (1950) and T. X. Barber (1969) have offered a variant of the White concept. Barber has stated that everything we see as hypnotic phenomena can be demonstrated with unhypnotized people motivated to work at accomplishing such phenomena. In other words, there really is no such thing as hypnosis. This idea would have to prove that people trying to remember what they think a hypnotized person should be accomplishing are *not* going to enter a hypnotic state spontaneously in the process. Suggestions involving a need to remember sensory stimuli and sequences of events are part of most hypnotic induction rituals. Sarbin and Barber apparently do not consider spontaneous trance behavior in the same category as induced hypnotic behavior.

Pavlov (1928) thought of hypnosis as a conditioned response where conscious associations are bypassed. He felt that this phenomenon occurs during sleep and that sleep was a sort of hypnotic state.

My observations suggest that deeper, perhaps stage III and IV sleep, as evaluated with continuous encephalographic tracings in sleep laboratories, are comparable to a hypnotic state. Thought sequences in deep sleep are very powerful and have a similar effect to posthypnotic suggestions during a deep trance state. The perceptions of people in lighter levels of sleep, on the other hand, are very much like they are when people are awake.

Bypassing cerebral activity certainly does occur in hypnosis. It also occurs in the presence of unexpected danger when there has been no formal induction of a hypnotic state. This seems to be a function that is carried out in the reticular activating system of the primitive brain. Reason dictates that this bypassing of higher cerebral activity must have survival value for lower animals where instant reaction to alarming sensory stimuli and release of epinephrine is preferable to losing time in selection of one of several options.

The epinephrine-imprinted reaction is fixed at subcerebral levels of neuronal activity and may be modified in accordance with differing initial sensory alarms and available means of escape at that moment. In a sense, the response to danger has been set as a sort of "macro," in computer language, and is not subject to higher cerebral controls.

Patients reviewing nighttime ideation have reported to me that the feelings they have at deep levels of natural sleep are very similar to what they have experienced during hypnosis. They differentiate this from their feelings when they are "just dreaming." Volgyesi (1966) studied with Pavlov and believed his understandings of hypnosis as bypassing cortical level brain activity have not been adequately recognized outside of the Soviet Union. Nevertheless, Pavlov gave us descriptions rather than a general theory to explain what seems to occur.

Pavlov apparently recognized that his research dogs became more responsive to suggestion when they were starved. There were many starving dogs in Russia in the famine of 1919, when he was doing his early work with conditioned responses. Experiments became more reproducible when the dogs were denied food. Some, on being unable to get to food shown to them, would go into a faint. The term "dog faint" was used by Milechnin (1962, 1967), another student of Pavlov, in a discussion of the "Pavlovian Syndrome" that he observed during World War II. Starving Russian prisoners in a Nazi compound would either become maniacal or would faint when they could not grasp the last piece of bread brought by the Red Cross trucks. Could this emergency type of resting state perhaps have survival value for animals when food is unavailable? Is this comparable to the "sleep state" of swifts when food is not available? That their subconscious awareness remains active at such times is shown by the fact that they return to activity when rain or increased humidity stimulates winged insects to fly.

Another facet of hypnoidal behavior has not been considered in most textbooks on hypnosis. This is the seeming insensitivity of animals and humans when recognizing certain death. It was shown by the Christian martyrs in Rome. David Livingstone (1858) experienced it when he was attacked by a wounded lion and furiously shaken. He wrote that he felt as do those under chloroform anesthesia "who know all but feel not the knife." The peaceful feeling he experienced led him to wonder if this state could be "a contribution of our benevolent Creator" to make dying less painful for animals that are killed by carnivora. This is an interesting concept. A neurologist, however, would limit consideration to the probable fact that the mechanism here is one of bypassing higher cerebral activity when all sensory perception is centered on the source of danger.

Volgyesi (1966) had this to say about the behavior of mice and sparrows that were placed in the cage of an owl:

> We had a horned owl that had strayed into the underdrawing of the roof and we tied it up with a cord by one foot. Before presenting it to the Budapest Zoo we amused ourselves with it. So that it should not go hungry we caught live mice and sparrows and set them before it free and unhurt. After staring at them for a few moments, the owl would grab them by the head and, in the most leisurely way, swallow them — five or six, one after another. I was astonished that the majority of the

victims let themselves be swallowed nice and slowly without the flicker of a muscle or slightest movement of wing, extremity or tail. . . . We have been witness to the way in which thousands, indeed millions, of human beings have been rendered passive by suggestion, and, stupefied into obedient fatalism, have gone unresisting to certain death on the battlefield, or to the finality of the electric chair and the gas-chamber.

Perhaps Pavlov recognized a relationship to the slower phenomenon known as hibernation for animals and dormancy for plants, but this was not clearly stated. In both states, hibernation and dormancy, the organism maintains responsiveness to the environment (Suomalainen 1960). There is a warming of the body for the true (homeothermic) hibernating mammals when the external temperature drops to a critical level.

The Australian psychiatrist Ainsley Meares (1960) feels that there is a shifting back to archaic behavior during a hypnotic state. This, again, is a description of what seems to happen without offering an underlying reason for such behavior.

Comment

I believe we must take a broad view of the varying phenomena occurring at differing levels of hypnosis. There is no simple way of categorizing all hypnotic variants that have evolved throughout the plant and animal kingdoms during the more than three billion years of life on Earth. My working hypothesis to explain hypnosis to my patients is as follows:

Hypnosis seems to be a mechanism for survival as we see it in humans. Variants of hypnotic behavior have evolved over millions of years to fit the needs of different species. The fact that there are varying manifestations of resting states does not negate the general principle of survival. Major characteristics of hypnotic states in humans are:

- Literal (childlike) understanding of ideas
- Flashback access to imprinted stressful experience
- Inhibition of physical activity
- Diminished ability to vocalize
- Diminished metabolic activity
- Decreased need for food
- Increased tolerance for painful stimuli
- Increased resistance to infection
- Homeostasis of coagulation mechanisms

3

Brief History of Hypnosis

Historical Notes on Hypnosis

I will consider here material that I believe is related to modern uses of hypnosis. The interested reader is referred to an excellent chapter by George Rosen in the second edition of *Hypnosis in Modern Medicine* by Jerome M. Schneck (1959) and to the more extensive history offered by J. Milne Bramwell (1930) in the third edition of *Hypnotism, Its History, Practice and Theory.*

Most historians limit discussion to the human uses of hypnosis. We need to be aware that hypnotic phenomena can be found throughout the animal kingdom. Many animals are capable of getting their food by a form of fascination, as told by Volgyesi in observing a captured owl (Chapter 2).

The mythological Perseus used his bright shield as a mirror when he killed the Gorgon Medusa, for it was known that a glimpse of her would turn men and animals into stone. This myth must have had its origin in the observations of nature.

The cobra is an example of an animal that mesmerizes its prey. One of its enemies, the mongoose, is usually the victor, however, when they meet in battle. Like Perseus, the mongoose never looks directly at the cobra. It presents the side of its body, scratching the dirt as though looking for food but repeatedly jumping just beyond reach of the cobra's striking distance. Gradually the cobra's agility decreases with repetitive, frustrated efforts to bite the mongoose. Finally the little ferret-like animal turns and bites into the back of the cobra's neck, just behind its expanded hood, as it reaches the end of its strike. That is the end for the cobra.

Volgyesi points out in his book *Hypnosis in Man and Animals* (1966) that Daniel Schwenter, a professor of mathematical and oriental studies at the University of Altdorf, described in 1636 the "bewitchment" of a fowl by attaching a wood shaving to the beak of a hen. This was ten years before Father Kircher wrote about the marvelous imagination of hens, reporting experiments in which a hen's head was pushed down to the floor and a chalk line drawn outward from the tip of its beak. In his case, as with Schwenter's, the fowl was first immobilized by a firm grasp that did not permit escape, but the immobilization that occurs with physical confinement of birds was continued by the unusual fixation of vision on the wooden twig on its beak or the chalk line.

Hudson (1893) in *The Law of Psychic Phenomena* in a chapter on mesmerism tells of European animal trainers who would stare into the eyes of a horse, elephant, dog, or other animal with their eyes rolled upward and slightly crossed. He said that apparently this type of gaze was so unusual that the animal would go into an altered state and accept any kind of suggestion of thought or words.

Deer, cattle, and humans on railroad tracks at night will become victims of locomotives, transfixed by fascination as they look into the headlight. Modern trains, to prevent this from occurring, have headlights that move from side to side. Folklore suggests using a light at night to fascinate frogs and fish. Humans have only picked up and used the lore of lower animals.

Hibernation

Hibernation, one facet of hypnotic-like behavior, occurs throughout the plant and animal kingdoms to permit survival when food is scarce and the climate unfavorable. Humans have discovered the value of brief hibernating states in emergencies. Travelers overtaken by blizzards in northern Europe know they can survive by digging into the snow and maintaining an airway with their upturned skis. I have been told by a Norwegian patient that her brother slept for four days in this way and came out of his resting state when the storm was over. He was not hungry and had not urinated or defecated during that period of time.

The healing power of continued, hibernation-like states was first observed by James Esdaile (1851/1902) after he learned to mesmerize his patients in an effort to help them bear the pain of surgery. He noted that bleeding was diminished and healing was by "first intention" (direct healing where sutures had been placed) instead of in the time honored way associated with "laudable pus" (meaning the patient had the capability to produce pus and might survive infection). Although all of his patients in India in 1845 and 1846 were subject to infection, his surgical mortality dropped from 50 percent to 5 percent after he trained his assistants to mesmerize all of his surgical patients.

No surgeon equaled this low mortality figure until Josef Lister in 1863 began using antiseptic methods of cleaning hands, instruments and the skin of surgical patients.

In his beautiful little book, *Mesmerism in India*, Esdaile tells of learning that the medicine men of the mountains in Assam had, from time immemorial, been using passes and breathing on the heads of sick people in just the ways that Esdaile had found described in the writings of the French mesmerist Deleuze. It is not always possible to be sure if something apparently new is really new.

At the end of the nineteenth century, Wetterstrand (1897) in Sweden found that prolonged periods of hypnosis permitted improved recovery from psychiatric problems and infection with tuberculosis. His patients were awakened once during the day to eat and go to the bathroom.

Hypnosis, with its accompanying openness to accepting suggestions, was used during the eighteen and nineteenth centuries mainly to coerce troubled people into good health. Hypnosis was used by physicians in major cities throughout Europe from 1880 until the first decade of the twentieth century. The reasons for this wide use and rather abrupt abandonment are not clear, but one of the reasons could have been that doctors were using authoritative techniques that left no way for the hypnotized subject to decide whether or not the suggestions were acceptable. Some people object to being ordered in hypnosis to get well; they may not be ready for that process. Symptom removal and positive assurances work for simple problems only.

The use of hypnosis to search for possible emotional factors in human illness seems to have originated with Josef Breuer (1957), a family doctor in Vienna in his work with the famous "Anna O" from 1880 to 1882. Breuer noted that there seemed to be some relationship between a traumatic experience and a state that he believed was much like, if not identical to, hypnosis. He called the traumatic causal experience "hypnoid" and was possibly the first to recognize what has later been called "state-dependent learning." He initiated the trauma theory for hysteria. He felt that artificially induced hypnosis might give access to causal events in psychological illnesses. He interested Freud in the possibilities of using hypnosis in the treatment of hysteria.

Breuer stopped his work with hypnosis, but Freud continued for a time. He visited Bernheim in Nancy, France, and observed the work of Charcot in Paris. He went to Stockholm to visit Wetterstrand. He interested Carl Jung and Ferenczi in the possibilities of using hypnosis as an analytic tool.

Unfortunately, both Freud in 1909 (1957) and Jung in 1913 (1975) decided to give up the use of hypnosis. Both were using authoritative techniques and ordinary conversational hypnosis. Both found patients reporting traumas that proved to be fabricated rather than factual. They felt hypnosis was an unreliable tool. Their stance set the cause of hypnosis back more than half a century because of their great influence within the field of psychiatry. Both of these gifted men searched for other, "more reliable" ways of learning about repressed or suppressed traumatic events. Freud invented psychoanalysis requiring one hour per day, five days a week; Jung searched for dream content in accessing amnesic material. His students continue searching for ways of getting through the cloud of amnesia for early life trauma. Playing in sand with various figures to represent meaningful people is one such method. Drawing pictures and modelling with clay are variants, as are tests of word association and Rorschach ink blot evaluations. Behavior modification and cognitive therapy are efforts to produce new adaptations instead of removing old maladaptive patterns of behavior. Then came the widespread use of mind-influencing drugs, based on the concept that disturbed mental behavior is chemical in nature.

Successes with any of the modalities now in use may be attributed largely to the placebo effects of trust and the therapists' enthusiasm for whatever is in style. We needed trustworthy methods of breaking the amnesia masking primary traumatic events. We needed better tools to work with.

Hypnosis came back into favor during World War II for the treatment of war neuroses near the front lines, but those capable of using hypnosis were few, and most of the psychiatrists used barbiturates such as sodium amytal and thiopental sodium to help soldiers relive a causal traumatic experience, to talk about it, and then to continue with ordinary conversational therapy.

Many dentists were using hypnosis after World War II (Moss 1952) for relaxing nervous patients. They found it helpful for treating abnormal gagging reflexes, for painless removal of teeth, and for controlling damage to teeth caused by bruxism (the clenching of jaws in association with troubled dreams at night).

Interest faded as dentists experimented with "white sound" and various combinations of short-acting inhalation anesthetics. Some dentists have continued its use for the purposes previously mentioned but have also demonstrated its great value in controlling hemorrhage in hemophilia patients. Harold Golan, D.M.D. of the Tufts University Dental School; Karen Olness, M.D., a pediatrician at Case Western Reserve Medical School in Cleveland; and Lillian Fredericks, M.D., Director of the Department of Anesthesiology at Albert Einstein Medical Center in Philadelphia have successfully treated hemophilia patients prior to surgery and at the time of already active hemorrhage. The hemorrhagic tendency due to absence of the special blood factor can be blocked by hypnotic relaxation. These doctors also taught such patients self hypnosis to protect them against emergencies when a qualified hypnotist might not be available. Fear and expectation of bleeding can precipitate life-threatening hemorrhage in patients with hemophilia. The appearance of a frightening epidemic of AIDS and hepatitis "B" in patients with hemophilia makes the need for safer methods of controlling hemorrhage even greater. The human mind is capable of controlling hemorrhage of all sorts, including that caused by emotional stress in combination with lack of the hemophilia factor.

Erickson (1901–1980)

The late Milton H. Erickson of Phoenix, Arizona, became interested in hypnosis when he was a student majoring in psychology at the University of Wisconsin. One of his professors was Clark Hull, the first person to try experimental studies to document what hypnosis can or cannot do. Hull asked Erickson to continue his research on hypnotic phenomena during the summer of 1923 and to report his findings in a workshop on hypnosis in September of that year. This was the beginning of Erickson's series of contributions to our knowledge of hypnosis. I believe these have been his major contributions:

1. He learned that people go into hypnosis when they are trying to remember sequential events (Erickson 1961).
2. He broke the amnesia of a comatose state caused by drugs and head trauma by repeated subconscious review of the experience (Erickson 1937). His patient had been beaten and left for dead two years before the interview.
3. He demonstrated the use of dissociative methods for pain relief. He would help a pregnant woman to leave her physical body in the process of childbirth while the astral self was across the room watching. He would have denied originality in the concept because it is a naturally occurring process when children are injured, but his many methods of accomplishing this were varied and unique.
4. He studied the variants of time distortion and stimulated others to continue research on this phenomenon (LeCron 1952b, Erickson and Erickson 1958).
5. He recognized that general anesthesia does not block the hearing sense.
6. He and his wife recognized that patients return to a hypnotic state when they carry out a posthypnotic suggestion (Erickson and Erickson 1941–1980).
7. He recognized that body image can be the cause of endocrine disturbances and that hypnotic techniques can be therapeutic in improving endocrine balance. August Forel (1907) and others had worked with abnormal uterine bleeding, but Erickson has gone beyond influencing endocrine function. He had impressive results with two women concerned about lack of breast development (Erickson 1960). These observations

deserve further research because of the recently discovered dangers from uses of foreign materials in breast augmentation surgery.

8. Erickson's great faith in the ability of his patients to tap personal resources was one of his greatest attributes.

LeCron (1892–1972)

Leslie M.LeCron attended the graduate school at the University of California in Los Angeles after a long career in business. He studied psychology under the direction of Prof. Roy Dorcus, one of the American pioneers in uses of hypnotism. He met Jean Bordeaux there and co-authored an excellent short book, *Hypnotism Today* (1949). He became a licensed California psychologist at the age of 52, began teaching uses of hypnosis to dentists, and in 1956 started the monthly Symposiums of Hypnosis, for which he co-authored the first edition of *Clinical Hypnotherapy* with me in 1968.

LeCron deserves a major place in the history of medical and dental hypnosis because he developed simple, safe, and rapid methods of uncovering causal events in psychosomatic problems. It seems reasonable that the cause of hypnotism would not have faltered at the beginning of the twentieth century if LeCron had been doing his investigations with ideomotor techniques in the 1880s. Freud and Jung would probably have continued to use hypnosis.

LeCron told me that he had learned about the use of a Chevreul pendulum for discovering unconscious information around 1929, but only after the beginning of the 1950s did he realize that the combination of light hypnosis with unconscious muscular gestures could break through the amnesia that masks memory of birth, the first years of life, and the experiences of people under general anesthesia (LeCron 1954). This was the beginning of his truly major contribution to our knowledge about cause-and-effect relationships in human illness as revealed by ideomotor or ideodynamic signaling. The techniques of searching are easily learned and are safely used by people in the healing arts who need not be psychiatrists. Therapists can do no harm as long as they maintain respect for the needs of the people they work with and obtain permission from their patients for each step of the search and reframing process.

It was LeCron's dream at the time of his death in 1972 that ideomotor techniques would gain general acceptance by psychologists, physicians and dentists. In 1993, I believe it is safe to say that his methods have gained wide acceptance in the United States and Canada, largely because of Ernest Rossi (1986, 1988), who pointed out the power of messenger proteins and the variations of their influence on cellular receptors throughout the body.

Rossi's influence has extended the interest in ideodynamic techniques to Europe, the Middle East, and Asia.

Because of LeCron's contributions, we now can explore the perceptions of infants during intrauterine development, the perceptions of anesthetized people, and the thoughts and reactions to thoughts when humans are in deep sleep states as well as when normally dreaming. We can discover and correct many sources of resistance that previously had interfered with successful psychotherapy. The entire process of psychotherapy has been accelerated, and the cost of psychotherapy has, therefore, been reduced.

4

Hypnotizability

Hypnosis: Susceptibility, Measurements of Depth, Challenges

There have been a number of studies regarding variations in susceptibility and ability to reach measurable depths of hypnosis. These have been described, compared, and summarized in an excellent, comprehensive book by Hilgard (1965) at Stanford. The better known of the scales that have been in the literature during the nineteenth and twentieth centuries are Liébault (1892), Bernheim (1895), White (1930), Davis and Husband (1931), Shore and Orne (1962), LeCron-Bordeaux (1949) and the comprehensive considerations known as the "Stanford, SHSS," based on studies by Weitzenhoffer and Hilgard (1959, 1962).

These are classic studies, and Hilgard's book (1965) should be read carefully. Ernest R. Hilgard, professor of psychology at Stanford University has done monumental work investigating the phenomena of hypnosis, variations of pain sensitivity, divided consciousness, and posthypnotic behavior, just to mention a few of his interests.

Susceptibility

As a clinician and a teacher for clinicians in the health sciences, however, I must point out that all the studies of hypnotic susceptibility reported by Hilgard have been done with volunteer students in university settings. The categories cannot apply to highly motivated worried, frightened, injured, or unconscious people.

For example, an injured and hemorrhaging victim of an automobile accident may have an imperceptible pulse and blood pressure and may appear to be dead. He may demonstrate catalepsy and be capable of turning off arteriolar bleeding and reversing the manifestations of surgical shock in response to some authoritative suggestions. That same patient in a quiet office setting later may test very poorly on the Harvard or Stanford scales of susceptibility.

Herbert Spiegel in a 1972 paper drew his conclusions on susceptibility from his clinical observations over many years. His findings were derived from personal experience. His conclusions have not been universally accepted by other clinicians. I have used his test with students in workshops on hypnosis and can vouch for its validity there, but I have found it makes me unfairly judge those who test poorly on his scale but prove to be wonderful hypnotic subjects when working on a project of great importance to them in my office.

I believe a research worker with volunteers must use one or more of the major scales in order to have results accepted for publication in a journal of psychology or hypnosis, but from the standpoint of practicality in clinical work the tests should not be used. My reason is that a test that would be understood by patients as classifying them as medium or poor hypnotic subjects will be understood as threatening and their diminished self-confidence could, then, block self-hypnosis.

Are Tests of Suggestibility Useful in Clinical Practice? My answer to this is that they are useful for the beginner studying hypnotic behavior. It is valuable experience for you to test your subjects' ability to respond to suggestions. By so doing you are diminishing your initial insecurity. You are testing the other people. If they do well or poorly it is their, rather than your, measurement of ability. When you initially start trying to get someone into hypnosis you may telegraph your insecurity to your subjects. They will then do poorly and you will feel troubled, thinking your technique is faulty.

Positive expectation gets through to your subject. It is common knowledge among people training animals that you must assume the animal is able to achieve the desired result or you will have trouble with that animal. Good teachers treat their pupils with respect for their ability to learn. David St. Clair (1974) has found that psychic healers "see" the sick patient as already cured before they attempt treatment. You will dispense with tests of hypnotizabilty with the passage of time and the accumulation of successful work with hypnosis. The test in itself reflects your question as to whether or not your subject will respond to your efforts.

Measurement of Depth

At present there is no universally accepted way of proving that a hypnotized subject is in hypnosis or, if hypnotized, is in any measurable depth of hypnosis.

LeCron believed that the subconscious mind of hypnotized subjects could determine at which level they were in at any moment. To set the parameters for such subjective reporting, LeCron would stipulate that "zero" was a normal awake state and "36 inches" on a "yardstick of depth" would be a comatose, very deep state. He would ask a designated finger to lift when his subject knew his or her depth and that the subject would report verbally what seemed right.

We gave up trying to establish depth of measurements because we recognized, as have many others, that hypnotized subjects will go as deep as they need to go for whatever task they have in mind.

Leonard Ravitz (1950–1959) has demonstrated ability to measure and correlate electrical field potentials with varying depths of hypnosis. He is a psychiatrist who has studied under the direction of Harold Saxton Burr and F. S. C. Northrop at Yale, and he is a pioneer in recognizing variations in electrical field potentials with varying depths of hypnosis. He was a founding member of the American Society of Clinical Hypnosis in 1957 and was highly regarded by Milton H. Erickson. His work deserves recognition.

Those of us who have used hypnosis under various circumstances have found that measurements of hypnotizability or of depth of hypnosis under laboratory or office conditions have no correlation with what we find under critical circumstances in life-threatening situations. *Depth of hypnosis varies from moment to moment. Hypnotizability varies also with motivation and need.*

Differing Depths Existing Simultaneously

It is apparent when we are using hypnosis clinically that a subject may be demonstrating one level recognizable as being "light" while at the same time carrying out activity clearly indicating a deeper level of hypnotic ability. A simple example of this can be seen when we ask subjects to have their fingers pull apart to drop a pencil when they "know subconsciously" that their left arm is numb, as though they had been lying on it. With this test we may find the subject does not drop the pencil even though the arm is found to be totally anesthetized at the end of the session. When we ask the subject to review the experience at a subconscious level we may find he knew at an ideomotor level that his fingers should be pulling apart, but there was a feeling that if he dropped the pencil he would be in some way losing control. Here, a higher-level integration was blocking the physiological level response.

This discrepancy can be revealed by asking for a designated finger to lift on the opposite hand when his subconscious mind "knows" the test arm is becoming numb. As we watch, we can see a trembling of the fingers holding the pencil as the designated finger on the other hand is lifting. The subject would have dropped the pencil if he had known that this action reflects his ability to achieve analgesia in the arm rather than being a sign of going out of control.

Tests with Converted Left–Handed People

I have found other subjects dropping a pencil when their designated arm is numb at a subconscious level. The designated finger on the opposite hand lifts at the same time to indicate this achievement. When tested, however, the arm is *not* demonstrably numb. Verbally, the subject says, "My other arm feels numb." This might be distressing to the hypnotist who does not know the subject is a left-hander converted to right-handedness early in life. The entrance into hypnosis shifted his orientation from learned right-handedness to his original orientation, making the "wrong" arm numb (Cheek 1978).

Experiential Variations in Skin Sensitivity

Another subject, giving identical signals, dropping the pencil and having a finger on the other hand lift, feels *no* numbness in either arm. On exploring the unconscious reason for this, I have found my test subject has been hurt by doctors early in life and immediately, but temporarily, brings back sensitivity when I test him. When I give him the test instrument, he finds his arm is numb. When he gives *me* the instrument again, the arm is immediately sensitive. He has identified me, a physician, with the one who hurt him in his childhood.

These are examples of the subtle subjective factors that individually determine results and do not lend themselves to statistical evaluation when we deal with groups of people in an experiment.

Are Tests of Depth Important?

They are useful for you in becoming acquainted with the phenomena of hypnosis when you are beginning your learning experience, but you will soon recognize that people go as deep as they need to in the process of reaching their goals. They will do this no matter what you are doing to make them go deeper or rise to a lighter level of hypnosis.

You can guess at the depth your patients have reached, but it will only be a very gross approximation and the depth will probably change in the moments between your observation and the conclusion you draw. The workings of the Lord are mysterious and wondrous and keep us puzzled and constantly humble.

Challenges with Hypnosis

Stage hypnotists use challenges to deepen trance states with volunteer subjects who have come up to the stage for entertainment. This is already a select group of highly suggestible people, willing to perform for spectators.

The Handclasp Challenge

The volunteers are told to clasp their hands, tighter and tighter until the fingers are sealed together, as though they are stuck together with glue. "Squeeze them tighter, tighter. They are stuck tight. Now try to pull your hands apart. The harder you try the tighter they are together!"

There will be a varying percentage of people who are easily able to separate their hands. They have proven they cannot be hypnotized under these circumstances. They are asked to return to their seats, and they do so with the satisfaction of feeling they have outwitted the hypnotist, whose reputation is usually well known. In fact, they have shown that they have difficulty using their imagination. It could also be that the behavior of the hypnotist was irritating to them.

Those who have had a little difficulty but are able to separate their hands are also culled and asked to go back to their seats. They would be good subjects if there were time to train them, but that does not suffice for the stage hypnotist who has to work under great pressure to entertain the spectators. The hypnotist thanks them before sending them back to their seats.

The handclasp test is an easy one to use. The hypnotist may use it with the entire group of spectators and select subjects for entertainment from those who could not separate their hands. The stage hypnotist will go on with another test or two, recognizing the unsatisfactory reactors and sending them back. In the meantime, he or she has convinced the finalists that they are wonderful subjects, and this has strengthened their expectation that everything demanded will work as ordered.

Eye Catalepsy

It is difficult for any person in a light trance to open the eyes if they have been closed. The difficulty can be augmented by adding a challenge with words like, "Close your eyes tighter and tighter, tighter and tighter. Now your eyelids are becoming stuck down. They are just *glued* down! Now you can *try* to open them, but the harder you try the tighter they will be sealed together. Go ahead and *try.*'' There will always be a range in reaction. Some will open their eyes immediately to show they are not hypnotizable. Some will blink a few times before opening them, and some will really have a hard time getting them open.

Arm Rigidity

This test can be used in a positive way to show subjects that they are stronger than they think possible. I approve of this kind of challenge. The challenge is to prove that subjects cannot bend their arm after they have accepted the idea of it being a rigid piece of steel from the shoulder to the hand. Suggestions are repeated about the strength of the steel and the impossibility of it being bent. The subjects are then ordered authoritatively to *try* bending the arm at the elbow, that it just won't bend.

Comment About Challenges

I do not like challenges of any kind unless they are followed by some sort of demonstration that the hypnotized subject can overcome the influence of the negative suggestions by using some new thought instead of *trying* to fight the old difficulty. The word *try* used with all challenges is telling the subjects that you do not believe they can do what they are trying to do.

Every new learning process from infancy onward is accompanied first by inability to perform, then difficulty in doing it as well as others do it. Many failures and experiences of feeling inadequate precede the final ability to remain dry all night, to walk upright without falling, and to tie a bow knot, as examples. The power is all on the side of failure and fears of failure. Every success is clouded by realization that all the older siblings and relatives have been doing this better for a long time.

Emile Coué referred to the differing values of will power versus fear of failure when he expressed his *law of reversed effect or the law of reversed effort.* He said: ''When the will power and the imagination (fear of failure) are at war the imagination will always gain the day.''

Since failure is such a major part of our experience during our formative years, it seems to me that challenges are not productive, and that they are even potentially harmful for vulnerable subjects. We should be building confidence rather than diminishing it with our patients.

Combining a Challenge with a Way of Beating the Challenge

There is an excellent way of teaching a patient the difficulty in overcoming a challenge and then demonstrating a way of getting around that challenge. This involves the postural suggestion test. A patient holds both arms parallel at shoulder height and is asked to imagine heaviness that would be felt if a heavy telephone book had been strapped to one wrist. He or she is asked to think, "My arm is heavy, pulling down toward the floor." This is followed by the command, "Now try to lift that arm. You will be able to do it, but it will take some work."

The patient usually will notice the effort involved when he or she tries. This is followed by saying, "Now, please put the telephone book down and imagine a bunch of balloons up there, tied to your wrist, lifting, lifting it upward toward the ceiling. Your arm can feel lighter and lighter." The effect of the heaviness is countered by the influence of the new thought of balloons, and the subject has learned a way to get around a difficulty without having to struggle.

This test demonstrates a variant of the dissociative exercises Erickson might use with patients suffering from chronic pain. The patient's attention is centered on heaviness followed by a sense of lightness in one arm. In the meantime the other arm is ignored. The patient would feel sharpness if you pricked the heavy/light arm with the point of a needle. At the same time, he or she would probably not notice a needle point if you tested the opposite arm.

Comment

The beginner in hypnotherapy must become familiar with what has been observed by authorities regarding susceptibility, evaluation of hypnotic depth, and the various challenges. With the passage of time, however, you will find that your respect for everyone being a good hypnotic subject will pay off in the results.

When LeCron, James Hixson, and I gave our first workshop together, our results the first day were not very good. We were a bit diffident. Certainly I was unsure of myself. I had never hypnotized a man before. By the third day our group was friendly and interested. All our demonstrations worked well.

Each of us seemed to have noticed this difference. At the next workshop a month later, we treated everyone as though this were already the third day and they were already enthusiastic and friendly. We had no further trouble with inductions of hypnosis.

Keep this in mind when you work with your own patients. Realize that everyone slips in and out of hypnosis every day. You are acting as a coach or a teacher who realizes the great potential of your patients. You are simply helping them recognize and use what they already know.

5

Inducing Hypnosis

There are three general ways of inducing hypnosis or bringing about the type of psychological behavior that we identify with hypnosis. It may take some emotional pressure off the beginner to realize that your prospective hypnotic subjects have been in and out of hypnosis many times before coming to see you and that you will simply be helping them use what they already know. It will be particularly helpful for you to find them giving a signal with a finger that they are "in a hypnotic state deep enough to use it helpfully with you" when you are thinking that nothing is happening. There is a tendency for beginners to underestimate the abilities of their subjects.

Hypnosis can occur spontaneously in a variety of situations, as will become clear throughout this book. It is important for the beginner to study the qualities of hypnosis as you sense them in your work, whether or not you use hypnosis in your work.

Spontaneous Hypnosis: Origins, Recognition, and Utilization

Hypnosis Occurring Spontaneously without Attempted Induction

The fact that hypnosis occurs without attempted induction is a very important consideration, and every professional in the health sciences should be aware of the situations in which hypnosis can occur spontaneously and be able to recognize the facial expressions, voice tones and general behavior that characterize a person in a hypnotic state. Understandings in hypnosis are literal and childlike, very different from the reasoning that occurs at conscious levels.

Hypnosis occurs under the following circumstances:

- At moments of great fear or great personal loss.
- When we are disoriented in time or space through trauma, general anesthesia, hallucinatory drugs or alcohol.
- With sensory deprivation, food deprivation, and oxygen deprivation.
- With sensory repetition. Hypnosis can occur spontaneously with disastrous results when a driver of an automobile or a pilot of a motor boat or plane is lulled by the sound of the engine, or when the eyes are drawn downward by interrupted, white divider strip markings on a highway, by raindrops, by methodical sweeps of a windshield wiper, by snowflakes or fog wisps coming toward the windshield, by evenly spaced shadows cast by poplar trees or the sun shining through the blades of a helicopter.

A physician, nurse, or emergency room person may need to take advantage of the benefit of a hypnotic state to help a patient in status asthmaticus shift from spastic to relaxed, abdominal breathing. A firm touch and a confident order to stop bleeding may be more valuable than hurried attempts to replace lost blood. Sincerely expressed commands can terminate surgical shock. Replacing a feeling of intense heat with imagery of coolness within a few minutes of a burn from molten aluminum (1750 degrees F) can change a potential third-degree burn to a second-degree status (Ewin 1986). Usually there is no time or reason to explain hypnosis or obtain permission for action when survival hangs in the balance. Emphatic commands to "take a deep breath," "open your eyes," "listen carefully to me" should follow the first steps of cardio-pulmonary resuscitation of a seemingly inanimate victim of drowning, electrical shock, or coronary occlusion.

Moebius (1957), Bernheim (1895), and Estabrooks (1948) have each recognized, as did Josef Breuer (1957), that a state indistinguishable from hypnosis occurs during serious illness, great pain, and great fear. Physicians, nurses, ambulance teams and "first responders" in the fire department need to have some organized, rehearsed protocols to augment behavior that is already in place because of the crisis (Jacobs 1991).

Direct Form of Induction

Hypnosis can be induced *directly*, meaning intentionally with the knowledge of the subject or patient. This section will describe direct induction in these ways: (1) spinning, chanting, dancing, rhythmic drums, and long-distance running; (2) mesmerism; (3) electronarcosis; (4) eye fixation combined with initiation of ideomotor signals; and (5) combined direct and indirect induction.

Spinning, Chanting, Dancing, Rhythmic Drums, and Long-Distance Running

Children seem innately to know that a trance state will occur when they keep spinning around in a circle. The religious ecstasy of the whirling dervishes is probably a derivative of childhood experiences.

Hypnotic states occur when chanting is continued. Those who work in circumstances of hardship and boredom resort to chanting to make the situation less stressful.

Methodical, continued dancing has been used throughout the world to induce hypnotic states in preparation for war, for heightening the perceptions of participants or making the expected wounds less painful or dangerous. Intricate drum rhythms are used to call in various orishas in the Candomble religious rituals in Brazil as participants slowly move in a circle.

I doubt if many joggers run for the express purpose of going into hypnosis, but it seems true that runners go into an altered state of consciousness somewhere between two and three miles from the start of their exercise. Some call it a "high." Others simply say they feel less tired or less pain after that stage.

Mesmerism

Repetitive mesmeric passes probably achieve their effect by having the hands of the mesmerist reverse the polarity of the electrical fields around the subject. Mesmerism, used by Deleuze in France, Elliotson in England, and Esdaile in India, had been known, according to Esdaile (1851/1902), for a long time in the mountains of Assam and probably in many other parts of the world by medicine men. He describes the method he used in *Mesmerism in India* pages 40 to 45.

First Experiment

Madhab Kaura, a hog-dealer, condemned to seven years' imprisonment, with labor on the roads, in irons, for wounding a man so as to endanger his life, has got a double hydrocele. He was ordered to be taken from the jail to the charity hospital, to be operated upon.

April 4th (1845)– The water was drawn off one side of the scrotum and two drachms (approximately two ounces) of the usual cor.sub. (mercury bichloride) were thrown in (injected). On feeling the pain from the injection, he threw his head over the back of the chair, and pressed his hands along the course of the spermatic cords, closing his eyelids firmly and making the grimaces of a man in pain. Seeing him suffering in this way, I turned to the native sub-assistant surgeon, an eleve of the medical college, and asked him if he had ever seen Mesmerism? He said he had seen it tried at the medical college, but without effect. Upon which I remarked, "I have a great mind to try it on this man, but as I never saw it practiced, and know it only from reading, I shall probably not succeed." The man continuing in the position described, I placed his knees between mine, and began to pass my hands slowly over his face, at the distance of an inch, and carried them down to the pit of his stomach. [This is the method he had read about. The operator sat facing the subject who was also seated. He placed his knees outside of the knees of the subject.] This was continued for half an hour before he was spoken to, and when questioned at the end of this time his answers were quite sensible and coherent.

He was ordered to remain quiet, and the passes were continued for a quarter of an hour longer — still no sensible effect. Being now tired (thermometer 85 degrees,)I gave it up in despair, and declared it to be a failure. While I rested myself, the man remained quiet, and made fewer grimaces, and when ordered to open his eyes, he said there was smoke in the room. This roused my attention, and tempted me to persevere. I now breathed on his head, and carried my hands from the back of his head over his face and down to the epigastrium, where I pressed them united. The first time this was done, he took his hands off his groins and pressed them both firmly down upon mine; drew a long breath, and said, "You are my father and mother and have given me life again." The same process was persevered in, and in about an hour he began to gape, said he must sleep, that his senses were gone; and his replies became incoherent. He opened his eyes, when ordered, but said he only saw smoke, and could distinguish no one; his eyes were quite lusterless, and the lids were opened heavily. All appearance of pain now disappeared; his hands were crossed on his breast, instead of being pressed on the groins, and his countenance showed the most perfect repose. He now took no notice of our questions, and I called loudly on him by name without attracting any notice.

In this first case, Esdaile remarks that the diarrhea this man was suffering disappeared after this period of mesmeric rest. Injuries to his skin healed without any indication of inflammation. In subsequent cases he observed that redness, swelling, and local heat disappeared when pain was removed with mesmeric passes.

Mesmerism may come back into use by friends and relatives of people too sick to think or respond to verbal hypnosis because of cancer, AIDS, head injury or the new form of drug-resistant tuberculosis. Deep hypnosis stimulates the immune system. The process takes from 45 minutes to two hours, but the profoundly deep trance can last several hours and can be therapeutic. Esdaile had this comment:

> I beg the reader not to do me the injustice to think me a Mesmeric doctor, for it would be as true to call me a rhubarb, jalap, or castor-oil physician. Mesmerism often comes to the aid of my patients, when all the resources of medicine are exhausted, and all the drugs of Arabia useless; and therefore, I consider it to be my duty to benefit them by it, and to assist in making it known for the advantage of mankind. (1851/1902, p. 33)

Electronarcosis

Electronarcosis is a variant of mesmerism. It produces analgesia, but the patient during the operation can talk and behave much as would be the case with hypnoanesthesia. A variable direct current of electricity passes through the eyes or from the roof of the mouth, through the brain to electrodes placed over the mastoid region of the skull. The method has been used in Russia but has attracted little attention in America because of the fear that damage to the eyes or to the brain might occur.

Eye Fixation Combined with Initiation of Ideomotor Signals

I use this method to teach patients how to experience a direct method in order to relax, get used to the experience, set up ideomotor signals, and, finally, to learn self-hypnosis.

An altered state we call hypnosis occurs directly when a subject is asked to sit back in a comfortable position with the arms loosely resting on the thighs and ankles separated slightly. People who initially fold their arms together or cross their legs will have an easier time entering hypnosis if they avoid these defiant postures.

This method involves setting up a signal that will tell the subjects when they are in a light trance. I couple this with a simple eye-fixation target that keeps my subjects' conscious attention while I am communicating with their unconscious perceptions.

This is how I present the material:

"Please hold this pen between your right thumb and index finger in such a way that you will know when it drops onto your lap or onto the floor. I am going to ask that your fingers pull apart when you are able to remember how your left arm would feel if you had been lying on it for a couple of hours during the night. Your fingers will pull apart at that moment but it will take a few more seconds before the message gets up to your conscious mind where you would know that the arm is numb or feeling like pins and needles.

"You give the orders to your subconscious mind in hypnosis and then you wait for an indication that the order has been carried out. This is comparable to ordering a meal in a restaurant. You don't follow the waiter into the kitchen to tell the chef how to cook. You wait for the waiter to put the food in front of you. Similarly, here you wait for your fingers to drop that pen and then wait a few seconds more until you consciously recognize what has already happened at an unconscious, physiological level of awareness. This keeps you from spoiling your results by trying to make things happen. Hypnosis should be free of effort.

"With your eyelids closed, please get the mental image of a lighted candle, now, on a table about 10 feet away. If you have trouble seeing it, just wait. Everybody is able to visualize at a subconscious level. If you can see the candle in your mind's eye, just nod your head so I can keep up with you. The flame of a candle is always moving. It gets larger, smaller, swings a little from side to side with the gentle convection currents of air in any room.

"While you are watching that candle flame, gradually relax the muscles of your forehead, neck, and shoulders. These are the muscles we tighten when we are scared, in pain, or depressed. It is very helpful to relax them but we usually have to take a little time to do that. Associating the sense of relaxing with each expiration is a good way to do it because our chest muscles and diaphragm contract as we breathe in; they relax as we breathe out. I am going to count from one to ten. With each number please think to yourself, 'relax, relax, relax.'"

With the average patient, the fingers will pull apart to drop the pen by the time I start counting, but, if nothing seems to be happening, I will announce firmly that I want the patient to come out of hypnosis in a few minutes when I count from ten down to one. This takes away the effort of trying to comply now. Even though the fingers have not dropped the pen, the patient is in a more relaxed state than before we started. It feels good to be slightly relaxed; therefore, there will be a slight degree of rebellion to being ordered to wake up. This seems to be the major reason for people dropping the pen when ordered to "wake up."

Dropping the pen helps the patient recognize that something is happening. Now it is possible to start the process of identifying symbol finger movements or "ideomotor signals."

When your inner mind knows that you are twice as deep and that left arm is twice as numb as it is now, one of your fingers on the right hand will lift to let us both know. Just keep on relaxing progressively with each breath out. (The process can continue, setting up signals on the same hand for "yes," "no," and "I don't want to answer."

Suggestions are then given for becoming more comfortable and going deeper each time this experience is repeated. I point out that learning to use hypnosis constructively is a skill and, like all skills, will improve with repetition.

Following this, I like to have the patient awaken and go back into hypnosis again as I count from one to ten. At the second time it is possible to proceed with whatever therapeutic project is indicated.

Initiating Hypnosis While Selecting Ideomotor Signals

For someone who has had no experience with ideomotor signaling we can start like this:

Children do very well with head movement answers to questions but adults do better with finger signals in hypnosis. Finger signals are more rapid and reflect information from a deeper part of your mind than can be reached when you nod or shake your head. We will need one finger to represent a "yes" answer, one to tell me "no," and a third one to tell me that you don't want to know the answer at this moment.

Focus your attention on that right hand on your lap and sort of wonder which finger your unconscious mind will select to represent a "yes" answer to some question. Just think "yes-yes-yes" until you see or feel a trembling movement of one of your fingers. Most people use their index finger for 'yes.' their middle finger for 'no,' and their thumb or pinky for 'I don't want to answer,' but your unconscious mind may want to use different fingers.

There is a 15-second interval before her index finger lifts in the typical way. By the time she has selected all three signals she is in a light hypnotic state that is reflected by the fluttering of her eyelids when she blinks.

I can, at this moment, continue with a search of her attitudes at birth and the earlier key experience of knowing when her mother learns that she is pregnant (see Chapter 20). Usually, however, I prefer to have her open her eyes and use her fingers in the process of learning self-hypnosis (Chapter 8).

For a Nervous Patient Who Cannot Set Up Ideomotor Signals

This is a type of induction that I have found very helpful for use with medical as well as psychological problems. Because most people focus their attention on a symptom while ignoring favorable sensations, I like to point out the value of concentrating on one source of stimuli while ignoring other sources. My presentation would be as follows:

"I would like to show you something about how our mind works. This is just a phenomenon about where we spend our attention. It can be on a pain, on an emotional trauma or on just plain fear. This is known as 'postural suggestion' and does not necessarily involve hypnosis.

"Please hold both arms out at shoulder height. Now close your eyes and focus your attention on your right arm. (I touch the hand of that arm to identify which arm is intended in case the patient is a converted left-handed person.)

"Imagine that you have a heavy telephone book hanging from a strap around your wrist, pulling your arm downward. Feel the weight pulling down. Pretty soon the muscles in your shoulder will feel too tired to support that book. (With repeated suggestions of weight and heaviness, the arm will start to move downward). That's fine. Now *try* to lift that arm. I think you can do it but it may be a little hard to do." (Usually you can see the combined activity of muscles trying to lift being opposed by those pulling the arm downward.)

The subject who can feel the movement of an arm downward or upward will recognize that muscles respond to ideas. He will then be able to sense movement when assignments are made of fingers to represent the three answers. It helps to touch the index finger while saying, "This is going to be your 'yes' finger after this. When I say 'yes' I would like you to move it purposefully. This attaches a conscious movement in association with the idea of 'yes.'" Have the patient respond consciously three times before you tell him to simply *think* "yes" repeatedly until that index finger trembles and lifts by itself, without his conscious movement. When this succeeds, you move on with the other two assigned fingers.

At this point I like to introduce the idea of a subconscious review. I want the patient to know how to search a nighttime of sleep for causal factors with problems. I word directions in this way:

"Please go back to the moment you fell asleep last night. When you are there, your 'yes' finger will lift. Each time you are dreaming, your 'no' finger will lift. (See Chapter 16 for ways to continue this type of exploration.) The review deepens the trance level. The results improve with each repetition. Very deep level thought sequences can be revealed and reprocessed when they are exposed to conscious reasoning.

Combined Direct and Indirect Induction

This is a rapid method for inducing hypnosis. I use it when a participant in a hypnosis workshop asks a question that reflects an unconscious need to discover the answer to the question. For example, a physician asked, "How can you be sure that a baby feels rejected when it can't hear its mother's voice at the time of birth?"

There is a strong probability that the doctor has been affected by my discussion about early life negative imprinting in the delivery room, imprinting that may prevent a child from believing subsequent maternal demonstrations of acceptance and love.

Ideas and interpretations associated with epinephrine will override those that are not associated with this stress hormone. For the same reason, any ordinary verbal answer to the doctor's concern will have as little chance of satisfying him as the nonstress show of love and acceptance by his mother after her recovery from the drugs and the stress of labor and delivery.

My response to him is, "Would you be willing to come up here and decide for yourself about fetal perceptions?" He appears to be at least 45 years old. His mother was probably delivered in a modern hospital and was sedated or anesthetized at the time of delivery. She was probably unable to greet her baby, and her baby would have had his vision disturbed by silver nitrate drops in his eyes. He would have been cleaned up and taken to a noisy nursery for examination by a pediatric intern before having a chance to meet his mother four or more hours later.

In a workshop the doctor would have already been exposed to the uses of ideomotor questioning methods. He is asked to check his finger by thinking "yes," "no," etc. He is then asked to orient to the moment of his birth and to have his "yes" finger lift when he is emerging out into the world. When this signal is given after about 20 seconds, I ask, "Is your mother awake and able to say something?" His "no" finger lifts after his face has already indicated some distress. I ask his "no" finger to lift when he knows how a baby feels under those circumstances. He murmurs, "Alone." I point out that this is the fault of modern obstetrics. It is not his mother's fault. She has been given drugs that prevent her from talking.

"Now, please go over that delivery as it would have been if your mother had learned to make her abdomen numb and had practiced until she was good at it. When you are delivering after an easy short labor, your 'yes' finger will lift. Tell me what she says when you can hear her voice."

After 10 seconds he smiles. A few seconds later he says, "I love you." He has reframed his original distressed subjective imprinting in the space of approximately five minutes.

Nonstress-Related Use of Indirect Induction

Milton Erickson used many forms of indirect induction of hypnosis. Basically, I believe his intent was to teach observers as much as he could about the subtle ways in which gestures, facial expressions, word timing and voice intonations could influence the human mind. Sometimes he used his inventions when willing subjects had experienced difficulties getting into hypnosis with other therapists.

Confusion Technique

The subject is asked to think momentarily about a time basis such as yesterday, "but two days ago this would have been tomorrow. Time is a very strange thing to comprehend. You can look forward to something happening next week and then all of a sudden you are in next month and it will be a bit hard to remember all the details of that experience last month."

Erickson was a master of this technique. He explained that he was asking for action of thought adjustment to so many different items that his subject would eventually escape into hypnosis in order to find relief. He would know when that occurred because of postural and expression changes shown by the subject and would then proceed with utilization of the trance state.

Accidental Confusion in the Beginning

Without realizing it, the beginner may be having so much trouble thinking of what should be said next, what sort of imagery would be appropriate, that the target person may escape into hypnosis trying to figure out what is expected. You will usually hear about this sort of confusion after you terminate the confusion you inadvertently caused.

Generally speaking, LeCron and I felt that there is so much confusion in the world today that we should avoid the indirect confusion technique, and we never advocated its use by our students of hypnosis.

The "Unhypnotizable Subject" Watching an Induction

Erickson frequently used this method. He would invite a student who had been totally unable to experience any facet of hypnosis to come up and carefully watch the behavior of someone Erickson was going to hypnotize in a demonstration.

In 1954 I unconsciously entered a hypnotic state in a workshop that LeCron had organized with Erickson and Aaron Moss, the originator of the term "hypnodontics." I had used hypnosis for ten years with patients but was sure I could not go into hypnosis myself. The dental assistant of one of the participants had volunteered to be a subject for demonstration but was unconsciously fighting every word that Erickson was using. I became so interested in the remarkable way he was using the young woman's resistances to help her get into hypnosis that I suddenly realized I was alone in the room except for Erickson and the woman. I had tunnel vision.

Using Induction Methods for Best Results

Probably the most important quality of the communication existing between a doctor and a patient, a hypnotherapist and a client or patient is subliminal. The way you look, speak, gesture are all important. Both clairvoyant and telepathic elements seem to be present in the subliminal elements.

To function at your best you should be feeling healthy, even if you are just practicing your skills at getting someone into a hypnotic state. The healers of Brazil all say you should not work with a troubled person when you feel sick or tired. Animal trainers will say the same thing.

Outline what you are looking for and what you wish to accomplish before you see a patient.

Refer a patient to someone else if you do not like him or her or do not believe the patient can get well.

Your honest faith can unleash very powerful resources for healing; no one knows the prognosis of an optimistic patient.

Maintain your humility at all times and be honest in all your thoughts about the patient you want to help.

Admit when you are puzzled and be willing to listen to suggestions made by your patient. Projection into a future time can help the patient discover changes that need to be made now.

Above all, remember that you are not treating a victim. Instead, you are working in a mutual relationship of trust and respect. Your patient is your colleague.

6

Trance Phenomena

Common Occurrences During Hypnosis

Heightened Perceptions

Perceptions of the hypnotized subject are keener than in the unhypnotized state. They border on clairvoyance and telepathy. Both would be assets to people in a time of great danger when speech would be dangerous.

Economy of Action

Humans in hypnosis progressively diminish the speed and extent of coordinated muscular action as their level of hypnosis deepens. This includes the muscular action involved in speech. There is increasing economy of motion until motion ceases in the deepest level of hypnosis.

Pseudodeath or Suspended Animation

T.J. Hudson (1893–1923) has described the pseudodeath states that were well known in the nineteenth century when difficulties of travel made it necessary to allow the dead to remain on dining room tables for many days, surrounded by flowers. "Dead" people have been known to have revived after many days of remaining cold, motionless, and apparently dead. Hudson interviewed several such people. All of them had responded to the pleas of a friend or relative.

He pointed out that people in this deathlike state are able to think and to hear. They feel comfortable and they will not spontaneously make the effort to come back unless someone vehemently insists.

Communication with unconscious and critically ill people is important to keep in mind. In such conditions the unconscious mind is open to forcibly given positive, hopeful instructions (Cheek 1969b). We can never assume a person is dead when we see an immobile body on the sidewalk or on the side of the road after an automobile accident. Physicians and nurses should know about this phenomenon of extreme economy of action, the "coma" level of hypnosis, when they respond to a "code blue" alarm in their hospital. While you think of what to do next, loudly say something like, "Take a breath now! Stay relaxed! You will be all right! I'm going to push on your chest!"

Patients in a state of apparent respiratory or cardiac arrest may temporarily have given up the will to live. They need to know you care. We have no right to insist that all people who want to die should be forced to live, but in emergency situations our responsibility is to respond positively. After near-death experiences, many suicidal people discover a genuine will to live when encouraged by people around them.

Reduction in Need for Oxygen
Reduction of Metabolism

Breathing and heart rate become slower as hypnotic depth increases. The skin becomes cooler. There are findings characteristic of fainting and hibernation.

Reduction of Inflammation

Esdaile in 1845 found that his mesmerized patients reduced signs of inflammation when they were in a deep trance state. He said the three cardinal signs of inflammation as described by Celsus (AD 35)—redness, swelling, and local heat—will disappear when pain is eliminated with mesmerism. Delboeuf in 1877 found that an arm hypnotically anesthetized after being burned healed quickly and without blister formation. The contralateral arm formed an ordinary blister (Bernheim 1895). Pain-relieving narcotics do not accomplish this reduction in inflammatory response; they work at more cortical levels of perception. The painful stimuli come through the brainstem and have their physiological repercussions within the midbrain.

Dabney Ewin in New Orleans in 1973 reported remarkable healing with third-degree burns when hypnotic analgesia was effected and suggestions of coolness were given soon after injury. He feels that a second-degree burn may increase to a full-thickness, or third-degree, burn because of pain and the resulting interference with circulation to the injured area.

Augmented Homeostasis Mechanisms

Bleeding diminishes in hypnosis, even when direct suggestions are not given (Solovey and Milechnin 1958). Authoritative suggestions have stopped massive hemorrhages from the uterus and even from smaller arteries. We do not know the mechanisms involved, but they may include changes in electromagnetic polarity of the vascular walls, blood cells, and platelets. It may be due in part to alterations of coagulation mechanisms, as seen with hemophilia, where there is a deficiency in a coagulation factor (Macfarlane 1961). Certainly it is true that peripheral capillary beds are constricted as hypnosis deepens. This occurs spontaneously with wounded people, but the process can be negated by the careless remarks of bystanders.

Contracted Visual Fields

When hypnosis is induced with the subject's eyes open, as with an eye-fixation technique, we can note a progressive constriction in the angle of visual field perception as the trance deepens. This can be tested by deepening a trance until catalepsy can be demonstrated. Set up ideomotor finger signals. Stand behind the subject and ask her to say "now" when she can see your finger moving as you carry out the simple test for visual field acuity in a horizonal plane.

Explain that you would like the "yes" finger to lift unconsciously when her inner mind "sees" the finger wiggling. The "yes" finger will lift immediately at the full range of vision. Her verbal "now" may not occur until this conscious field of vision has been reduced to about 20 degrees.

It would be hard to make sense out of calling this simply a phenomenon of hypnosis without considering its survival value involving all the senses at moments of life-threatening stress. The spot on the wall used for starting the eye fixation might, in nature, be a hungry carnivore requiring alertness and responsiveness if attacked. There is a need to focus sensory input on a threatening adversary. Global awareness at such a time would also seem necessary for the threatened animal to know about a possible avenue of escape. Survival could depend on avoiding other predators on one side.

Augmented Healing and Augmented Immune Capabilities

Augmented healing and immune capabilities are phenomena of the deep hypnotic states observed by Esdaile in India. It seems logical to conclude that his trance inductions using repetitive passes altered the electromagnetic force field of his patients in a way comparable to how Becker and Seldon induced anesthesia with salamanders by stroking them with a nylon brush

(1985) and later producing anesthesia by reversing the polarity of the brain with an electric current passed from front to back of the head. Studies have shown that hibernating groundhogs are insensitive to surgical manipulation as long as they are not alarmed by a human sneeze or voice. They have survived removal of their liver until they come out of hibernation. Similarly, their bone marrow and circulating blood cells have shown no changes after lethal doses of irradiation until they have come out of hibernation (Lagemann 1957). There is no previous model of exposure that would prepare the groundhog for withstanding these experimental assaults.

These findings seem to suggest that there is some process involving the primitive brain during induced hibernating-like states with mesmerism that resemble the protective mechanisms available to mammals during hibernation.

Literalness of Understanding

Literalness of understanding is characteristic of hypnotic ideation. Because of this literalness, hypnotized subjects may miss the humor in a play on words or punning. Like children, they have difficulty processing negative statments. "Don't play with matches" may be interpreted as meaning a parent expects that child to play with matches or the command would not have been given. All statements to hypnotized people and those you suspect might be in a spontaneous trance state due to injury or anesthetic agents should be positively stated. If asked for a verbal statement or an answer to a question, a hypnotized person will speak in the most economical way. If asked, "Do you feel all right?" he might answer "No" or may only shake his head silently. It will be necessary for you to ask for the reasons he does not feel all right. These features probably relate to the more primitive part of the mind's activity before the advent of higher, cortical-level associations of thought that include a complex vocabulary.

Anatomy
If you ask a hypnotized subject to reduce sensations throughout his body, he will neglect to make his arms, legs and head numb because you have not mentioned them.

Sleep Ideation
If you want to know about "dreams or thoughts last night," you must mention both dreams and thoughts. Hypnotized subjects may not tell you about the "thoughts" going on at deeper levels of sleep. "Dreams" are the connected experiences with symbolism that occur at rapid eye movement levels of sleep. Hypnotized people seem to differentiate the two.

Continued Ability to Hear and Remember

Patients continue to hear and remember while unconscious, in comatose hypnotic states, or in deep levels of natural sleep. Amnesia will block out conscious memory for such information, but memory can be retrieved through repetitive retracing of the event using ideomotor signaling. It is helpful to remember this fact if you become troubled on recognizing that your subject refuses to come out of hypnosis. This seldom happens. When it does occur, the subject usually has some resentment for what has gone on during the session or feels there is further information needing attention. The subject will respond with finger signals and will come out of the trance when you have explored the trouble. Examples given by Hudson (1923) and Quackenbos (1909) show that people in a pseudo death state will respond to suggestion, as will a person who is near death with pneumonia. They are paying attention although they may show no outward signs of comprehension.

How People Look When Hypnotized

It is not always easy or possible to recognize hypnotic behavior but there are some characteristics we may be able to see.

Eyelid Flutter

Eyelid flutter, an early sign of light hypnosis, may be distressing for patients wearing hard contact lenses. Ask about contact lenses and let your patient remove them before you start a formal induction.

The lids flutter at a rate of approximately 12 per second when people are in a light state of hypnosis. You may notice it when patients first come into your office. The lids will vibrate as they blink their eyes. It reflects some nervousness relating to the reason for visiting your office.

During a formal induction with your subject looking at a spot on the opposite wall your first indication of entering a hypnotic state will be the flutter of the lids when she blinks. As the trance deepens it will not be necessary for her to blink, but you can ask her to close her eyes when you see the flutter. Stage hypnotists will use their fingers to close the subject's eyes when they see this lid flutter. I prefer simply to ask for eye closure.

This phenomenon seems related to the repetitive impulses of alpha rhythm in the brain. It is an action that seems associated with every thought. It makes a pendulum swing to reflect an answer to a question. It is the signal that tells you the trembling movement of an ideomoter finger signal is truly reflecting an unconscious thought.

Economy of Muscular Action

There is increasing economy of muscular action as depth of hypnosis increases. Facial expressions diminish. The eyes, if open, will appear dull. Movements are slower. Modulation of voice diminishes, as does its intensity. Adjectives and adverbs are left out. Eventually the subject may speak only in monosyllables or the response to a question may be a slow nod or shake of the head without a verbal response.

Children move very quickly in and out of hypnosis. When they are trying to remember what happened next in a movie they have seen, their facial expression will iron out. Their gaze will leave you and their eyes will look off into the distance about 20 degrees above the horizon.

If your adult subject is standing with his eyes open and fixed on yours, he will remain with his body stationary but his eyes will follow you if you move to one side. If you continue talking from one side, he will slowly shift his body to face you. If he enters a deep trance, he will remain looking straight ahead as though you had not moved. This decreasing mobility probably is derived from the tonic state animals go into in the presence of great danger.

Alarm at Flashback Phenomenon

About 10 percent of people exposed to a formal induction may show some alarm in their expression. Some will open their eyes and, without knowing the reason, ask if they can use the bathroom. They may suddenly decide not to go on with the procedure. It is important for you to recognize the signs of distress before your patient decides consciously to terminate the interview with you.

The reason for this association of distress with entrance into hypnosis relates to the fact that hypnosis is a state-dependent phenomenon. Because it has occurred at some critical time of stress in the past, the causal experience of that time will be remembered instantly as you induce hypnosis for any unrelated purpose. We noticed that the doctors who showed such discomfort during an introductory group induction exercise would not include hypnotic methods in their clinical work until we helped them realize that they could go into hypnosis comfortably and not have to repeatedly confront some troublesome past experience such as a tonsillectomy in childhood.

When you see your patient is looking distressed, stop the induction and shift to use of a Chevreul pendulum and ask if she was reminded of some past experience when she was frightened or injured. Help her discover the origin and then ask, "Now that you know this, will you be able to go into hypnosis comfortably and to use it helpfully in the work we are doing?" I have found this helpful in overcoming initial resistance to hypnosis (Cheek

1960c). The correction is seldom necessary when you have explained the flashback phenomenon *before* you start an induction of hypnosis.

Logic tells me that this type of "instant replay" at an unconscious level of awareness has biological survival value. The animal confronting a dangerous larger animal needs to have instant retrieval of information relating to a similar situation in its genetic past or its more recent experience.

Continuation of Motion (Catalepsy)

In selecting pendulum responses to represent the three answers, you may find the pendulum continuing to follow the direction it had selected for a previous response. If you suspect this, you may stop the swing yourself or ask your subject to do it and then ask for the next signal.

This phenomenon is well known to long-distance runners. After two or three miles of regular pace they begin to feel less tired. Some have said they feel elated, a nondrugged "high." They have entered a hypnotic state that has raised their tolerance for pain and fatigue.

A logical deduction would be that this is another way for hypnosis to conserve energy for animals like wolves or coyotes needing to travel long distances between meals.

Stationary Catalepsy

The tendency to hold a position, even one that is uncomfortable, is a phenomenon of a medium trance level. You can test for this by gently lifting an arm from its resting position, holding it for about 20 seconds and then lowering your supporting fingers, one by one, until you sense that you can take the support away. As you test by withdrawing your fingers, you will feel the arm becoming less heavy. If it starts to get heavier again, the subject has become analytic and is now in a lighter stage of hypnosis. Give the arm a quick shake and then hold it steady again.

Catalepsy may be a reflection of "freezing" to be less visible when an animal is in the presence of a hungry, larger carnivorous animal. I have found catalepsy present with injured and unconscious people after an automobile accident. Bernheim (1895) saw this phenomenon with moribund typhoid victims.

Comment

To look at human hypnotic behavior as something produced only by one human impinging on another is disrespectful to the vast extent of hypnotic-like states found everywhere in nature. Resting states clearly have been evolved throughout the history of life on Earth. Viruses, bacteria, plants, and the majority of animals in all the phyla will go into some sort of resting state when weather is not clement. They all know when it is time to come out of the state when the weather is favorable.

I offer the concept of hypnosis as an animal survival mechanism occurring spontaneously under varying circumstances. I believe the concept needs to be followed by pointing out the value of the hypnotic mechanism for rapid access to causal events in life and the way in which maladaptive behavior can be modified. I keep these points in mind in my work:

(1) Hypnosis is a biologically evolved mechanism for survival.

(2) It occurs spontaneously:

- With mesmeric passes continued for more than an hour
- With lulling, repetitive sensory stimuli.
- When a person is trying to remember sequential events
- When a person is frightened or seriously injured
- When disoriented in time or space (ejected from a wrecked car)

7

Principles of
Suggestion

In this chapter we are mainly concerned with ideas and how a therapist can best communicate ideas to a hypnotized subject. We need to know a little about the differences between conscious and unconscious understandings.

Differences in Understandings

Conscious Understandings

We have learned the conscious mind is capable of understanding a play on words, punning, and humor. It is capable of recognizing symbols. It can use logic in formulating an action. When we talk about nighttime we mean, generally speaking, the time between dusk and sunrise. "Last night" refers to the entire night. When we talk about "the body" we include head, arms, and legs as parts of the whole.

Subconscious Understandings

The subconscious mind understands words literally. In common conscious communication a person stating, "It's pretty late now. I'm going to split, go home, and crash," would be recognized by another unhypnotized person as talking about going away from a location and the people there, going home and going to bed. A hypnotized subject would be confused and frightened by the implications of a friend splitting in two parts. "Crash" might be interpreted as meaning an accident is expected to happen on the way home.

A student in a normal, conscious state responding to "Would you tell me when you were born?" would give month, date, and year of birth. A daydreaming student or one in a hypnotic trance state would simply respond to the question with a nod of the head, meaning, "Yes, I will tell you my birthday." Verbal communications are economical and very literal. If we want to know whether or not a hypnotized subject is feeling pain, we must be specific. Mention head, arms, and legs to get a meaningful response.

There is a great difference between conscious logic and the logic of a hypnotized person. The conscious person who has been told to go open the door when the speaker takes his glasses off would refuse to do something that makes no sense. The hypnotized subject who has accepted a post-hypnotic suggestion will invent a logical reason for opening the door. The invention would include a rationalization for the act of opening the door. The hypnotized subject will use no critical judgment in deciding whether or not to accept the posthypnotic suggestion. When the signal is given it will be necessary to find some understandable reason for the action of opening the door. The hypnotized subject may suddenly feel very warm and uncomfortable in order to have a reason for opening the door to reach cooler air outside.

The Power of the Positive

Positive Versus Negative Suggestions

It is an interesting fact that our subconscious mind has great trouble processing negative ideas. Even in our everyday communications we need to keep this fact in mind. "The successful hypnotherapist will always use positive thoughts." Compare the effect of this statement with its negative mate: "The successful hypnotherapist *never* uses *negative* suggestions" (two negatives).

Some professional people commit the sin of saying, *"Not infrequently"* such and such will happen. You almost always have to go back and read what has been said in order to realize that the writer was troubled by having to admit that *"fairly often"* such and such will happen. The "not infrequently" puts a hurdle in the way of the free flow of ideas.

Parents are constantly pounding *don't* and *never* words into their children's understandings. Negatives are usually understood by the child as directives, meaning that my mom expects me to do what she says not to do.

Optimistic Versus Pessimistic Suggestions

Commensurately, the expressed or implied feelings of the person giving suggestions are an important factor. Again, this consideration applies to everyday communication as well as our communications with frightened or hypnotized people. Physicians have a dreadful tendency to be so afraid of being wrong about a stated judgment that they inactivate the effect of an optimistic statement. The patient who has asked, "When will I go home after this operation?" may receive this watered down assurance: "You are in good condition. *If everything goes well*, you will be home in five days." "If" in this sentence translates subconsciously into *"He thinks something could go wrong."* *If* is a negative, pessimistic word because it is conditional.

Pessimism Overrides Optimism

We have known for many years that pessimistic ideas will take priority over optimistic ones. Now we know that feelings of guilt, rejection, and unworthiness can be registered and remembered from the time a mother realizes that she is pregnant. They continue throughout pregnancy. Any distress over outside threats such as poverty or a husband's insecurity about the pregnancy will create a feeling of being responsible and/or a feeling of being rejected. These firmly fixed ideas will influence perceptions and judgments in later life. They will remain unrecognized during ordinary conversational methods of analysis and psychotherapy.

Putting the Power of the Positive into Action

There are many attitudes and techniques that will help you use the power of the positive to the advantages of your patients.

1. *Use positive ideas and repeat them often.* The reason for this is that words directly or tacitly implying negative ideas have a very powerful impact on a hypnotized subject. Repetition is important in all phases of hypnotic communication with others. It is a different matter when you are using self-hypnosis. Do not repeat ideas at that time. Your own subconscious mind gets the idea the first time around and resents having you repeat your suggestions.

2. *Convince yourself that what you ask will be accomplished.* You will be increasingly successful with each experience in teaching a patient to use hypnosis. You are using a skill with words and a skill with presenting thoughts. That skill grows with practice and work. Notice, when you are starting to use hypnosis, how much your confidence or lack of it is transmitted in some way to your subjects. Your subjects will enter hypnosis more quickly and go more deeply when you treat them from the start as experts in using their own hypnosis.

You do not have to struggle. Set up ideomotor signals as discussed in Chapter 11. Tell your subjects to wait for unconscious signals and then begin your exploration for sources of their problems. All hypnosis is autohypnosis. You are helping patients use their own hypnosis.

Some people are critical of their abilities at first and may seem to be resistant. When this occurs, it is helpful to give them a relaxation exercise and then return to a formal induction before moving into using ideomotor responses.

3. *Say "please" instead of "I want you to."* All of us are rebels when we are commanded to do something for which we can see no good reason. Please offer suggestions in a way that indicates your respect for the subject's right to accept or reject what you are saying.

4. *Practice with the help of playback from a tape recorder.* It is helpful to try out giving suggestions to an imaginary subject while you record your words, timing, and voice tones. Give directions aimed at relaxation in two ways. Notice how you react when you listen to a playback of your voice saying: (1) "I want you now to relax more and more as I talk." Wait a few seconds before saying it this way: (2) "Please focus your attention on relaxing your shoulders progressively each time you breathe out."

5. *Introduce challenges appropriately.* A stage hypnotist will tell a highly selected hypnotic subject, "Your right arm is as heavy as lead. It is pulling right down. You can't resist. Try as hard as you can to lift that arm. You cannot do it!" In a place of entertainment this approach might be appropriate. In your office, however, challenges can be presented in softer terms and can be used to help a patient recognize forces that have been harmful in the past. Difficulty reacting to the challenge should always be followed by showing the subject how to get around a challenge, inventing imagery that can get the job done unconsciously. The following is an example of a permissively introduced challenge:

> "See if you can imagine a very heavy weight, like a New York City telephone book, hanging by a strap around your right wrist. Think to yourself, 'My arm is heavy, heavy as lead' until you notice that it is in fact heavy and is pulling downward. (Wait until you see the arm moving downward before saying . . .) "Now *try* to lift that arm. You can probably do it but will notice that it is not easy because of that negative word *try*. Go ahead and try to lift that arm."

When the subject recognizes the power of the challenge, he can be asked to imagine putting the telephone book down and substituting the sensation of having a large bunch of balloons tied to his right wrist. Add the thought of their lifting the arm higher and higher until it begins to move upward against the normal pull of gravity. This is a positively introduced lesson in finding a way around a challenge.

6. *Use permissive rather than authoritative suggestions.* Permissive suggestions are more likely to succeed with private patients. Authoritative suggestions often arouse feelings of rebellion and resentment. Authoritative commands are needed and are necessary when you are working with frightened, injured, or comatose people in emergency situations, but that is a restricted group.

7. *Use your normal voice as opposed to a monotone or crooning.* Most beginners are so concerned with what to say next that they speak in a low monotone. Often they sound sickeningly obsequious. Your patient may think you are courting him. It is helpful for you to go into a light trance state as you work with a patient, but avoid going so deep that your voice trails off and you go to sleep. Your patient will resent your seeming lack of respect.

Make your statements during an induction or during utilization of hypnosis with your normal voice. That is the voice your patient has known in relating to you. Don't change your modality.

8. *Control the timing of your words.* Leave space between your words to allow the meaning to sink in. Some hypnotists are like the famous Pat Collins, who is an excellent psychologist who talks so rapidly that her subjects have to go into a trance in order to follow her. Erickson, on the other hand, was a genius in presenting ideas with evenly spaced intervals between his words. Most of us tend to speak with an uneven tempo—saying some words more rapidly than others. Erickson's words were so evenly spaced that it is possible to understand him when his tape recording is running at twice normal speed.

9. *Use periodic silences to permit your subject to drift deeper.* Beginners have a tendency to say more than their subject wants to hear. You can safely use periods of silence lasting as much as 15 seconds. Repeating a phrase once or twice during that time will emphasize its impact. If you ask your patients for comments after a hypnotic session, you will often hear them say, "If you would stop talking I could relax more."

10. *Believe in the value of your suggestions and project this belief.* Telepathy seems to play a very important part in our communications with people just as it does when we are communicating with animals. This means that, like the door-to-door salesperson, you must first convince yourself about the value of your product (suggestion) or you will not get your foot in the door to demonstrate your wares. Tentative suggestions will probably be ignored.

Telepathy is only a part of the communication. If you believe in what you are saying, your voice inflection, intonation, and facial expressions are all sensed. In the early days of the telephone, operators were trained to smile as they ask, "Your number please." The human voice sounds pleasant when we form a smile with our facial muscles.

11. *Honestly believe that your patients will act on your suggestions.* Project your respect for your patients in thought, words, and gestures. Your belief in your patients' resources has a powerful effect in helping them overcome inner doubts. Envelope them with your confidence that they can use your suggestions and will probably invent their own suggestions to back yours up.

Keep this idea in mind even when you are practicing with friends and colleagues. I was unable to get consistent, verifiable accounts about operating room conversations until I phrased my questions as though I knew that something important had happened and I knew the patient could recall the details. Hypnotized people do not fabricate information at deep, ideomotor levels of perception and response. They will, however, shake their head or verbalize a "no" if you ask, "Do you hear anything while you are in the operating room?" Hypnotized subjects do not want to put out work.

An example of the lethargy and unwillingness to put out energy while semiconscious or while in a hypnotic state was the woman who slowly shook her head from side to side when the anesthetist said, "Can you hear me, Mrs. J.?" as we moved her out of the operating room. Obviously she heard. Later she explained that she knew some demands would be made if she nodded. She did not want to be bothered. This is another example of the differences between conscious and subconscious thinking.

Emile Coué's Laws of Suggestion—Reversed Effect

Coué made "autosuggestion" a household word during the first 20 years of the twentieth century. He was one of the first to point out what he termed the *"Law of Reversed Effect."* He said that when the imagination (fear of failure) and the will (I want to) are at war, the imagination will always win. He discovered this for himself when he was trying to stop a headache by saying to himself repeatedly, "My headache is going away." Instead of going away, it got worse. Finally he recognized the fact that he knew much more about headaches than he knew about removing them.

The reason for this law of reversed effect or reversed effort is probably related to the fact that every skill we learn as infants and children is preceded by many failures. When we finally succeed, what of it? Everybody else has been doing it much better.

The Teleology of the Unconscious Mind

Coué conjured with this concept of autosuggestion after watching the wonderful results effected by his friend Liebault, a physician who used very simple suggestions of well-being with his hypnotized subjects. Coué began to see positive changes in people who simply came to his meetings and listened but did nothing else. It occurred to him that there must be an underlying drive toward good health and survival in all of us and that the energy transmitted by groups of optimistic people in an environment of hope allowed this force of teleology to be activated. It is just our negative belief systems that create difficulties. In essence this teleology is ready to work for us when we direct our thoughts toward a goal. We need to remove the more superficial feelings of guilt, doubts and negative learnings.

The Concept of a Psychological Automatic Compass

Coué told his patients to get the mental image of a goal and to use his techniques to mobilize an automatic compass toward reaching that goal. He said, "Think of your unconscious mind working like the automatic compass on a ship. Set the destination course. Your unconscious mind will keep you on course, no matter how much the wind blows toward one side or the tide moves you the other way."

Coué was amazingly successful with the sick and troubled people who flocked to his home for treatment. His way of accessing the potential for their healing was to expose them to optimistic patients who already were getting well. He would come in after the crowd had absorbed an almost religious hopeful anticipation. He would talk quietly about resting well at night, having pleasant dreams, eating thoughtfully and having good elimination from kidneys and bowel.

He would then instruct them to keep repeating rapidly to themselves this statement: "Every day, in every way, I am getting better and better." He instructed them to say the words very rapidly in order to avoid paying attention to them consciously. He wanted them to carry out this ritual at night on drifting off to sleep and the first thing in the morning on awakening. These are times when the mind is more suggestible, he said. Coué wrote very little, but his work has been described well by Baudouin (1920) and Brooks (1922).

The statements in this chapter will take on more meaning for beginners after reading the rest of this book and after practicing simple inductions of hypnosis before moving on to therapeutic uses of hypnosis. I hope the statements are just allowed to simmer in your unconscious mind, rather than making you feel you must work at understanding them.

8

Self-Hypnosis

Hypnosis comes from within at times of danger, with lulling stimuli and with the help of others on the outside, but a valuable aspect of hypnosis is what we can learn to produce for our own use.

People can learn to review nighttime ideation to discover the origin of symptoms that are there when we awaken in the morning—asthma, headaches, abnormal bleeding, the feeling that makes us think we are "coming down with a cold."

Hypnosis and Pregnancy

Self-hypnosis can help pregnant women prepare for an easy, short labor. I have learned that the coaching in the office (Chapter 20) will not be of much value unless the patient practices turning on and turning off analgesia of her back and abdomen at home between office visits. Especially is this needed during the last four weeks of pregnancy. The exercise needs to be repeated four or more times a day until the woman has absolute confidence in what she is able to do.

Feto-Maternal Telepathic Communication

The fetus has been reading its mother's mind since conception. It tries to communicate with its mother but she is usually too concerned with her external world unless she puts herself into hypnosis and opens communications that can be very important for her peace of mind.

Fetal Movement

A baby often stops moving when it senses that the mother is worrying about something in her external world. The woman who is disturbed on noticing that her baby is not moving should put herself into hypnosis and visualize (tune in to) her baby before she calls her doctor or midwife. She can do this subliminally by asking for an ideomotor answer from her fingers to the question, "Are you all right in there?" This type of communication occurs at a very deep level of perception. In my experience since teaching patients how to ask, starting in 1960, there has never been an incorrect response. Patients have told me that they feel this effort seems to be much appreciated by their baby. It is another way of commencing maternal infant bonding prior to delivery. (For more on feto-maternal communication see Cheek 1992.)

The second-best action when the baby is not moving is for the mother to put herself into hypnosis with relaxation suggestions during a space of 5 minutes. Maternal relaxation seems to reassure the fetus and it will begin to move actively.

Case Example

A woman in the last month of her pregnancy was threatened by her doctor when she refused to let him induce labor. He had told her that she could not come into his hospital if she did not comply with his decision to take action. She was weeping when she called for advice. I pointed out that she had been an excellent hypnotic subject and said to her, "How about going home, putting yourself into hypnosis and having a chat with your baby?"

She called the next day immediately after giving birth. "He said that he would be ready tomorrow morning. We have just delivered." Until the moment of communicating with her baby she had not known he was a male.

Help with Postpartum Adjustment

Two to five minutes of self-hypnosis four times a day can help overcome fatigue and prevent the onset of postpartum "blues," especially for mothers of twins or a second baby. An older sibling can make excessive demands for attention. Such mothers will still be feeling composed and energetic in the evening.

Lost Articles

Self-hypnosis is valuable at a time of great anxiety over inability to find keys, jewelry, important documents or a valued book. It is also useful in anxiety-provoking situations in which sustained attention is important.

If questioning with a pendulum indicates that you are not punishing yourself or someone else and if it does not reveal the place to look, then is the time for a 10-minute period of self-hypnosis after asking the subconscious mind to lead you to the time and place you last held that object in your hand—or hands (remember the literalness of understanding in hypnosis). Ask your "yes" finger to lift when you are at that moment and for the thought to come to you consciously when your finger lifts. Ask for outside help if this much is not enough. Sometimes people convince themselves in frustration with the thought, "I'll *never* find it!"

Our attention begins to fade in the classroom or when we are working at learning something from books. When we try to continue with attention past a 20-minute limit, we are doing so with a tired mind. Self-hypnosis has proven its value when I have worked with attorneys who have failed their state examinations. It has been much appreciated by graduate students of psychology and medicine.

I teach each individual to be able to go into hypnosis very quickly—usually within 20 seconds.

1. I instruct them to time their reading or their studying with an electric timer as a reminder to put the book or notebook face down on their lap while they review what has been covered.
2. They then review the 20 minutes of information they have absorbed subconsciously. They are told to avoid the effort to remember details consciously.
3. They are to have their "yes" finger lift at the beginning of the first page of reading. The "no" finger is to lift unconsciously each time they come to something that would be good to remember, and their "I don't want to answer" finger is to lift when they have reached the end of the 20-minute segment of reading.
4. They are to scan the 20-minute period *three times* because there will be additional material related to the original dominant ones during the second and third review.
5. With a little practice, the review of 20 minute study or reading will take as little as 2 minutes that are well spent because the material will be firmly set in subconscious memory, ready for retrieval at a later time. In addition, the reader has been recharging energy and will be totally

alert instead of tired during the second and subsequent 20-minute segments of study.

Self-Hypnosis as Taught to Surgical and Obstetrical Patients

It is virtually impossible for people who have never experienced hypnosis to teach themselves hypnosis. We all have been heavily indoctrinated since birth with the idea that no new learning can occur unless someone teaches us. Any effort to try without training seems to evoke Coué's Law of Reversed Effect. Someone else, using any form of induction needs to help students of self-hypnosis overcome their fear of failure and then build confidence in going back into hypnosis unaided.

This is the method I have used after a patient has experienced a light to medium level of hypnosis and has an idea how it feels. Finger signals are selected by the patient if this has not already been done: "yes," "no," and "I don't want to answer." The signals will all be given by the fingers of one hand. I like to have the right hand used for this because pressure between the tips of the left index finger and thumb will later be used for immediate entrance into hypnosis and the right hand will be used to answer questions or specific fingers on that hand will lift to indicate jobs that have been completed.

I ask the patient to hold a pen between the finger tips of the right hand. These are my directions:

1. "Always, at first, ask permission from your subconscious mind. You can just think to yourself. You do not have to speak the words; 'Will it be all right for me now to go into hypnosis for 2 minutes from the time I drop this pen?'

   "Wait until your 'yes' finger lifts. It usually will lift within 20 seconds. The interval between the question and your answer allows you to mentally shift gears into a readiness for hypnosis. If a finger says 'no,' you can stop and come back later. This might not be a good time to do it."

2. "When you feel your 'yes' finger lifting, add this thought: 'When I am deep enough to use hypnosis *helpfully*, I would like my fingers to pull apart to drop this pen. Two minutes from the time it drops I will awaken *feeling good.*'" Do not repeat the suggestion. Repetition is good when you work with somebody else but a subconscious mind is paying attention the first time. It will resent a parental sort of nudge with repetition. You have had that a lot when you were a kid."

3. "After thinking this statement, get a mental image of a lighted candle as though it were on a table across the room. Watch the slight

movements of the flame until your fingers pull apart. When the pen drops, let your mind go anywhere it wants to."

4. "The purpose of this exercise is simply to have you relax and to recharge your energies. Later you will be able to go quickly into hypnosis without dropping anything. You could have your 'yes' finger on the other hand be your signal for being in and it could lift to let you know when the time is up. When you sense that your selected time has come to an end, open your eyes to break the pattern of hypnosis. Otherwise it might feel so good that you will just fall asleep and take a nap. Your subconscious mind is pretty lazy when you are in hypnosis. I want you to use just short times for hypnosis so that you get a lot from brief moments in this state."

The specific uses of self-hypnosis for obstetrical patients are outlined in Chapter 20; for surgical patients in Chapter 21. In a general way it can be used for diminishing the physical and emotional fatigue that can occur with humans who do not or cannot break the tempo of their day with an after-lunch siesta.

A cardiologist in Seattle told me that results of fragmentary rest periods in self-hypnosis had greatly improved results with his postcoronary patients. He had made them take ten-second "breaks" in self-hypnosis whenever they had a few moments of freedom from activity. The only suggestion used by them was associated with the word "relax" as they pressed their left thumb and index finger together as a signal to relax.

Is Self-Hypnosis Habit-Forming or Dangerous?

I believe the answer to this question is that we are all pretty expert in unconsciously using self-hypnosis to impress ourselves with our unhappiness, our lack of loving understanding from our peers. Thurber called this type of self hypnosis "circular brooding."

Self-hypnosis is not habit-forming in the sense of being harmful. It does not weaken the mind of the user.

Risk of using self-hypnosis harmfully to ourselves is possible, just as with poorly constructed meditation. The risk is minimal if we word our instructions to include the "helpful" use of hypnosis.

9

Is Hypnosis Dangerous?

Just twice in my nearly 50 years of using hypnosis have I felt that hypnosis might be dangerous. In both cases the danger was personal, my own. The cause was my failure to recognize unconscious distress before the reason for distress reached consciousness.

Dangers of Touch Induction

With the widespread recognition that hypnosis can be used for stress management, athletics, and a host of other possibilities there is an exploding population of hypnotists who have very little knowledge of potential dangers in its use. Males and females who have been physically or sexually abused as children can "freak out" during an induction of hypnosis, particularly an induction that involves the hypnotist touching the subject.

I have seen demonstrations of so-called "nonverbal inductions" that are traditional for stage hypnotists and unlikely to be dangerous for the adroit hypnotist who is working in front of an audience. Hands-on inductions could be very risky, however, to an inexperienced enthusiast trying it with a client in the privacy of an office. It is potentially dangerous, regardless of the sex of the client.

It is unwise to touch anyone before stating what will be done and obtaining permission for the action. All of the nonverbal methods depend on confusing the subject by manipulations of fingers and wrists and unusual positioning of the arms. When the operator finds catalepsy occurring, he or she knows that the subject will uncritically accept suggestions. This can tempt the operator to take advantage sexually of a seemingly passive subject, who will later be furious on awakening and can either involve the

operator in a civil suit or be the cause of his or her losing a license to practice. Audiotaping of such an induction and conduct of therapy would be
no protection in court.

Danger of Induction Triggering Disturbing Associations

What I am saying about actually mistreating a patient or client is easy to
understand. What is much more subtle is what can happen to a perfectly
innocent hypnotist who does not know that a rape, traumatic childhood
molestation or satanic ritual has occurred.

In the first of my two disturbing experiences, I assumed, incorrectly,
that the woman who referred a patient to me would have mentioned that
I might use hypnosis to help with her problems. I have learned that I can
never safely make such an assumption. In the second case, a dentist in an
advanced course on hypnotherapy asked me to help him discover what had
happened during a "blackout" on a training mission in World War II. His
request came from his conscious mind; I failed to ask his unconscious mind
if he would permit me to help him recover the memory after he had entered
a medium hypnotic state.

Since these two uncomfortable experiences prior to 1960, I have been
very careful to watch respiratory movements and pulsation of neck vessels
during inductions of hypnosis (Cheek 1960c). I am careful about asking subconscious permission for each step of an exploration.

Reaction must be swift, however, because there is a very short time lag
between physiological expressions of stress and the moment a frown and
tightening of jaw muscles become visible. By that time the potentially
dangerous thought associations are very close to conscious awareness.

A Way of Diminishing Chance of Unpleasant Identification

On seeing accelerated breathing and pulsations of neck vessels, I back off
and ask the patient to come out of hypnosis. This is when a pendulum is
very helpful because the patient is no longer in hypnosis. The time orientation is to the time of interview. My verbalization is as follows:

1. "You looked troubled just now. Let me ask the pendulum, 'Were you
   remembering some troublesome experience before I asked you to come
   out of hypnosis?'" This question clearly defines the time boundaries.
   The patient and I are here in my office. The troublesome event is back
   there in the past. The answer will either be "yes" or "I don't want to
   answer." The next question:

2. "Would it be all right for you to know what bothered you?" The answer is usually "yes" with the pendulum. The next question is:
3. "Would it be all right for you to leave that experience back there and use hypnosis comfortably up here while we work here in my office?" (This shifts the time orientation away from the original event.)

These steps have worked very well with my patients over the years. The goal in this questioning procedure is to have the patient work as a colleague in a therapeutic process and avoid having him or her feel pressure to produce information for an authority figure.

Uses of ideomotor questioning techniques will be discussed throughout the remainder of this book. For the moment, see if you can picture the situation I will be describing in these two cases. Put yourself in my position at that time.

Case #1

A 32-year-old married woman I will call "Jackie" (not her name) is suffering from low back pain, fatigue, severe menstrual pain, chronic vaginal discharge, and pain with intercourse. The gynecologist in her city had decided, after months of futile standard care, that it would take a hysterectomy to bring about a cure. A former patient of mine who had moved to Jackie's city wanted her to get a second opinion from me before having such drastic surgery.

The history Jackie gave me strongly suggested the major cause might be her relationship with her husband rather than a physical disability. The physical examination substantiated my speculation. I could find no justification for removing her uterus. Consequently I suggested some psychological evaluation at another appointment. Jackie seemed to approve of this idea and appeared to be friendly and cooperative. I explained that back and pelvic muscles react very strongly to emotional stresses. Further discussion after she dressed gave additional information that she had been finding her work situation stressful.

I made some notes in her chart while she went out to make an appointment with my secretary. I looked into the waiting room for my next patient, who had not yet arrived. Thinking I might at least show my patient a little about muscle relaxation and about turning down the volume of pain, I returned to the secretary's position in the office. Jackie was turned with her back toward me. I touched her shoulder to attract her attention as she was given her appointment card and said, "I have a moment before the next patient comes in. I would like to show you something about muscles. Please hold your arms up (I demonstrated how she should do this.) Close your eyes and pay attention to the feeling of your right arm. Imagine you have your purse hanging on your wrist, pulling that arm down toward the floor.''

She complied with that suggestion. I added, ''Give your own suggestion, 'My arm is heavy, pulling down, down toward the floor.''' Her right arm began to move slowly downward. I could see her eyelids start to flutter (a sign of her entering a light hypnotic state).

Then, she clenched her jaw muscles and turned on me with fire in her eyes, saying, ''I came down here to get some help with my pain!'' She stormed out of the office, slamming the glass door as she left. My secretary and I were stunned. Neither of us could understand the reaction.

Two weeks later I received a letter of apology from Jackie. She said that while standing in my office she had suddenly been overwhelmed with a feeling of mixed fear and hostility toward me. It was not until she had nearly reached her home that the image of herself as an 11-year-old youngster, crossing an empty lot on the way home from school late in the afternoon, had entered her mind.

She said that she had heard someone running behind her, felt a hand grab her shoulder. She knew that this must be a sexual attack. She fainted, and her appearance must have frightened the man, she said, because he ran away.

She was reporting a 22-year-old flashback emotional experience that had been triggered by the combination of my touching her shoulder just as she started to enter a light trance while imagining a weight on her right arm. She identified me with the stranger and reacted angrily instead of fainting during this state-dependent moment. She went on in her letter to ask, ''I wonder if I went into hypnosis at that time?''

I wrote a thank-you letter in response and told her that her guess was probably correct. Jackie referred two other patients to me, but she did not keep her appointment and did not communicate further with me. Apparently there was residual hostility that she could not remove. I wondered if some of her physical problems might have related to this imprinted sexual fear rather than poor communication with her husband but did not have a chance to search further.

Case #2

The dentist at an advanced workshop asked me to explore his two-hour black-out while pilot of a bomber in flight. He had landed successfully but was having troubled dreams about what could have happened during that blank period of time.

This seemed like a good opportunity to show how ideomotor review methods can break through conscious amnesia. At the next part of the program I asked him to come up on the platform and sit next to me.

He explained his blackout, saying that he was pilot of a bomber plane, part of a squadron being transferred from Texas to Salt Lake, Utah. They were not carrying oxygen because they anticipated a simple journey at 12,000 to 15,000 feet elevation. Soon after takeoff, however, they ran into clouds. It had appeared to the dentist that the clouds represented a thunderstorm and that the squadron should have turned back but the commanding officer ordered them to climb. At 18,000 feet he saw clouds rising much higher ahead. It is dangerous to fly higher without supplementary oxygen which no one had in their planes.

The commanding officer ordered them to maintain the elevation but to separate in order not to collide with each other. At this point the dentist said he could not remember what happened after that.

I used a simple induction of hypnosis involving eye fixation and suggestions of relaxation. He entered hypnosis easily and set up finger signals. I asked him to go to the moment he was ordered to deploy in the cloud bank. He immediately began to look angry. His finger lifted to indicate the moment. He said, "Another plane comes out of the darkness and zips right across my path. I am shocked! This is not supposed to happen. That's when I black out."

By this time he was growling. He pulled away from me as I asked him to go on and wait for further impressions to come up to where he could talk about them. He clearly was identifying me with his commanding officer. It seemed wise to discontinue the regression and ask him to come out of hypnosis.

The dentist recognized what had occurred. We talked about it. He continued to add that the "S.O.B. flight commander should have ordered us to return to base." Six of the planes crashed, he said. Then he added "He got his—he crashed in France and broke his leg."

This experience turned out all right, but the dentist was angry with me until the third day of the workshop. He taught me an excellent lesson.

Comment

An unexpected abreaction can disturb a neophyte but is not really a danger. The pros and cons of calculated abreaction as a therapeutic process are discussed in Chapter 12.

There really are minimal risks of danger to the patient when we are using permissive tactics in our communications and are careful to ask permission for each step of the procedure. Authoritative, manipulative therapy can make a patient angry and resistant.

Physicians and surgeons who are not using hypnosis are at greater risk of doing harm to their patients when they perform treatments that have not been adequately discussed and have failed to be aware that their patients might be troubled by the chosen course of action. With the exception of emergencies such as a ruptured tubal pregnancy or an appendicitis it is wise always to give patients plenty of time and an opportunity to obtain other opinions before scheduling surgery.

10

An Orientation to Medical Hypnosis

Factors in the Concept of Therapeutic Hypnosis

A working concept about the meaning of hypnosis might be that it is a state dependent phenomenon occurring in all forms of life. It appears to have evolved to maintain species survival in the presence of danger and privation. An animal facing danger from predators goes into a state resembling hypnosis. It will be storing information about how it responds to the sensory stimuli coming into its nervous system at that time. The patterned behavior will vanish if escape efforts fail and it succumbs. The behavior will instantly be called back into action, however, if similar stimuli occur in the future.

The awareness of danger is the state phenomenon. Evolutionary needs in humans seem to have decreed that the state we call hypnosis will cause a flashback of subconscious memory to frightening experiences during which a trance state has occurred spontaneously. It is this state-dependent phenomenon that makes hypnosis such a valuable tool in psychiatry and in our search for better understanding of psychosomatic diseases. Memory patterns that are permanently stored in subconscious memory in association with real or imagined danger are the sources of most human problems of disturbed adaptation.

Therapeutic hypnosis is not a mysterious force exerted by one person to manipulate another person. It is a valuable tool for discovery and for the reassessment of maladaptive behavior. It is a force that permits troubled people to use their powerful resources successfully in the pursuit of good health.

Much more than this is the fact that the functions of immunity, healing and regulation of hormonal balance in the body are enhanced when humans are deeply hypnotized. Suggestions for this need not be given. We give suggestions, however, because this act projects our confidence in the patient being able to use these built-in regulatory mechanisms.

Connectedness to Environment at All Times

It now seems clear to us that the subconscious mind retains connections with external environment during sleep (Oswald 1960), unconsciousness from trauma (Erickson, 1937) or chemicals (Cheek, 1959a), after fainting, and even during a catatonic state. The connection may be telepathically but certainly involves the eighth cranial nerve mechanisms of hearing and position sense as well as a tactile, vibratory sensitivity.

Hibernation, a Survival Mechanism

We reason that hibernation is also a form of hypnotic behavior occurring spontaneously in nature. All plant and animal species, including forms in a nether world of fungi, bacteria and viruses seem capable of entering a resting state to bridge periods of privation. Hibernating or aestivating forms of animal life "know" when conditions are more favorable and will resume normal activity. Deciduous trees become dormant by "knowing" in some way that winter is coming as was demonstrated by Burr (1972) in his studies of the electromagnetic force fields of trees. Short-lived plant forms put out seeds that seem to know when to germinate; other plants store food in bulbs that sense when the weather will become favorable for regrowth. Primitive, dipnoid fish of Africa, South America, and Australia can dig into the mud at the end of the rainy season and remain safely for several months without food, water, or appreciable amounts of air. We do not know what their communications are, but they, like humans in a hypnotic trance, are immobile, with lowered metabolism and the capability to reactivate energy when favorable signals are perceived from the environment.

Lulling Stimuli and Hypnosis:
Mesmerism and Nursing

Hypnosis can occur spontaneously with repeated, unimportant stimuli such as the hum of an automobile engine on a straight road on a warm day. It can occur with highway driving in fog, when it is raining, or when it is snowing. The driver may go into a trancelike state watching wisps of fog coming in at the windshield, or the windshield wiper swinging across his visual field, or snowflakes pulling his eyes downward as they come down toward the windshield. Highway hypnosis is dangerous because the driver's reactions are slower, the visual fields are diminished, and the driver may ignore warnings such as a car slowing down in his lane or another moving in from the side. These are phenomena shared with those found when hypnosis is induced artificially.

Lulling auditory and tactile stimuli are valuable for a newborn infant while being nursed by its mother, whose appearance and relative immobility at this time are typical of hypnosis. Herbivorous mammal mothers lick their newborn infants from the head to the genital region and carnivore mothers lick their young again after each nursing period. Ashley Montagu (1962, 1971) has written about the importance of skin stimulation.

Spontaneous Hypnosis Caused by Danger

Humans enter a hypnotic state spontaneously in the presence of great danger, when they are disoriented during an earthquake or an explosion, or when losing consciousness under any circumstance. At such times they may be immobile with their eyes open or closed. They may be unable to speak. If we gently move their arm, it may remain in a cataleptic immobility when we take our hand away.

If left alone at such a time, free of frightening sounds or conversations, the physiological responses to the catastrophic stress will be useful. Bleeding from a wound will stop; respiration and pulse rate will be slow or imperceptible. If the individual is moving, his movements will be slow, his head will be bent forward, and his back will be curved forward. Although appearing unresponsive on the outside, the unconscious or dazed person is always highly responsive to touch and to verbal communications. A remark such as "This one won't make it" may precipitate massive bleeding and may even be lethal. If you touch a shoulder firmly or put your hand on the forehead of a seemingly insensate person, you can attract his attention to your directions for constructive action in the future, saying something like, "You're going to be all right. The ambulance is on its way. Keep on relaxing," as is discussed in the chapter on emergency uses of hypnosis. An apparently unconscious person who has been alarmed by bystander remarks and starts bleeding can stop a hemorrhage within seconds when an ambulance driver orders him confidently to take a deep breath and stop that bleeding (Jacobs 1991).

Protective Power of Deep Hypnosis that Blocks Subconscious Pain

James Esdaile (1851–1902) taught us that the hypnotic state he induced in the mid-1840s to permit painless surgery had powerful healing qualities also.

He noticed that swelling, redness and local heat disappeared when pain was removed by his mesmeric passes over the face and body. His 50 percent surgical mortality from hemorrhage, shock and infection dropped to 5 percent, long before the advent of sterile surgical preparation and use of drugs to diminish anxiety in surgical patients.

A human exposed to freezing temperatures will fall into a hypnotic like resting state before freezing to death. This state can also occur with other conditions where death seems imminent, as was pointed out by Livingstone (1858) when he was being mauled by a wounded lion. As discussed earlier, he commented on what seemed to him was a "merciful provision by our benevolent Creator" for lessening the pain of death. Certainly it is true that those who have had near death experiences have all recognized the peaceful experience and the effort it takes to come back to the living.

An opossum caught in its natural environment by a dog will struggle awhile and then suddenly appear to be long dead. Its skin temperture drops to that of its surroundings, its eyes glaze over, and it loses all reflexes except that of its prehensile tail. The effect of this sudden change is to shock the dog and cause it possibly to drop this disturbing, cold thing and go looking for the real opossum that seems to have escaped. Though seemingly insensate, the opossum knows when the dog has gone far enough away for it to reconstitute circulation and escape into the forest or up a tree. It probably senses the Doppler effect of vibrations caused by the distancing canine footsteps.

Shock and Coagulation Mechanisms

This response of the opossum is probably comparable to surgical shock, in which there is massive intravascular coagulation at a time of great stress. Release of fibrinolytic enzymes from platelets and endothelium digests coagulated blood to permit the circulation to recommence. McKay (1965) and others have suggested that human shock as found in eclampsia, placental separation, and the generalized Schwartzman-Sanarelli phenomenon are all due to intravascular coagulation. John Hunter reported on the interesting fact that human beings who are killed suddenly will have fluid blood in their vessels and that this blood does not coagulate when removed from the body. His report on "The Blood and Gunshot Wounds" was published by the British Royal Society in 1794 after his death. The fluidity of blood observed by Hunter was caused by massive release of fibrinolytic enzymes.

Cadaver Blood Bank in Moscow: Its Significance

One century later, Yudine (1935) in Moscow created the first cadaver blood bank using the blood of people who had been killed suddenly at a time when they might have been fearful before dying during the purges ordered by Stalin. The value of his rather isolated contribution is that about 18 units of blood can be removed from a large donor. When this blood is transfused into a patient, there is only one possible reaction of immune response. With 18 units drawn from 18 separate donors there would be 18 chances for the recipient to react harmfully against the blood he received. There would be a greatly diminished chance for infection from a hepatitis virus or one of the viruses causing AIDS using blood from one donor.

Varying Manifestations of Hypnosis: Clinical Significance

Hypnotic phenomena are widely diverse. We have resting states, limitation of motion, high pain tolerance, increased immune responses, augmented coagulability of blood and massive intravascular coagulation followed by rebound fibrinolysis. Now we should think about threatening situations present with human beings while asleep, while unconscious with an anesthetic, or while hearing careless conversation in the operating room. We can begin to understand how pregnant women can hear about problems a friend is having with a pregnancy and include worry about this matter in her dreams, with a resulting pyramiding stress reaction that can threaten the existence of her unborn child. We can begin to understand the dangers of unfavorable identification with significant relatives who have had heart attacks, emphysema, asthma, and so on.

Familial Disease: Clinical Versus Subclinical, Fact or Fancy?

There is reason to believe that some, if not all, of the so-called familial diseases could be due to the continuing beliefs that "because he or she has it I will have it also." Tuberculosis was once thought to "run in families" as though it were a genetic tendency.

There is clear evidence with truly genetically transferred potential disease such as psoriasis or hemophilia that the potential does not manifest itself unless evoked by external stresses. Hypnosis is helpful in revealing the source of causal stress. The victim of genetically transferred absence of a clotting factor can learn to control his hemorrhaging tendency and thus avoid the risks of type B hepatitis or HIV infection from human blood transfusions of plasma containing the missing coagulation factor.

Significance of Imprinting

Konrad Lorenz (1935) has pointed out that greylag goslings, conditioned by the mother's answer to their lost piping sound after hatching, will imprint on and follow a moving piece of wood on a string as they enter the water. They will not follow the mother thereafter. Lorenz called this phenomenon, a short-term learning process that does not fade with time, "pragung," meaning stamping in or imprinting like striking a coin.

Imprinting has engaged the interest of ethologists, zoologists, and psychologists (Sluckin 1965). Survival of fledglings among ground nesting birds depends on their recognition and following of the significant parent. Going to the wrong parent in a feeding area may be fatal. Imprinting seems also to occur with mammals (Hess 1958). Imprinting definitely occurs with humans and seems to be a fundamental factor in maladaptive behavior. Spiegel (1960) has compared a causal imprint to a classical posthypnotic suggestion. There is a compulsion to carry out patterned behavior, amnesia for the original stimulus and rationalization for the compulsive action.

Epinephrine: Imprinting of Memory

The role of epinephrine in fixation of a patterned response to a frightening stimulus has been clinically clear during age-regression studies using ideomotor search methods (Cheek 1975). McGaugh and colleagues (1984) documented information regarding the role of epinephrine in the learning process, substantiating what we have known clinically.

There is now evidence from studies of anesthetized rats that epinephrine imprints an avoidance response when coupled with painful muscle stimulus and a sound (Weinberger, Gold, and Sternberg 1984). The response of avoidance will be evoked by the sound after recovery from the anesthetic if an injection of epinephrine has been given prior to the combined muscle shock and sound. It will not occur when epinephrine has not been associated with the combined stimuli.

It is beginning to appear likely that experiences or misunderstandings of experiences at birth, at times of great stress, and during periods of unconsciousness may be single-impact producers of patterned behavior. These may be harmful to the human instead of helpful as they seem to be for lower orders of animals. With the tools available now, with better understanding of ideomotor activity, we seem to be approaching sources of learning that are identical with or very similar to the imprinting of Lorenz. We are learning how to communicate better and are opening wide horizons for research into the physiological and psychological interconnections of mind and body. We are learning from patients how best to communicate hope and what mechanisms and uses of words can destroy hope and crush the will to live.

Mimicry and Learning

The feature of mimicry as a learning process is seen in all birds and mammals that care for their young. At times of danger the young become silent and immobile. They turn to the parent and mimic the behavior of the parent, or they remain immobile while the parent either attacks or leads the enemy away. These facets of restricted attention, immobility, silence, and mimicry for animals in danger are classical features of hypnotic behavior.

Subconscious Pain Perception

A boil in the skin is intensely painful. The center is devoid of circulation and is surrounded by lymph fluid containing protective white cells and fibrin, effectively walling off the infection from the general circulation. If the boil is painful enough, the surrounding muscles may be rigidly contracted to further diminish the spread of infection. The very same tissue reaction will be found in an abscess of the liver or the brain, and yet there may be no sense of pain. The brain has had no training for painful stimuli in liver or brain.

George Crile, Sr. and W. E. Lower (1914) observed that a general anesthetic does not interrupt noxious stimuli. There seems to be total body awareness. The human brain seems to monitor every tissue of our body at all times, whether we are awake, asleep, or unconscious. Cheek (1962d) has called this subliminal awareness of tissue damage "subconscious pain." Hilgard (1975) has called this "the hidden observer." It appears to be the reason for once injured tissues to retain a hypersensitive, smoldering, subliminal awareness that breaks upward to consciousness in cyclical way in recurring back pain, bursitis, rheumatism, and hemorrhagic colitis.

We as therapists can help troubled people recover from physical disease as well as emotional problems when we give them the courage to fight back, to find the sources of maladaptive responses, to correct negative early life impressions, and to hold on to a selected future goal of good health.

11

Uncovering Methods

Carl Jung has said in reference to the ideas of Freud, "We know that in the mind of a creator of new ideas, things are much more fluid and flexible than they are in the minds of his followers." This is a thought we should hold.

Methods of treating psychosomatic illness, neurosis, and other emotionally caused conditions are by no means standardized, nor can they be claimed to be as successful as therapists wish. We have close to 200 methods available to us, each with its own language, each with its gifted originator. The followers may not be as gifted or as aware that all people have the resources to heal themselves and that psychotherapists are there to offer encouragement and to help remove obstacles. They cannot *always* remove the obstacles. The number of therapeutic successes will diminish, therefore, with any new formula of treatment. Every conscientious therapist will be more depressingly influenced by failures than by the grateful patients who improve. This fact will have a dampening influence on the unconscious messages a therapist transmits to new patients while using someone else's method of treatment.

For many years, since the beginning of this century, Freudian concepts have been accepted, mainly in English-speaking countries. Eventually some of Freud's ideas have been modified and some discarded. Many therapists do not believe, as Freud did, that everything is based on childhood conditioning, with emphasis on sex. They look more to present happenings as the genesis of many conditions, and they attempt to modify troubled behavior in various ways. Some of these efforts to work with the "here and now," such as operant conditioning, cognitive therapy, behavior modification, reciprocal inhibition, and psychodrama, have been widely used.

Freud, Otto Rank, and Nandor Fodor seemed to be aware of the importance of birth trauma in subsequent human behavior, but conversational hypnotic techniques of search and the analysis of dreams were not adequate for the job of discovery and the consistent reframing of birth memories.

LeCron's contribution, the use of unconscious gestures to permit scanning of information available below conscious awareness, has reopened the idea of trauma as causal in production of human maladaptive behavior and will, I believe, greatly simplify the treatment of human dis-ease. Before enlarging on this point and the methods of therapy derived from the work of LeCron, we need to look at some other avenues of information.

Projective Techniques

Hypnotized patients will sometimes reveal valuable information when they are asked to imagine sitting in a theater watching actors in a meaningful scene from the viewer's life. The mechanism has eventually shifted to watching scenes on a television screen, but a lighted stage with living actors seems to have a more powerful effect. The hypnotized subject is safely watching the action with the audience in a darkened theater.

Revelations and their effect are subjective. There is no adequate means of learning about their validity. Are they fabricated to please the therapist? Are they screen memories to obscure the real sources of trouble?

Projection into the Future

Hypnotized patients who may be blocking efforts to discover an initial imprint experience can sometimes hallucinate a future time when they have been perfectly well and free of fears that an illness might return. They can signal when this time orientation has occurred and then look back at how it happened. LeCron used this pseudo-orientation with an excellent hypnotic patient who was anxious and depressed. Therapy was not progressing.

At the next visit, LeCron shifted him forward 10 years and said, "It's been a long time. I don't have your record here with me. What was it I did to help you become completely well?"

His patient rattled off a number of comments about the progress of his therapy while LeCron wrote them down in his record. He gave the man an appointment for the next week. His patient had total amnesia for having talked to LeCron about this. When the patient came back, LeCron helped him get into hypnosis and then gave back to the man the detailed statements he had committed to notes in this man's chart. The man's recovery was rapid and permanent, but the value came from the patient's sifting and reorganizing what LeCron had been doing; it did not reveal causal events in the man's life.

Automatic Writing

Automatic writing can be useful in gaining access to otherwise inaccessible information, but it is a skill that is not readily learned. It is a most interesting phenomenon, consisting of placing a ballpoint or fine felt-tip pen in the hand of a hypnotized subject while his mind is diverted from the hand. This allows his subconscious mind to take control of the hand. In automatic writing the subject may not consciously know what is being written until he reads it later. He may read something while the hand busily writes.

Automatic writing may be very rapid, with the hand racing across the paper, or it may be very slow. The handwriting never looks like the person's normal writing. Rarely are words separated. They will be run together. Further economy of action involves omission of dotted *i*'s and crossing of *t*'s. This makes the writing difficult to read. Sometimes the letters are not clearly formed. The subconscious mind takes shortcuts and may write cryptically. The word *before* might be written "B4"; a figure 2 or the word *to* may appear for any of its three meanings. The writing may be performed in a normal way from left to right or might be upside down, backward, mirror writing, or a combination of all these styles.

Anita Mühl (LeCron 1952), a psychiatrist, was the leading authority on automatic writing and used it continually in her therapy. She claimed to be able to teach it successfully to 80 percent of her patients, though this might require 20 or 30 hours of practice. Others have not had such good results or have felt the time and effort involved in the training were not justified.

In our workshop demonstrations, we started with the development of arm levitation and a graduated series of directions of subconscious energy from the mind, down the arm to the hand and fingers. The process started with first writing in the air and watching the after-image as though writing with a sparkler on a Fourth of July night. When this was successful we placed the subject at a table with a large piece of paper held in place with masking tape. The subject was given a felt-tip pen to hold in his normal writing hand. He was asked to initiate the process by making an *x*, leaving the pen at that spot and allowing subconscious energy to flow down the arm and eventually move his hand to write something about a subject such as "mother."

We asked the subject to imagine the sensation he might have had in school practicing penmanship exercises when the teacher is gently guiding his wrist. Very good hypnotic subjects do well with automatic writing. I have found only a third of my patients able to learn, and some who learn are not motivated enough to work with this skill at home.

Automatic writing at home can be done at an optimum time for the subject and costs him nothing. In addition, each period of 10 or 15 minutes devoted to the process allows the patient to relax and mobilize information that can be used at the next office visit. I instruct the patient to start with

a brief autohypnotic relaxation period of a minute or two and the suggestion "I would like my subconscious mind to write something helpful about
(name the topic) after I make a mark on this paper. I will awaken from hypnosis at the end of (x number of minutes) feeling comfortable and relaxed."

Even under the best of circumstances, however, automatic writing can
have the same pitfalls as the time-honored conversational techniques of
psychotherapy. The patient in hypnosis at home may block on accessing
significant material and may spend hours writing about nonsense or may
spend the time writing depressing or self-deprecating thoughts.

Group Hypnotherapy: Hypnodrama

J. L.Moreno developed the use of group therapy into what is now called
hypnodrama (1950). Moreno, a psychiatrist trained in Europe before World
War I, was a master of the techniques he developed for having troubled
people witness their actions and feelings as they were acted out by another
member of the group trying to play their part. He would turn the situation
around to have the patient play the part of himself or herself, interacting
with other members of the family, who would trade positions. Hypnosis
occurs spontaneously without any formal method of induction during these
sessions. Remarkable insights would occur. Other members of the group
also enter hypnosis while watching the action. I remember being oblivious
to the fact that Moreno's wife, a consummate actress, was without one of
her arms as she took on the part of an adolescent son of the demonstration
father.

Ira Greenberg (1977) has put together an excellent book about hypnodrama. This form of searching for causal events in life, however, is the
province of gifted, psychically endowed people. Even under the best of circumstances, I believe, the primal causes of maladaptive behavior will escape
discovery. The value of the modality appears to lie in helping people deal
with interpersonal communications and interpretations of the present time.

Ideomotor Questioning Methods

LeCron (1954) believed that ideation reflected by unconscious gestures, or
ideomotor responses, was the most valuable means of rapidly uncovering
significant causal experiences in emotional and psychosomatic problems.

Sources of resistance can be discovered and corrected during the first
interview. The persistently resistant patient can be spared continued un-
productive and costly therapeutic efforts.

The technique consists of wording questions in such a way that they can be answered with simple, "yes" or "no" unconscious symbol answers with a pendulum or fingers. LeCron explained that this mechanism is similar to the ordinary way we nod or shake our heads when we agree or disagree with someone. The movements of our head in this instance are always repetitive and we are consciously unaware that we are using this means of communication.

There are differing levels of perception and response that can be observed when we talk to unhypnotized people during a friendly visit. For example, "Will you have lunch with me next Wednesday?" may evoke a verbal "Yes" while your friend is unconsciously moving his head from side to side in contradiction. In such an instance you will usually find that "something has come up" and there will be no friend there on Wednesday. Another form of differing communication is the verbal one of saying, "I will *try* to get to that meeting of the Tiger Lodge tomorrow." Any secretary trying to improve attendance will know immediately that this person will fail to appear. We do not use the word *try* when we honestly agree to be present at a meeting.

A level of response is shifted deeper into subconscious zones when we move away from the head and depend on hand and arm movements with a pendulum or finger movements. We trust the pendulum when it disagrees with head movements or verbal communications. We trust finger signals if they contradict the pendulum.

A light object such as a finger ring, an iron washer or a paper clip on an 8-inch-long thread can be used as a pendulum. The thread is held lightly between the thumb and index finger of either hand. The elbow is allowed to rest on the arm of a chair or on a table top. It does not matter which hand holds the object because the response is an imperceptible movement of the total body. The pendulum picks up direction because responsive body movements are always repetitive.

Four basic movements of the pendulum are possible. These are clockwise, counterclockwise, and straight movements at right angles to each other. Straight movements shifting like points of the compass are too hard to remember so we need to have them at right angles, like north and south, east and west on a map.

LeCron initially had his subjects select four separate movements for "yes," "no," "I don't know," and "I don't want to answer." After induction of hypnosis he would have the subject use the right index finger for "yes," the left index finger for "no," and the thumbs for the other two answers. When we watched each other during workshops we soon recognized that polite subjects too frequently would subconsciously give an "I don't know" response rather than seeming difficult with an "I don't want to answer" signal.

This could be readily revealed if we asked, "Is your inner mind willing to tell me what you don't know? We eventually eliminated the "I don't know" signal with the pendulum and finger movements. We did not want our subjects to get away with an "I don't know" if they really were afraid of confronting an unpleasant experience. "I don't want to answer" basically means "yes-but-I-am-not-ready-yet-to-know."

Initial Subconscious Total Age-Regression to a Traumatic Event

An initial "I don't want to answer" signal with a pendulum or finger movement may mean that the patient is initially unwilling to confront an unpleasant event. Repeated experiences with this evasive action suggested to us that the patient's subconscious mind had instant access to a stressful experience as a total age-regression or "revivification." The patient was on the scene as though it were just happening. This called on the natural defense of not wanting to talk about it or know about it. We found during demonstrations that the wave-off signal often changed to a "yes" while we were pausing to decide what to do next. Here is an example:

Q: *Does* this happen before you are two years old?

A: (Pendulum or finger signal) I don't want to answer (IDWA). After 20 seconds): Yes (Y).

We learned to recognize this emotionally protective response and to soften its impact by changing the time viewpoint into a more distant perspective. Using *did* for *does* and *were* for *are* could avoid the "IDWA" signal. Distancing could also occur if we just waited. To save time, however, the questioning could immediately shift to something like this:

Q: Would it be all right if you look back at that experience from today, here in my office?

A: (Immediate) Y.

Shifting Hand Dominance Can Confuse Interpretation of Responses

It was frequently evident that signals with the pendulum and fingers would reverse themselves. We found that this could be very confusing until we learned that all signals should either be checked frequently for their meaning or, as in the case of using finger signals, be limited to one hand. If a shift occurs to the opposite hand, the signals will retain the same meaning.

Nearly half the population of American people are born left handed but only about 7 percent remain stubbornly left-handed. Gentle, repeated coercions in the kitchen before the origin of conscious memory convert the rest (Cheek 1978). The primordial handedness orientation is usually revealed by the thumb that is uppermost in a handclasp test where fingers are interdigitated. The 2 or 3 percent of people who have shifted from original right handedness to use of the left hand are exceptions to the rule, as are those who are truly ambidextrous at birth.

I have found that subjects will shift to their pristine handedness orientation as they enter hypnosis. It is wise to ask for a handclasp test and avoid confusion when you use the Chevreul pendulum. Time is wasted when the pendulum is used with a converted left-handed person because the unhypnotized person holding the pendulum can slip in and out of hypnosis without having this be apparent to the therapist. A circle swing will be one way when the subject is in a normal state; it will go in the opposite direction when he or she slips into a light hypnotic state.

Answers will always be consistent, however, when finger signals are used as described here. For these reasons, most workers who are experienced in use of ideomotor questioning techniques will limit use of a Chevreul pendulum to the first interview and will shift to use of finger signals as soon as they can be obtained during the first visit.

The pendulum has great value when a therapist wishes to use hypnosis with a patient who has no knowledge of hypnosis and has come for an ordinary consultation or who might have reservations if you mention hypnosis. A brief explanation can be given that our unconscious mind often has information that is not consciously known about a problem. The patient will quickly recognize that she nods or shakes her head when she agrees or disagrees during a conversation. The therapist can show how the pendulum picks up tiny body movements in response to the word "yes" before handing it to the patient.

As the pendulum starts moving involuntarily, it will usually interest the patient and evoke exclamations of surprise. Try this technique yourself. You will find your responses are quickly established. It is not necessary for the questions to be stated audibly. The patient is told to think them in her mind.

Differentiating Voluntary from Subconscious Movements

In trying to be cooperative, a patient may lift a finger or move the pendulum voluntarily. Close observation will quickly detect this. Movement of the hand holding the pendulum is hardly perceptible when the pendulum swings in response to a subconscious thought; hand movement is obvious when the person is consciously thinking what the answer should be. A conscious thought will override the unconscious movement of the pendulum. This confusion can be avoided if the subject pretends that someone else is holding the pendulum and that he is curious to know what will happen.

Unconsciously activated finger signals are usually slow to appear and are always vibratory and repetitive. In contrast, voluntary responses are quick to appear, may be large or small but are given only once.

Should the Eyes Be Open or Closed During Questioning?

With the pendulum, we have found that answers are more quickly obtained and are less likely to change in direction when the subject is looking at the weight on the chain or string. The subject's mind may wander when the eyes are closed.

Finger signals can be obtained while the subject's eyes are open but will tend to appear more readily if the eyes are closed. It is also easier for the subject to deepen a hypnotic state when the eyes are closed.

What If a Patient Cannot Get Finger Signals?

An inability to get finger signals may simply reflect initial resistance to the use of hypnosis, but more commonly it is the result of critical thoughts such as "I don't think I can do this."

Martin Reiser (1980), psychologist for the Los Angeles Police Department has found it helpful to designate the index finger to lift when the subconscious answer is "yes," the middle finger on the same hand to lift to answer "no," and the thumb to lift for "I don't want to answer." Reiser then ties in a conscious reaction of lifting the finger meaning "yes" every time he says "Yes." The key words are spoken in a rather loud, authoritative voice in order to impress them on the memory of his subject. The consciously directed symbol responses will soon move unconsciously when Reiser then asks the subject to think the words but refrain from consciously moving the fingers.

Assignment Versus the Patient's Unconscious Selection of Fingers

The Reiser technique for obtaining responses works very well to start the process of questioning. The patient may continue to use the assigned fingers. It is wise, however, to say later, "I have given you these signals but you might prefer to select your own answers. Please think 'yes,' and so on." Cooperation is usually better if we offer options to our patients.

Our Mental Makeup

The workings of the human mind are complicated. We will probably never fully understand what is happening and what part of the brain is functioning at any time. The research of Karl Lashley with rats during the 1920s revealed the interesting evidence that every cell in the rat brain seemed to have some information regarding the pathway to food in a maze. Lashley removed various parts of the brain of an educated rat. After recovery, the action became progressively slower but the result was the same. Karl Pibram (1971) extended this concept of the holographic brain.

Enormous interest has been drawn to the functions of the brain since ways have been discovered for recognizing the sources of releasing substances and messenger molecules or "information substances" and their sites of action within the nervous system and throughout the body (Pert 1981, 1985; Rossi 1986; Rossi and Cheek 1988).

Clinical experience has been teaching us how much our emotions can influence labor, lactation, digestion, renal function, circulation and coagulation mechanisms. I want to share my experiences as an obstetrician/gynecologist in the hope that the reader will extend the possibilities in his or her sphere of work.

It is apparent now, from the work of Candace Pert and many others, that our mental makeup must comprise every cell of our body as well as our brain and that Mind and Body must be considered as one.

12

Ideomotor Search Methods

My introduction to the effectiveness of ideomotor questioning techniques occurred during the first Hypnosis Symposium in September of 1956 when Leslie LeCron helped a doctor locate the cause and realize his ability to stop the embarrassment of a severe gagging reflex that prevented him from having x-rays made of his molar teeth. He would sometimes vomit when he brushed his teeth.

The total experience lasted about 20 minutes and was effected with the help of a Chevreul pendulum. Yes, no, and I-don't-want-to-answer signals were set up. The doctor quickly became so interested in the answers that he slipped easily into a light hypnotic state. LeCron asked the doctor if he knew the cause. While he was shaking his head and saying, "No," his pendulum was saying "yes." The problem had been there for as long as the doctor could remember, so LeCron asked if the cause was an experience in the past. The answer was "yes." The questioning continued:

Q: Was it something that happened before you were 40 years old?

A: (Pendulum) Yes.

Yes was the answer to before 30, 20, 10 years of age but a "no" occurred at "before 5 years of age."

Q: Were you 5 years old?

A: No.

Q: Six years old?

A: No.

Q: Seven years old?

As the pendulum began swinging to say "yes," the doctor put the pendulum down. Each question had required a subconscious search of the causal experience. As the questioning continued, the doctor was successively raising the information toward higher levels of perception where it could be reported verbally.

The causal experience he believed was a complication of his tonsillectomy at the age of 7. An arteriole in the tonsil fossa had begun bleeding during the night. The intern on duty put some sort of clamp against the bleeding area that was held in place until the surgeon could arrive and control the bleeding.

At the moment of completing his account, the doctor shrugged his shoulders to indicate that there was nothing more to report. LeCron asked him to hold up the pendulum to let his subconscious mind answer this question:

"Now that you know this, can you be free of this problem?"

The pendulum gave a big "yes" answer. A tongue blade was produced by a member of the class. It was moved around in the back of the doctor's throat without any gagging. Skeptical about the result, the doctor took the tongue blade himself and wiggled it all around his throat without any discomfort.

At another meeting several months later, the doctor told us that he had started to gag the next time he went to his dentist. It started as the dentist used a mirror to examine a molar tooth. The reflex stopped when the doctor recalled that he really did not need to do that any more. That was the last of his problem.

Seven Approaches to Causal Events

1. LeCron's "seven keys"
2. Retrograde search, as outlined in the gagging case
3. Chronological search, moving from prenatal time toward the experience to be recognized by the patient as causal
4. A direct approach, going immediately to what has been thought to be a significant experience and then looking earlier for a sensitizing event
5. An indirect approach with "Christmas tree lights" and "auras"
6. Past life therapy
7. Spirit depossession therapy

These are the major approaches to causal events as they evolved after that first Symposium on Medical and Dental Hypnosis in San Diego. The latter two are controversial and may not seem usable by you nor acceptable by your patients. I will discuss them in this chapter and refer to them with examples in the chapter on resistance because they have proven their value when therapy has failed to bring about constructive change. Past life therapy and spirit depossession are still considered rather wild ideas in the Western world but can be valuable aids when used with a friendly patient who is open to the possibilities.

Here are the methods that will be discussed briefly before we move on to the applications of ideomotor techniques in psychosomatic problems:

The Seven Keys

LeCron identified the "seven keys" as (1) conflict, (2) motivation, (3) identification, (4) masochism, (5) imprints, (6) organ language, and (7) past experience.

Conflict

A conflict occurs when there is a wish to have something that is not to be had, something that is taboo. Life's prohibitions start soon after birth. Opposing forces are responsible for many human problems, "I want" collides with "you can't." Infants have many frustrations in not having their desires fulfilled. There are many sources of conflict. One of the most common concerns sex. Conflict may be a source of strong guilt feelings, particularly if the person acts against moral codes. A conflict may originally be at a conscious level but later may be repressed and the person then is consciously unaware of it. Often there is no repression and the conflict is consciously recognized but is not resolved. Patients, while in hypnosis, can more easily talk of their conflicts and problems than they can in ordinary conversation. They can more easily bring to consciousness a repressed conflict.

Motivation

Does an illness or symptom serve some purpose? Here there can be much variance. A simple motive would be if the ailment or symptom gained sympathy and attention. This would be immature behavior but might be entirely at a subconscious level of awareness. Most of us have immaturities along some lines.

A motive in hysterical blindness could be that the condition prevents the person from seeing something unpleasant or could serve as punishment for having seen something about which the person feels guilty. As an unconscious means of escaping from hated housework, a person might develop an allergy to detergents. These are merely possible motivations, the condition thus serving some purpose.

The motive behind a symptom or illness frequently is defensive, the condition acting as a protection. An example would be migraine headaches that are used as a defense against unacceptable feelings of hostility and aggression, emotions that are almost invariably found in migraine patients.

Motivations are sometimes deeply hidden but much more often can be located through the questioning technique. Often insight alone is enough to overcome the condition. In other words, the origin is reframed in the light of more mature understandings.

Identification

Anyone who has children in the family has noticed how a child tends to copy the parents and at times tries to be like them. In early childhood we all identify with those close to us, and this can be carried over into adult life.

Identification means dramatization. It may be difficult to know whether some trait or even illness is inherited or is merely a result of identification. If a mother, or perhaps the father, is greatly overweight, the children probably will tend to be overweight for their age. There may be some hereditary tendency for obesity, but certainly identification plays a role.

Children identify with parents or other loved ones for several reasons. Love for the person is a strong motive but even a hated parent may be the object of subconscious identification. Children may wish to be like a parent because they want to be big and strong and powerful, as the parent seems to be. They have a need for power. Children may be told repeatedly that they are just like one of their parents, that they take after that side of the family. This acts like a posthypnotic suggestion.

We should keep in mind the rather strange fact that when there is a choice between identifying with a good quality or a bad one involving habit, characteristic, or illness, the unfavorable trait will take priority.

Masochism

Self-punishment due to strong guilt feelings is a very common form of unconsciously damaging behavior. Most of us will exhibit masochism at times in minor ways, but it may be so exaggerated that it includes self-destruction.

Some people have such an exaggerated conscience that they will punish themselves severely over minor transgressions or unacceptable thoughts. Sometimes one part of the subconscious mind will compel a person to behave in an unacceptable way while another part is simultaneously demanding punishment for the offense.

Extreme masochism can lead to suicide or fatal illness. The alcoholic frequently uses his drinking as a means of self-destruction. While there is an instinctive need for self-preservation, sometimes the will to die will win.

When self-punishment is located as a cause, insight is seldom enough to end the problem. The reasons for guilt feelings should be explored. These often center on sex and may originate long before birth. The therapist needs to reassure the patient and explain that feelings of guilt are probably unwarranted. No one wears a halo and everyone does things they regret but now it is time to reframe the causal experience, leave its negative imprints behind, and move forward.

Sometimes we can appeal to the patient's willingness to get well for the sake of a loved one. We can point out that we punish the people who love us when we punish ourselves. People will often do nice things for other people that they would not do for themselves.

Imprints

Psychotherapists unfamiliar with hypnosis and the effects of suggestion are rarely aware of single-impact imprints, which often seem to explain the cause of a problem. An imprinted experience may seem consciously trivial yet may prove to be of great importance. An *imprint* is an idea that has become fixed in the subconscious part of the mind and then is carried out in exactly the same way as a posthypnotic suggestion. Spiegel (1960) has pointed out that many neuroses may be of this origin, with compulsion to act out behavior for which the causal stimulus has been forgotten.

Moebius (1957), Breuer (1957) and Estabrooks (1948) each recognized that great emotion produces a state very similar, if not identical to hypnosis. Bernheim (1895) describes hypnotic-like behavior of very sick patients with typhoid fever. There is similarity in thinking between hypnotized people and those who are unconscious during general anesthesia (Cheek 1962b). Something said at the time may register in the subconscious mind and it is as though a posthypnotic suggestion has been given.

Thought processes become childlike and literal, just as in hypnosis. There is no doubt that everyone is subconsciously affected by emotionally charged imprints, or "engrams." These engrams may be helpful or very damaging.

We are concerned here with semantics. Words used by a surgeon in the operating room may not be understood by the patient as they would be by a nurse or an assistant. LeCron called powerful words "command statements." They can be worded something like this: "You'll *never* get over this," "It *can't* be helped." If such an idea is set up, therapy will be unsuccessful until the imprint is removed. Of course such phrases would have no effect if the person were not emotionally distressed at the time of hearing it.

Organ Language

Organ language is an interesting source of physical difficulty. We often speak of something unpleasant, saying something like: "That's a headache to me," "That makes me sick at my stomach," "I can't swallow that," "It's a pain

in the neck to me," "I'm itching to get out of this." The actual physical condition mentioned may develop from such an idea. Many a chronic headache,
nausea, back pain, oesophageal spasm and dermatitis may have its origin
in organ language. The repeated thought creates the problem.

Past Experience

Experiences of the past may be involved with some or all of the Seven Keys.
Essentially they are imprint memories.

Comment

The Seven Keys used by LeCron are helpful for beginners in the uses of
hypnosis and ideomotor techniques. It has been my experience, however,
that most of the events that are located as the beginnings of a problem have
been preceded by earlier events that made the patient vulnerable or sensitized in preparation for what is brought out during the questioning.

Often this is not a matter of concern as long as a problem clears in the
process. A recurrence of the problem, however, at a later time demands a
more exhaustive search. For this reason, I gave up the use of these keys
in my practice and worked with the remaining four major strategies.

Retrograde Search

The retrograde search method, also devised by LeCron, immediately permits distancing from a potentially disturbing primary trauma. The patient
using a pendulum or finger signals has no conscious awareness of the causal
event in the beginning but each "yes" ideomotor response (to indicate the
event occurred before each designated age) requires a subconscious review
of the primary event.

This way of searching is protective because the patient is remaining in
the present and is not forced to confront a traumatic event as though it were
just happening. He can be subconsciously using present-day knowledge and
perspective on life events to reframe initial impressions before the information is raised to conscious levels of awareness for discussion.

Questioning continues until the answer is either "no" or "I don't want
to answer," to indicate that the event was either during that specific age
or at some time between that age and the next older bracket, as is shown
in the case of the doctor and his troublesome gag reflex.

An "I don't want to answer" really means "yes but I am not ready yet
to know what it is." It usually will change to show willingness if again we
remind the patient to remain at the time of the interview while looking back
at the time of the incident.

A very important question should be asked following discovery of the first reported incident. Always ask, *"Is there an earlier experience that could have made you vulnerable or sensitive to what you have just told me?"* Failure to ask this question may lead to a mistaken conclusion and failure of the therapeutic process. Discovery and treatment of a peripheral or satellite trauma will probably require a follow-up, more exhaustive search into the past.

This retrograde search is safe for the beginner in uses of hypnotherapy because the patient is going through a form of desensitization while subconsciously answering each question. The questions are permissive rather than coercive. We have not encountered sudden abreactions with the retrograde search. Abreactions can be very disturbing to an inexperienced hypnotherapist.

After locating the earliest source of trouble, we can then ask, "Now that you know about this, does your inner mind know that you can be well and stay well?" This question will reveal possible sources of resistance to therapy that will need removal.

Chronological Search

Searching by moving forward in time has evolved from our recognizing that patients will frequently have trouble when they are doing the retrograde search going back in stages of time from the present. A particularly stressful experience will lead to formation of screen memories that will interfere with reaching the key experience.

I noticed during explorations of traumatic surgical experiences under general anesthesia (Cheek 1959a) that screen interference is avoided by going to the moment the patient loses consciousness and moving forward to the moment something important is happening. The patient may suddenly react with a great display of anguish in an abreaction when this abrupt meeting with trauma occurs. You must be prepared for this or else do not use this technique until you are comfortable handling abreactions.

The starting point for a chronological search was extended eventually back to the first emotional experience a pregnant woman encounters. This is usually when she is being told she is pregnant. My studies have convinced me that this moment of maternal emotion is observed and recorded by the embryo. Hypnotized persons can very quickly orient themselves to that time and sense their mother's reaction to the news (Cheek 1990). Her reaction, positive or negative, sets a permanent world view that may last a lifetime.

Here, as with the surgical experiences, the hypnotized patient, arriving at a possibly stressful moment, has had no time to set up screen memories for defense. The result can be a disconcerting abreaction that could discourage beginners. For them, we recommend the retrograde exploration until they have learned how to handle abreactions.

How do you handle an abreaction? Abreacting patients are usually willing to move past the event to a time of comfort and can then look back and reevaluate the situation. Sometimes, however, they adamantly continue their reaction.

Keep your poise when this occurs. The patient is very attentive to the way the therapist is reacting. Keep your voice sounding calm, even if you do not feel calm yourself. Tell your sobbing patient to keep reviewing the event. Ask for a "yes" finger when it starts and a "no" finger each time the event is concluded. By designating an end to the traumatic part, there is tacit communication that there will be an end to the effect of the trauma. Ask for the review to continue until "the experience is no longer a source of distress."

Direct Approach

Time is often a matter of importance in the constraints of teaching physicians, dentists, and psychologists how to use hypnosis in their work. LeCron and I found that it saved much time during a demonstration if we moved beyond the safe, gradual approaches to traumatic events and told the volunteer to go immediately to something we had learned might be important. The subject was asked to have his "yes" finger lift involuntarily when he was on the scene but to know about what was happening as though looking from the time of interview. This "bifocal" view was chosen in order to diminish the chance of a spontaneous abreaction that might happen if the regression were a revivification (a total age-regression) of the event.

During a few experiments with this direct approach, it became clear that we had previously been underestimating the resources of our hypnotized patients and volunteer subjects. We had assumed that it would take time and a gradual approach. Several subjects reported after an interview that they were bored by our method because they had immediately oriented to the key moment while we were droning on with our routine.

With a direct approach it is still necessary, however, to ask if there might be some earlier experience that could have set the stage or created the vulnerability to the initially selected trauma.

A "yes" response to this question always requires a retrograde further search until the original, sensitizing trauma is discovered. We feel that beginners in the uses of hypnosis, no matter how experienced in dealing with psychiatric and physical problems, should work with the slower methods: the Seven Keys and retrograde searching. The reasoning involved here is two-fold: First, if you are tentative and not sure that a patient can go directly to a traumatic event, this message transmits to your patient. You will be disappointed with the result. Second, your patient may start abreacting in a disturbing way.

I take the opening comments of my patients as clues to the direct orientation when I am working in my office with patients having psychosomatic problems. I shift my initial approach depending on the behavior of my patient while I am taking a routine history. The patient who ʋays, "I've wondered if something way back is hindering me in relationships to men" will perhaps be directed immediately to the moment her mother knows she is pregnant. From there we will move chronologically with, "Please let your subconscious mind go to the first moment in your life that had to do with a boy or a man. When you are there your 'yes' finger will lift." This sequence of questioning will frequently reveal a sexual molestation for which there had been amnesia or an imprinted impression of having been abandoned by a father or an attractive but aloof male.

An Indirect Approach ("Christmas Tree Lights" and Auras)

Hypnotized subjects using ideomotor level access to physiological memory are able to use imagery of lights and of auras to diagnose problems in their own body (Cheek, 1989).

The method for learning about and experimenting with this method is simple. Hypnotized subjects are asked to "see" themselves standing in front of a full-length mirror. Their "yes" finger is to lift when the image is subconsciously clear. They are asked to imagine tiny Christmas tree lights of different colors to represent feelings. They are to see one in their forehead to reflect the feelings of their head, meaning the surface and all of its contents, that is, their brain and their impressions of themselves. After reporting the color and intensity of this light, they are told to shift attention to each of their extremities and eventually to look into deeper structures, lungs, heart, and so on.

Subjective meaning of each light is reported and noted on a line drawing of the body marked for left and right sides. If some light reflects pain or some other indication of abnormality, the patient is asked to go directly to a time before that light changed from a "normal and healthy" color to the moment some other colored light is put there. When the signal for this is given, the color of the light is again noted because it may have been different from the one initially reported to you. Other experiences may have modified the first abnormal light. The patient is asked to "look around" and tell me what might have caused that new light to appear in place of the old one. With this method I have learned about an unruptured tubal pregnancy that I had failed to notice during a pelvic examination. I have learned (Cheek 1962d) about the persistence of subconscious pain caused by an injury that happened at an early age but had been forgotten. A woman who saw a "black light" in the area of her left ovary recognized that a suppressed memory of a sexual molestation by her father was responsible for development of an endometrial cyst on that side, the side he was on when he put his finger into her vagina.

Seers have for years been able to read auras and diagnose various types of illness, physical and emotional. I have found that hypnotized people in front of the full-length mirror will report the color of the aura they see around the reflection of their head and shoulders. They will know, at a level reflected by finger signals, whether this color is healthy or unhealthy. The shade of color closest to their skin seems to be the most important. I let them assess the meaning of the colors because subjective impressions of colors vary with the individual who owns them. We have no right to use our personal criteria for this evaluation. It is helpful to learn what these personal aura colors are at birth and at various times during life.

Most of my knowledge about Christmas tree lights and auras have come from children who have been my patients. Children are great teachers when we pay attention to their spontaneous observations. James Hixson, the dentist who was a permanent member of the Hypnosis Symposiums faculty, had learned, from a young patient's observation, a simple way of developing effective anesthesia for dental work. This youngster said he could get the idea of numbness by thinking of turning off electricity to his hand. He visualized wires from his brain going down to his hand, a different color for each finger. He imagined a little Christmas tree light of the same color as the wire for each of his fingers. He had a switch that he could turn off for each finger. The finger would get numb when he turned off the light; the sensation would come right back when he turned the light on again.

When Doctor Hixson asked the child to make his jaw numb the same way, this little patient moved his hand up to the side of his face and "ran" the numbness out of his hand and into the area he was touching. It was easier to do this with touch than it would be to just "think" it being there.

LeCron had also learned another way of using imagery from a child he was hypnotizing. He had considered using a television as a projective approach to learning something about the child's relationship to a sibling. His little client could not "see" his brother there in the television picture. After a few moments he said, "I have to turn it on first." With that, he reached out and turned an imaginary knob before offering comments about his brother.

Children talking among themselves will use colors to describe feelings they have about people. Lyall Watson in his delightful book *Gifts of Unknown Things* tells of a Malay child using colors to describe the calls of birds and the sound of thunder and lightning.

It occurred to me that the colors children use to describe people might reflect their ability to see the electromagnetic fields of life (Burr 1972), the etherial energy surrounding all living things. Auras have been known about for thousands of years. Harold Saxton Burr observed from his largely ignored classic observations with trees, various animals, and eventually with humans during the 1940s that measurable differences in voltage and polarity of these fields would occur with circadian rhythms, with changes in weather, with disease and even with malignant tumors. The electrodes used for this were not in contact with the skin or organs. They were placed at a distance, just as the electrodes for evaluating heart action and brain waves with the electrocardiogram and the electroencephalogram are distant from the heart or the brain.

Leonard Ravitz, a psychiatrist and founding member of the American Society of Clinical Hypnosis, was a student and a colleague in the research done by Burr, who was then professor of anatomy at the Yale University School of Medicine. Ravitz (1959) measured the force fields of subjects who were sleeping, were under anesthesia, and who were in varying levels of hypnosis. His findings demonstrated that there were similarities in all three conditions and that the depths of hypnosis could be quantified with the very sensitive equipment he used. Ravitz's pioneer observations need recognition and further testing.

Robert Becker (1985) an orthopedic surgeon, has studied the electrical forces involved in regeneration of limbs in salamanders and in the healing processes of fractured bones and has been able to accelerate healing with direct current energy. During the 1980s it became clear that the energy around the step-down transformers from high power electric lines can be causal in the development of leukemia in children and connective tissue tumors in adults.

All these observations lend credence to the possibility that the imagery of children may be tuning in to energies that are invisible in the ordinary sense. I have learned that children can see auras around people and seem to associate the colors of the auras with personality. We can hear children say, "Oh, Aunt Susie is a pink person but sometimes she is gray." If psychically endowed people can diagnose illness by looking at human auras, could it be that all children have a similar potential that can be enhanced?

Past Life Therapy, Fact or Fiction?

LeCron, James Hixson, and I agreed that we should keep an open mind about the matter of reincarnation. We believed anyone who sincerely believed that past life traumas had recurred and caused trouble in the present life should have a chance to evaluate the data and decide for himself or herself.

In our symposiums between 1956 and 1972, roughly 50 percent of our physicians, dentists, and psychologists said they believed in reincarnation.

We explained to the nonbelievers that children had convinced Ian Stevenson, professor of psychiatry at the University of Virginia, enough to investigate possibilities of reincarnation among the Eskimos and the people of Egypt, Sri Lanka, and India. His first book, *Twenty Cases Suggestive of Reincarnation,* is worthy of study. One of his cases seemed to have a very brief interval between the sudden death of a 20-year-old man and the appearance of his spirit in a child who was comatose. (This case might qualify for consideration in the next category, spirit attachment, to be discussed.)

Stevenson has found that children under 4 years of age in the cultures he studied would spontaneously blurt out that they are not the child that is being scolded or physically abused. They give their name, tell about where they lived, and can recognize people they have known in the life before their death. Apparently epinephrine frees the memory.

We wanted to know more facts about the patients who were sure about their past lives, so we went along with exploring their memories. Sometimes their report and reframing of their disturbed impressions were followed by an improvement in health. Often, however, their reports, given in most convincing and detailed manner, were little more than a ventilation of emotions.

I have searched for past life traumas when I have run out of pathways in trying to help a patient and have met with continuing resistance to my treatment strategies. A therapist can spend many hours discovering one sad or exciting life time after another. At one time, during my initial excitement about this subject, I was dictating exhaustive notes that ran on, page after page. My secretary asked in a plaintive voice, "I wonder if it could be possible for your patients to decide to leave their past experiences, to cut the strings that attach them to the past?"

This was a most attractive idea. I tried it and have found that patients do very well without having to dig up terrible details from the past. I explain to them that past lives are really not "past" at all. Time is circular or globular. It is not linear, like a railroad track. We do not need to be wrapped up in the strings that connect us to those "past" lives when we have the opportunity to make the most of the one we are presently living.

My advice to clinicians is to reserve the idea of searching past lives for those patients who ask for it. When you are concerned because a patient is not progressing in therapy or is dramatically improved for a day or two and then suddenly reverts back to old difficulties, you can try this question: "Is it possible that some experience in another lifetime could be interfering with what you and I are trying to do in this lifetime?"

This question does not condemn you as a "kook." You are only considering the unconscious convictions of a colleague in your therapeutic process. The answer is a finger signal indicating "yes" or "no."

Spirit Depossession Therapy

Is spirit depossession possible? Is it a metaphor? Can the concept have treatment value?

In 1985 I went with a team of professional people to visit the healers in Brazil. At the Spiritist Center in Saó Paulo I watched teams of volunteer mediums who have worked for four years to learn their skills. There are usually three trance mediums with one specially trained medium who is able to take on a spirit from the patient and verbally report the spirit's feelings and wishes. This special medium knows how to protect himself or herself from serving as a new host in case the dialogue carried on by the other three is unsuccessful in releasing the "earthbound" spirit.

At the Center there is a working hypothesis that people who are killed suddenly will be unable to move on toward another incarnation. They are earthbound. They will try to enter a living person who is sick, unconscious, or under the influence of chemicals. It is believed that the protective energy field, or aura, of such people is shrunken or cracked in some way and it permits entrance by these lost, often frightened, spirits.

The job of the mediums is to remove invading spirits that have carried over their problems to the new host. They feel this type of treatment has a two-fold value: (1) It gives the spirit of the dead person permission to move "into the light" and toward a new life; and (2) it also relieves the troubled spirit host. The belief is that invading spirits will drain strength and immune capability of the host and that many diseases can stem from spirit attachment.

Convincing cures from emotional and physical diseases appear to follow successful removal of earthbound spirits. Of course, we must keep in mind the power of belief, the power of the placebo. On the other hand, the voice of the spirits, their accounts of how they died, how old they were, in what part of the world they lived is pretty impressive.

Edith Fiore (1987), a psychologist in Saratoga, California, has discovered that the subconscious mind of a hypnotized subject can do the same sort of channeling that a special medium does. Using ideomotor questioning, she has found that her resistant clients can reveal the presence of a spirit and that the spirit seems able to express its understandings and feelings through the voice of her hypnotized client.

Although she has natural doubts about the validity of such revelations by her patients, she has found that progress in therapy can follow the release of spirits. Her book and her methods make interesting reading. She uses this technique only when all else has failed to produce results or physicians have referred patients specifically for this sort of therapy. It will probably not be successful as a treatment modality if offered to someone whose cultural and religious beliefs are negatively biased.

Temporary Out-of-Body, Surgical, and Near Death Variants

Moody (1975), Ring (1982), Ritchie (1978), and many others have written about out-of-body experiences. Their writings do not prove that this spirit attachment could follow if the owner's body actually died and its spirit was unable to get back. There are some curious facts, however, that might lend some credence to the Brazilian work being done at the Spiritist's Center and to Fiore's experiences.

Many reports have come to us from people who have survived drowning, electrocution, cardiac arrest, and life-threatening illness. Their descriptions are peculiarly similar. Crile (1947) tells in his autobiography about a patient who had survived a cardiac arrest. She had not been told about the event. At hospital rounds one morning she wanted to know about a dream she had been having since her operation. She said that at some point she rose upward from her body and looked down from the ceiling and watched while he and his assistants were doing something to her chest. She said that she got back into her body at the time her doctors stopped what they were doing and continued with the operation.

Comments

Some of the ideas presented here, such as considering the perceptions and understandings of the infant at birth, were being explored during our workshops and our private practice. LeCron and I felt, however, that we should refrain from writing about these matters until their therapeutic value had been established by other observers. I believe this time has come.

I accept responsibility for the section on spirits and their possible impact on the people they target for attachment. I will state, however, that consideration of past life experience and earthbound spirit attachment should be limited. We need to understand and respect the cultural and personal beliefs of the people we treat. We need to avoid presenting ideas that may seem bizarre and unusual to our clients and patients.

I will give one summarized case example of work with a past life and one of spirit attachment in the chapter on resistance (Chapter 27) to show how the presentation is made to a patient. The ideas are offered as a means of helping patients feel less troubled by their unconscious sources of resistance.

There would be few problems with communications about past life experience or spirit involvement in South America. In North America we must be careful if we want to avoid having our patients complain about us to authorities. Members of licensing boards could also be biased if they were unaware of our reasons for considering these matters. Here is some sage advice by William James (1958) from his book *The Varieties of Religious Experience:*

> Perfect conduct is a relation between three terms; the actor, the objects for which he acts, and the recipient of the action. In order that conduct should be abstractly perfect, all three terms: intention, execution, and reception, should be suited to one another.
>
> The best intention will fail if it either work by false means or address itself to the wrong recipient. There is no worse lie than a truth misunderstood by those who hear it, so reasonable arguments, challenges to magnanimity, and appeals to sympathy or justice, are folly when we are dealing with human crocodiles and boaconstrictors. (pp 275–276)

13

Biological Considerations:
Animal Models

Amnesia

Why is memory of a traumatic experience suppressed or repressed? We have known about conscious amnesia for traumatic events. This phenomenon has troubled psychiatrists and psychologists who have searched for causes of mental disturbances. It has also been a handicap for those interested in the somatic manifestations of traumatic experiences in life.

It has not been generally recognized that there might be a phylogenetic need for such amnesia throughout the animal kingdom. Human survivors of a serious accident, a fire, or an earthquake may have vividly clear memories for details during the next few hours. Their memory will then rapidly fade from consciousness but will remain to haunt the victim's unconscious mind during sleep, during a similar time of day, or when entering a similar location. The triggering stimulus may come into the brainstem reticular activating system (RAS) by way of any sensory channel. Epinephrine, the adrenal hormone released during stress, seems to be the cause of imprint type of learning as well as of the forgetfulness that is associated with trauma (Weinberger et al. 1984). We have observed this relationship clinically but recent research with animals has supported the association.

Consider this phenomenon in the light of what we can learn from animals. Consider the behavior of herd animals on the great plains of Africa. Zebras, hartbeests, antelopes all show the same behavior in a crisis. They are not restricted to any territory. At the approach of danger, they will rush wildly together to escape from the limited territory of the predators. Behavior changes rapidly when safety is reached.

Within seconds, herd (hoofed) animals are grazing as though nothing had happened. Is this because evolutionary adaptive factors have demanded conscious forgetfulness for a recent danger? Does crisis amnesia serve a biological purpose in nature? My impression is that the answer would be "yes." Amnesia must have survival value in nature. Constant worried alarm after a crisis would be harmful. Feeding would be curtailed. Water holes would be avoided. The young would not be nursing. Procreation would diminish.

Amnesia is important but escape behavior is instantly ready for action should the threat reappear. With herd animals the triggering mechanisms may be telepathic, visual, auditory, or olfactory. The stimulus and the response are state-dependent. Mental activity involved at a time of danger seems to concentrate within the primitive hind brain and midbrain (Magoun 1963). The reticular activating system surrounding the spinal cord and the brainstem relay sensory messages upward for action. The rostral portion of the RAS apparently decides which stimuli are important and which can be suppressed to ensure economy of the evoked physiological and motor responses to danger.

Humans have not yet learned to block out what Thurber used to call "circular brooding" over threats and recent dangers. We will relive traumas during repetitive cycles of deep sleep until accumulating stress hormones cause havoc with physical and emotional balance (homeostasis). Like the lower animals, however, humans will have conscious amnesia about important, causal events in their life that have set the stage for the damaging effect of recent stress (Cheek 1962c, 1963, 1965c, 1966b).

Triggering, flashback stimuli with humans become less and less closely related to the primary imprint experience but the primary response tends to remain unchanged. Any recall system depending on verbal communication may fail to reveal an experience that caused great fear or pain during intrauterine life or the years before origin of conscious memory. The amnesia of catastrophic experiences after the dawn of conscious memory may block access to significant information for the same reason. Conversation depends on thought associations in higher zones of perception in the cerebral cortex. We need more effective tools for discovery of information stored at deep, subverbal levels of awareness.

LeCron and I believed that ideomotor techniques offer the tools to reach primary causes of maladaptive behavior. Patients often recall significant information during an ordinary hypnotic interview, but the "ah ha" memory is usually a recent one. This is when the approaches discussed in Chapter 12 permit rapid and often verifiable discovery of an original trauma or imprint memory. The economy of the human subconscious mind seems always to throw out a recent "trauma" and retain a defense against finding a primal trauma, almost as though hoping a therapist will be satisfied and will reduce pressure in the recovery and reframing process.

State-Dependent Memory

Hypnosis seems to be a "state." A person who goes spontaneously into a hypnotic state at a time of great danger may become disturbed and refuse further search at the outset of an innocuous formal induction of hypnosis (Cheek 1960c). Similarly, any of the causes of spontaneous hypnoidal states discussed in Chapter 1 or 10 will call out responses that were set into a fixed pattern by a truly traumatic event. This phenomenon is state-dependent in the same sense that learning associated with drugs and alcohol is state-dependent. Donald Overton (1978) has written extensively about the general subject of state-dependent learning and its application to human chemical dependency.

The remaining chapters will be concerned with application of ideomotor search and reframing techniques in a limited number of considerations about health and disease. It was our purpose at the time of the first edition to present information in specific areas that could be used by readers whose specialties and interests are in other spheres. I am adding material that was not available to us in 1968 and writing about some considerations that we were thinking about but did not think it wise to put into print. Because matters of past life therapy and spirit attachment are controversial, I have placed them in the chapter on resistance because I have found them valuable when ordinary therapy was failing to progress.

In concluding this chapter, I wish to stress the importance of using appropriate medical and psychiatric consultations and to constantly keep in mind the dangers of overlooking physical causes of outwardly psychological problems.

Some Dangers to Be Avoided

We must always keep in mind that our enthusiasm for considering the mind as the root of physical and emotional problems may blind us to the fact that emotional and organic problems may exist together or that an initially psychological problem has led to a disabling organic disease.

Ask for a medical consultation if your patient comes to you with a complaint of recent origin and has not had a medical consultation since the beginning of the trouble.

There have been tragic mistakes made with the lives of very nervous people. Metastatic thyroid cancer can occur from a small thyroid nodule. Anxiety and insomnia may be the only symptoms.

There is no collateral circulation for the appendix and the gallbladder. Bacteria can penetrate the wall of the appendix or the gallbladder because of contraction of the blood vessels during a time of prolonged stress. Emotionally troubled adults and children have died or suffered long, disabling illness from a ruptured gallbladder or appendix because their family had decided that their abdominal pains were "only" psychogenic.

Sudden change in personality and shifts from previous behavior may be caused by a brain tumor or metastasis from an unrecognized lung, breast, adrenal, or kidney cancer. Personality changes, dizziness, and visual disturbances can be caused also by previously unrecognized syphilis or AIDS.

We have a tendency to think all headaches are stress related and emotional in origin but headaches can be caused by hypertension or cancer in one of the sinuses or in the brain. A benign tumor of the meninges (meningioma) may have been present for a number of years before the gradual onset of symptoms. Headaches, ringing in the ears, and hearing loss may be the result of nervous clenching of the teeth (bruxism). Ask about consultation with the patient's dentist.

Sudden appearance of headache, blurred vision, and irritability in a young person may be signals that an aneurysm of the Circle of Willis around the pituitary is bleeding. Delay in treating this condition surgically may be fatal for the patient. Always remain alert and willing to ask for medical consultation.

All of us working in the healing arts must keep ourselves informed of new methods of diagnosis. We need to remember that none of us is an authority about all forms of human distress. We best serve our clients and patients when we are willing to ask for help from those who have special knowledge about the problems we treat. We need especially to remember that the troubled people who come to us for help not only can lead us to the cause but can also, with our encouragement, find the resources to cure themselves. We are in the role of co-workers with our patients in this process.

14

Fetal Perceptions: Maternal-Fetal Telepathy

Since publication of the first edition of *Clinical Hypnotherapy*, I have extended my evaluation of patients to include their regression in hypnosis to the moment their mother was given the diagnosis of pregnancy in the doctor's office. This is an emotional moment. The pregnant woman is happy, disappointed, angry, frightened, or ambivalent. These emotions are keenly perceived by her embryo. If they are interpreted as meaning that its mother does not want to be pregnant, this threatening impression seems to become permanently imbedded in the memory of the embryo and will not be softened or reversed by subsequent maternal show of loving acceptance during the pregnancy or at the time of birth. Although this will appear to be an overly strong statement, the evidence given me during more than a thousand age-regression studies with male and female adults has substantiated that statement.

An Example

A German psychologist, living in Hamburg, asked me to place her in hypnosis and try to find out the reason she and her mother had never been able to get along with each other. She was born in Berlin in 1943, the first child. Her mother was now aging; her father had died. She loved her mother but was feeling constantly irritated in her mother's presence during her occasional visits home, yet she felt her mother's loneliness and increasing needs for comfort and care. The conflicts were troubling her.

Work with Hypnosis

The psychologist was a good hypnotic subject. It took only a few moments to establish ideomotor signals with her fingers. She gave permission for me to help her review her birth and early life with her mother.

I asked her to let her inner mind go back to the moment her head was emerging into the outside world at the end of her mother's labor. Her "yes" finger lifted to indicate this time orientation. Head movements and the recognition of which arm came out first were indications that she was getting physiological memories (Cheek 1974).

Q: Is your mother able to speak at the moment of your birth?

A: (Finger signal) Yes.

Q: How does your mother feel when she sees you?

A: She is very happy. She says I am a beautiful baby.

Q: How does the baby feel?

A: (The psychologist now shrugged her shoulders and uttered a sort of grunt that indicated a lack of interest in the excitement shown by her mother. It appeared that she did not believe the demonstration of pleasure. This reaction had to be secondary to some earlier imprinted memory.)

Q: Please go back to the moment your mother realizes that she is pregnant with you. When you are there, your "yes" finger will lift. As it lifts, please tell me how your mother is feeling when the doctor tells her.

A: (As her finger lifted). She is scared. (After 15 seconds of silence:) She doesn't want me.

Q: That sounds strange to me. Go to the moment she tells your father that she is pregnant.

The psychologist now said that her father was not there, adding, "He's on the eastern front fighting the Russians." (This came from her adult knowledge.) She had looked puzzled and unhappy while searching for her father's reaction, as much as to say that he must also not want her.

I said, "This is a terrible time in the world. A war is going on. Of course your mother would have been scared. She did not know what the future would bring. She did not know if your father would live to come home." I said, "Ask your fingers about this. Is there a part of your mother that is happy to be pregnant?"

A: (Finger signal) Yes.

Now I asked her to come back and review the labor and the reactions of her mother during that terrible time when Berlin was being bombed at the time of her birth. This time she showed genuine pleasure on sensing her mother's happiness.

On coming out of hypnosis, the psychologist smiled as she commented on having a very different feeling now about her mother. That night she put in a long telephone call with her mother. She told the class about the sudden change in her feelings and the happiness she sensed in her mother's voice on learning that this distant and often angry daughter had been wrong in feeling her mother did not want her. Her mother had verified that she really was happy to be pregnant but was frightened about the outside world.

Comment

Uncovering early life negative attitudes shown by a mother does not always end so happily. I have been told by patients that their mother really would have had an abortion if she could have, that their mother never showed love at birth or at any other time. It is important then to impress the patient with the fact that this attitude on the part of the mother was her problem and was probably based on the mother's early relationship to her parents and her siblings.

Sometimes it is possible to have the patient review the moment of her unhappy mother's diagnosis of pregnancy and have the mother think to her little embryo the kind of feelings that would have made her baby feel welcome. This is turning the concept of the baby into being the mother. It curiously is possible for troubled patients to hallucinate the sensations of really feeling welcome and nurtured when there was none of this in the early experience.

At the end of March 1989 I received a stimulating letter from Doctor Charles Wallach, which I will quote in part:

Dear Doctor Cheek:

Your fine letter to the *Brain/Mind Bulletin* (March '89) struck a responsive note here. For twenty-odd years, I was a member of a multinational research team, originally funded by a British foundation, investigating the neurophysiological mechanics of mental telepathy.

Based on irrefutable evidence that telepathy is a real and demonstrable phenomenon, as hard scientists we were forced to make the assumption that it was not a spiritual or metaphysical manifestation, but rather mediated by certain areas of brain cells, and that these were connected to exteroceptor and interoceptor nerve fibers to discrete organs of reception and transmission.

Over the years, we were quite successful in identifying the biomechanics of telepathy, and incidentally of several other related parapsychological phenomena, and localizing this activity to a lower gyrus of the right cerebral hemisphere after the age of two years; before that age, the function appears to ascend through the triune brain in the same manner as judgement of spatial relationships from more primitive quasi-cognitive levels.

Our work provided us with definitive evidence that all normal human infants have an essential telepathic link with their mothers from the fifth or sixth month of gestation (if not earlier), and (with a few notable exceptions) begin to turn off this communication channel for very good reasons at around 18 months of age—when more effective verbal skills begin to develop.

We believe this is an evolutionary trend which would not have developed unless it had positive survival value. . . .

Sincerely, (signed) C. Wallach

Warm-blooded animals, birds, and mammals must care for their young until their children are able to survive on their own. It seems reasonable to assume that warning messages and commands for appropriate behavior at a time of danger would be communicated telepathically and would demand instant and complete obedience. It seems further reasonable that the mechanisms for this type of communication must be in place and rehearsed before bird eggs are hatched and before a mammal is born.

The recognition and use of maternal-fetal communication are ready and in place for mothers and their obstetrical attendants. F. Rene van de Carr, a physician in Hayward, California, has been instructing his obstetrical patients and their husbands about singing and talking to their unborn child (van de Carr and Lehrer 1988). I feel certain that much of what is accomplished in his "Prenatal University" is telepathic in nature and has valuable power in the bonding process between parents and their babies.

Of course, we will have to admit that healthy, normal women have been using this sort of communication with their unborn child for hundreds of years. My concern is for the women who have had years of infertility, repeated miscarriages, or other obstetrical tragedies. In my experience as an obstetrician I have found that such women are afraid to think about a living child at term. They do not paint bassinets in readiness before their baby is born. They seem superstitiously unwilling to "count their chickens before they are hatched." They will not be able to hallucinate the blackboard stating the date of delivery, sex of their baby, weight of their baby, and length of labor until they are subconsciously very sure that their baby is developing normally and all is well. This means that their baby has had very little telepathic information about its mother's desire to have a baby, very little encouragement. This may be the secret of babies who miscarry or die before birth. We must keep these matters in mind.

A chapter on fetal perceptions would not be complete without mention of the pioneer research of Stanislav Grof (1985), which began in 1956 in Czechoslovakia using lysergic acid diethylamide (LSD). Later, in America, he resorted to the continued deep breathing advocated by Wilhelm Reich when he could not continue with the LSD research. This, like deep hypnosis, seems to access the memory reservoirs in the primitive brain.

Grof is a spiritually gifted and intuitive psychiatrist who has had the courage to explore realms of consciousness that culminated in the origin of transpersonal psychology. His book *Beyond the Brain* is a wonderful resource of information about the world of the unborn child and the scope of the resources the human mind can tap in pursuit of health and the understanding of mental activity that has often been called schizophrenia.

15

Hypersensitivity Disease

Hypersensitivity disease is a hard group of maladaptive problems to define. There are many different types of hypersensitivity. All of them, however, have these qualities in common:

1. They stem from an initial target organ sensitizing experience, either personal or by identification with someone else.
2. They stem from a form of unconscious fear and need to protect self from a threatening source of injury or unhappiness.
3. They are usually cyclical in appearance, with intervals of relief between episodes.
4. Victims can cure themselves if feelings of guilt, need for self-punishment, and passive acceptance of disease or bad luck can be eliminated with help from someone else.

Treatment

The approach that seems to offer the best prospect for control and eventual cure involves the following steps:

1. Offer hope by informing the sufferer that cure is possible.
2. Discover the primary source of vulnerability and help the patient reframe associated assumptions with that source.
3. Teach the patient how to use self-hypnosis to temper and eventually eliminate auto-immune–type reactions against the triggering sensory or emotional stimuli.
4. Check for sources of unconscious resistance with the question "Does

your inner mind know that you can be totally well?" If the ideomotor level answer is "yes," try for an hallucinated date of "cure" that is subconsciously visible on an imaginary chalkboard, saying, "When that appears, your 'yes' finger will lift. As it lifts, please tell me the month, day, and year." Freedom to move forward is shown when all three are reported—month, day, and year. Resistance is indicated when one or two items are absent.

5. Sources of resistance are considered in Chapter 27 and must be addressed before moving to step 6.

6. Help the patient find a simple, "macro-like" signal or "anchor" to initiate or intensify the symptom involved. This action is to be reversed by some other anchor. I usually designate pressure between the fingertips of the left thumb and index fingers to start and those of the right hand to diminish and eventually remove the symptoms. The fingers separate on the left hand when the removal anchor is used on the right hand. This is suggested in order to keep from giving both signals at once. It seems wise to diminish the symptom in stages such as to ask the "yes" finger to lift when the symptom is "half as uncomfortable." Failure to lift or a long delay reveals unconscious resistance of some sort. It may be because of the "too good to be possible" phenomenon. Point out that the subconscious mind "knows" it can turn a symptom off if it is able to turn it on with a thought.

7. Build reinforcing confidence by exercising the patient in altering such physiological reactions as hunger, thirst, or bowel activity (See Chapter 21), and then reversing the sensations.

8. Insist that the patient use neutral, brief periods of self hypnosis four times a day. The time can range from two to five minutes. Explain that these rest periods help keep a balance of energies and endocrine production that will remove pathological reactions against the environment. Insistence on this daily practice is very important. The patient who fails to do it or claims lack of time is revealing previously unrecognized resistance or a serious lack of motivation.

9. Warn the patient that there will be recurrences of the symptoms at some point. Each recurrence will be a signal to orient back to the moment a stimulus triggered the recurrence, have a "yes" finger lift on its recognition and then use the "removal anchor" to get rid of the symptom. In this way a recurrence will be a constructive learning process rather than a defeat. The patient is to call on the telephone if help is needed in locating the causal stimulus.

10. Set two more definite appointments at equal intervals.

11. Close the first interview with the question "Have you thought of anything or learned anything today that can be useful to you?" The answer requires a review of the positive elements of the interview. The response to this question can be very helpful in pointing the way to using the information for further therapy.

(Comment: The patient will be unlikely to make an actual call on the telephone if he or she knows you will be there at that moment or will return a call to help locate the problem. Your willingness to be available allows the patient to work out the problem without calling.)

Diseases Related to Unconscious Factors

The diseases listed in Table 15-1 are just a few of the potentially disabling disease patterns that seem related to troubled personal interaction with family and the external environment.

Although they are all complex problems, we can be of greater service to the sufferers if we treat the patients with respect for their ability to compensate for difficulties that have often started long before the origin of conscious memory. Some hypersensitivity diseases, as you will note, involve viral infection (herpes and possibly with interstitial cystitis). Some are due to or are associated with bacterial infection (sinusitis, urinary tract infections, colitis).

Psoriasis is a congenitally transferred skin vulnerability but it may not become a clinical problem unless the person is suffering from troubled sexual self-image, such as believing he or she should have been of the opposite sex.

TABLE 15-1 Partial List of Hypersensitivity Diseases

Allergy
Headaches: vascular, migraine, muscle tension
Skin sensitivities: psoriasis, neurodermatitis, "atopic" dermatitis, herpes simplex
  (facial and genital)
Sinusitis
Chronic bronchitis
Recurring urinary tract infections, acute cystitis, acute pyelitis when obstruction
  of urethra and ureters can be ruled out, interstitial cystitis
Collagen diseases, including dermatomyositis, scleroderma, lupus
  erythematosus and disseminated lupus, rheumatoid arthritis, rheumatic
  fever, Hashimoto thyroiditis
Maternal Rh and AB-O factors incompatibility (Chapter 20) Menorrhagia,
  dysmenorrhea, polycystic ovaries in Stein-Levinthal syndrome, en-
  dometriosis, stress-related cervical dysplasia (Class 1-3) Hemorrhagic colitis,
  hyperactive bowel syndrome
Anorexia nervosa and/or bolemia
All phobias
All habit problems. (Addictions, including obesity, are too complicated to include here)

We will do no harm with the sufferer from any of the hypersensitivity diseases if we work on releasing unconscious information regarding their origin and tap the resources of the patient in the project of recovering totally.

ACTH and Cortisols Versus Our Own Means of Diminishing Inflammation

In 1944, Hensch (1954) at the Mayo Clinic found that cortisone gave relief to sufferers from rheumatoid arthritis. The initial responses in relief of pain and reduction of inflammation were dramatic. In time, however, there were side effects of water retention, "moon facies," and depression that had to be contended with. It was discovered that quiescent lesions of tuberculosis that had been walled off could suddenly release active bacilli into the bloodstream to cause fatal miliary tuberculosis. This was in the days before the advent of antitubercle bacillus chemicals.

Cortisone and related steroids diminish inflammation and are widely used with allergies, the other collagen diseases, colitis, bursitis, and tendonitis. Their use, however, is limited by the side effects that accompany them.

Hypnosis has no side effect to mar its antiinflammatory potential. Notice that infection was present with all of James Esdaile's surgical patients in India in 1845–46. He observed that redness, swelling, and local heat, the reflections of infection, were reduced or removed when mesmerism was used to relieve pain.

The cortisol-like response produced by hypnosis improved, rather than diminished, the immune capabilities of Esdaile's patients. His surgical mortality rate dropped from 50 percent to 5 percent. No one equalled his statistics until after the advent of chemical anesthesia and antisepsis.

It is time now for allergists, orthopedists, rheumatologists, gastroenterologists, dermatologists and internists to study and use the values of continuing periods of deep hypnosis as were used by Esdaile in India and Wetterstrand in Sweden. It is important for them to recognize that patients can learn to use their own resources with self-hypnosis to ameliorate or cure their problem.

16

Significance of Sleep
and Sleep Disorders

Sleep is a fascinating subject. In this chapter I want to outline some features of sleep and the thinking processes during sleep that are pertinent to psychology and maladaptive behavior. I am particularly interested in sleep ideation that may cause potentially serious physical and emotional problems. This matter has been discussed elsewhere (Cheek 1963, 1965c, 1969a) based on evidence revealed by ideomotor review methods that give access to previously unreachable zones of memory.

During my research into the auditory responsiveness of people under general anesthesia, it became clear that attention is paid to meaningful information, as understood by the patient. This attention is directed toward the anesthetist after losing consciousness, then toward the surgical team after the incision is made, and to both surgical team and anesthetist at the end of the operation. The methods used by research aimed at proving people do not hear while anesthetized either ignored the need for test sounds to be meaningful or attempted to ask with inadequate search techniques whether or not patients remembered test information (Cheek, 1981). It may be that much could be learned about the zones of "dreamless" sleep with the help of ideomotor techniques.

We have known in an unscientific way that a caring mother will awaken at the sounds emitted by her sick baby; her husband will continue to sleep. If husband and wife are asleep in the cabin of their boat, the husband will awaken in alarm while his wife sleeps on if the anchor is disconnected from its grasp on the bottom by wind or tide. The mechanism involved for shifting attention and subsequent arousal appears to be the reticular activating system, as was demonstrated by the classical work of Hernandez-Peon, Scherrer and Jouvet with cats in (1956).

There is a curious cyclical nature to sleep, which is found with all birds and mammals that have been tested. The reason for shifts from deep sleep to near awakening at regular intervals may relate to evolutionary need for alertness to danger, but this would not explain the regularity in the frequency of these cycles. It may have something to do with lowering of the blood sugar level, but this could not explain why, for example, a baby awakens at three- or four-hour intervals instead of every 60 to 90 minutes.

In the last decade of the nineteenth century, G. T. Ladd, professor of mental philosophy at Yale, reported his observations (1892) of cyclical eye movements during sleep. There were no sleep laboratories at that time. Apparently he first noted his own eye movements when he was dreaming and then was able to corroborate this observation while watching his wife's eye movements during sleep. He was able to distinguish between times the eyes were motionless, in apparent "dreamless sleep," and times when they were moving. He said he was "inclined to believe that, in somewhat vivid visual dreams, the eyeballs move gently in their sockets, taking various positions. . . ." He went on to say, "In a dream we probably focus our eyes somewhat as we should do in making the same observation when awake" (Kleitman 1960).

Since the early 1950s, Nathaniel Kleitman, a pioneer in dream research working under sponsorship of A. J. Carlson, professor of physiology at the University of Chicago, has contributed to our knowledge of sleep physiology. Volunteer subjects were studied in the laboratory while they were sleeping. Electrodes were placed on their scalp and connected with wires to a constantly running electroencephalograph.

The characteristics of the EEG tracings changed in a cyclical way. Kleitman with Aserinsky in 1953 learned about and described the association of rapid eye movements with the ascending phase of stage 1 sleep. In 1957, Dement and Kleitman reported the connection of rapid-eye-movement (REM) sleep with dreaming. Dement and Wolpert (1958) extended the studies to correlate dream content with external stimuli.

Schiff, Bunney, and Friedman (1961) found rapid eye movements occurring when subjects were carrying out posthypnotic suggestions that they dream. Continuing research has shown that sleep walking, night terrors, enuresis, and snoring occur in deeper stages of sleep as measured on the electroencephalographic tracings.

It has long been believed that there are periods of "dreamless" sleep that were correlated with stage 3 and 4 EEG sleep but studies (Rechstaffen, Verdone, and Wheaton 1963, Foulkes 1966) have shown that there is considerable ideation during non-REM levels of sleep.

Dreaming is characterized as occurring in the ascending phase of Stage

1 sleep when the sleeper's eyes are moving rapidly as though focusing on moving objects. Eye movements are slow, roving independently of each other during other stages of sleep. When volunteers in sleep laboratories are awakened during the REM phase of sleep, they report connected ideas that appear to be real. It is much more difficult to get any sort of connected thoughts from subjects who are awakened during Stage 2, 3, or 4 sleep when the eyes are not involved in focused attention. There might be very important connected thoughts in the so-called non-REM (NREM) phase of sleep if those doing the research could use ideomotor techniques of exploration combined with light hypnosis.

I have found that patients with emotional and physical problems are often able to recognize that something was happening during the night before the symptom appears, but they usually will remember only a garbled dream that seems unimportant. After setting up finger signals and reviewing the entire night of sleep, I have found that the real beginning of their symptoms closely followed a much more real and often alarming sequence of thoughts that has been difficult for them to recall. These thoughts were apparently transposed and made to seem funny instead of alarming. The amusing report is what the patient will say is a "dream." The patients know what a dream is like. They will say the causal sequences were "thoughts" and were not dreams.

I have believed that REM dreaming was less important than what I would call NREM phases of sleep. A review of reports from sleep laboratories since 1956 has led me to speculate that the ideation of REM sleep has two components: (1) intensely real "thoughts" that cause physiological disturbances and, (2) the secondary, nonstressful transformation into what are described as dreams. The dreams can be remembered on awakening, but the intensely real thoughts are forgotten. I believe emotion and adrenal hormone secretions stimulated by disturbing ideation could cause amnesia, just as is the case with classical trauma. I hope that the elite observers of sleep ideation will be able to substantiate or reject this simplistic view.

During regression studies of sleep ideation my patients have emphasized that thoughts are deeper and dreams occur at lighter levels of sleep. They are very literal in their understandings about when thoughts or dreams are occurring. I must say "last night" for the time before midnight and "this morning" for occurrences between midnight and final awakening in the morning.

Severe Preeclampsia Traced to Deep-Level Thoughts

Case Study

An excellent example of the importance of recognizing that an ordinary dream may have a deeper precursor is given by an obstetrical patient. I will call her Barbara. She was in her seventh month and was feeling very well.

I saw her on Friday. Her blood pressure was normal. Her urine test was negative for protein and sugar. She showed no evidence of edema in her legs. On Saturday afternoon she gave a going-away party for friends of her husband who were being transferred to another section of the country. As the guests arrived, two of her women friends commented on how pretty she looked. They were surprised that she appeared so slender for a woman seven months along. The first friend said, "Why, Barbara, you don't even *look* pregnant!" A few minutes later a second friend came up the stairs to compliment her and added, "Barbara, you don't even *look* pregnant." Barbara had no reason for alarm at this point. She had been told that everything was going as intended and that her physical condition was excellent.

She was flattered by the compliments of her friends. She thought she slept well Saturday night, but in the morning her legs were swollen and she had gained three pounds. On Monday morning she awakened after a fitful night of sleep. Her legs and her hands were puffed up. She had gained another three pounds. She called and was told to come immediately to my office.

Now her blood pressure was 172/110. Her pulse rate was 92. She had pitting edema (pressure with a finger would leave a dimple) from her feet to her knees. Her urine tested 4+ for protein. This was a fulminating preeclampsia, carrying an increased risk for her baby as well as herself, but I knew from my resident training and subsequent experience that hospitalization may allow a drop in blood pressure temporarily because the patient feels she will be helped. The causal emotional factors will not have been altered, however, and within 24 to 48 hours there is a rapid increase in the blood pressure, leading to emergency caesarean section. The reason for this is what I call "hospital anxiety." Blood pressure testing and questions about new symptoms such as headache or pain in the upper abdomen tend to cause pyramiding alarm. For Barbara, a caesarean at 26 weeks would not be a productive solution. This was an important pregnancy. I wanted good results and a term-sized baby.

I explained the alternatives. She decided to follow my advice which was to go home and stay most of the time in bed *for a few days* in order to mobilize fluid and electrolytes and permit her kidneys to work more efficiently for her. I told her to insist that her *husband take that time off to be with her at home.* I would see her there twice a day *until her blood pressure returned to normal.* (These directions conveyed to her that there was an end point to being in bed "a few days," that she would have her husband's support full time during those days and that her blood pressure would "return to normal". Before she left the office, I placed her in a light state of hypnosis and began questioning her about the sequence of events during the weekend. Barbara was a good hypnotic subject. She knew about finger signals and had been practicing self hypnosis. The search moved quickly.

D.C.: Has your sleep been restful and comfortable last night?

Barbara: (finger signal) No.

D.C: Please go over your sleep last night. As you fall asleep your 'yes' finger will lift. Each time you are dreaming, as you know dreams, your "no" finger will lift. When you are finally awake this morning your "I don't want to answer" finger will lift.

It took approximately 60 seconds for her to review the seven hours she said she had slept. I asked her to go over the night again and to have the "yes" finger on her other hand lift any time she came to something that made her feel uncomfortable. Her "yes" finger lifted. Then, a few seconds later, her "yes" finger on her left hand lifted to indicate something distressing. The same signal of distress lifted three more times synchronously with the dreaming signals. I started searching again.

D.C.: Is it the same dream each time your "no" finger lifts?

Barbara: (After a brief unconscious scanning of the data) (f.s.) Yes.

D.C.: Do you know yet what you have been dreaming about?

Barbara: (Verbal) Yes. I have been dreaming that I have a baby that looks like a grasshopper.—That's pretty silly!

D.C.: Let me ask your fingers. Is there some idea or series of thoughts at a deeper level of sleep that come before the dream and might have something to do with the problem that brings you in here today?

Barbara: (f.s.) Yes. (An expression of distress appears before her finger lifted). My finger is lifting but I don't know what it means. (This is a typical response. The unconscious knowledge has moved the finger but has not yet reached higher levels of perception.

D.C.: Please go over that thought or series of thoughts until you know what it is telling you. As it starts, your "yes" finger will lift and when it ends, your "no" finger will lift. When you know it well enough to talk about it your 'I don't want to answer' finger will lift.

Barbara: (After six sweeps over the data) The thought has to do with a very disturbing sense of seeing that the baby I have just delivered is abnormal and cannot survive. That has been going through my mind ever since Saturday.

D.C.: Just tune in to your baby, Barbara. I'm going to ask your subconscious mind, 'Is this little baby all right?'

Barbara: (f.s.) Yes.

At this point I went over the sequences involved when she will, in the future, go into labor and deliver a healthy, full term infant. She hallucinated the time of labor starting. She recognized her ability to turn off feelings in her abdomen and then bring the feeling back to normal. She "saw" her baby, a healthy, full-term infant, and then read off the date of delivery, the sex of her baby, the length of labor from the time her contractions were five minutes apart. (This use of a pseudo-orientation into the future helps me know the patient is free of resistance when all parts of the imagery are reported. It also helps set a subconscious mental picture that is associated with optimism.)

Comment

Barbara's blood pressure and weight were back to normal within 24 hours. Although she continued to excrete protein in her urine, she delivered a term-sized healthy infant a few days after the hallucinated date for delivery.

The only reason we could find for her unusual reaction to the comments about her looking pretty and looking as though she was not pregnant was that she had been a very sensitive child who carried that sensitivity into adult life. She was married to a man who tended to be overly critical of her when anything failed to meet with his wishes. The idea of not looking pregnant was subconsciously sensed as a criticism as though she really should look more pregnant. Some people carry their infant protruding forward and some carry them in their abdomen without appearing very pregnant. We talked this over in order for her to use her conscious-level understandings to reframe the original conversations with the friends.

One other patient suddenly developed a similar severe preeclampsia with marked proteinuria. She and her husband moved into a motel near my house. There they could be together and I could see them both, twice daily.

While her husband was picking up lunch for her at a restaurant, she reported a repeated dream that her baby would be abnormal. During a quick search for the reason, she recalled the advance made to her by her boss who had been drinking too much at a Christmas party when she was in her second month of pregnancy. He had pulled her into a room in order to have sex with her, but she managed to talk him back to his senses and got him back to the party. In subsequent months, however, he would jokingly ask, "How's my baby doing." This was the source of her unrealistic dream that the baby would look like her boss. After recognizing the source and exposing the information to conscious reasoning, she returned her blood pressure to normal within 36 hours and delivered a normal child at term. She was relieved to see a white patch on the back of the baby's head, identical in its place to the similar patch of white hair on her husband's head.

There is genuine clinical value in helping patients discover what they believe in hypnosis to be the origin of their problem. It could be an acute anxiety attack, a postoperative bowel obstruction (ileus), severe pre-eclampsia, massive postpartum hemorrhage, thrombophlebitis, or an acute asthmatic episode. I have worked with each of these problems and found that the troubled patients can quickly reverse the stress response when given a chance to recognize the enemy.

Those doing research on these matters, however, need to consider *all* the revealed thought content with techniques that are adequate for the job. They must not ignore possible information because they do not know how to access that data.

Outline of Sleep Disorders

The ways of treating the common sleep disorders can be simple. The initial treatment should involve a psychological search for possible cause-and-effect relationships. This takes very little time. If no change in behavior follows, there is still time to refer the patient to a university center were special studies and treatments can be carried out. Common sleep disorders are:

Children

Night terrors: Incidence from birth to about 10–12 years
Enuresis (bedwetting). Organic and psychological
Sleepwalking (somnambulism)

Adults

Insomnia (difficulty getting to sleep): two types
Narcolepsy: Undesired falling asleep with or without cataplexy sudden loss of muscle tone]

Hypersomnia (continued need for sleep—15–20 hours)
Consciously unrecognized stressful ideation

Sleep Distubance in Children

Night terrors, bedwetting, and somnambulism (sleepwalking) all are more prevalent in boys than girls, they occur during the first part of the night and all occur during non–rapid eye-movement (NREM) stages of sleep. Again, here are abnormalities in sleep that originate when the child is deeply asleep, suggesting as I have said earlier in this chapter that we will learn more about these complaints when ideomotor search methods are used for their exploration.

Night Terrors

The condition of night terrors with children seems to be time limited, usually ending before the age of 6 or 7 but occasionally 12 at the latest. A child will awaken screaming with fear without knowing the source of fear. The child will not be comforted by parental efforts. The child's eyes will be open but seeming not to see. After an interval of 5 to 20 minutes the child will fall asleep and have no memory of the event on awakening in the morning. Symptoms suggest deep trance phenomena.

I have not had the opportunity of treating such children. I believe, however, that any child above the age of 4 years might be able to discover the stimulating imagery that triggers each event and would probably trace it back to frightening stimuli during the labor or delivery. Treatment would be to have the child rehearse the sleep ideation and the start of a fear reaction. He or she would be given a reversal anchor, turning off the fear by pressing the right thumb and index finger tips together. This would be repeated until a finger would lift to indicate confidence that the child will now be able to sleep restfully and comfortably all night.

Two mothers have reported their observation that their infant awakened screaming in fear at precisely the time of the night when delivery was by forceps because of fetal distress. This would be an imprint memory that would be triggered by a diurnal rhythm. I have advised them to go to the baby while it is peacefully sleeping. They are to nudge the infant slightly to bring it to a nearly awake state and then to give soothing suggestions of love and assurance that sleep will continue to be peaceful all night and that he or she will awaken feeling happy and smiling in the morning. Babies are tuned to a mother's thoughts at all times but the moments of being almost, but not quite, awake seem to be the best for suggestions.

This was a form of treatment used by Emile Coué with parents of infants with various problems. The method seemed to work with these two infants, but the problem could have been related to external noises in the street at a specific time. It also might have cleared spontaneously without maternal treatment.

Enuresis

Bedwetting has frustrated parents and doctors alike. All sorts of treatments have been tried, ranging from repeatedly awakening the child with orders to walk to the bathroom and urinate to having electrodes that would shock the child when the sheets are wet. Children in Germany have been humiliated by having a wet bed set off a loud alarm that would tell neighborhood children about the sad state of their friend. This was intended to motivate a child to stop the problem in order to save face.

Enuresis occurs more frequently in boys than in girls. It is associated with deep, NREM sleep and usually is outgrown during the first four years of life. Doctor Raymond LaScola (Chapter 23 in this book) has discussed this problem and his success in using hypnotic techniques with positive reinforcement.

Parents should keep in mind, however, that children can insert foreign objects into any and all orifices of their body. The urethra is no exception. Inflammation of the urethra can be a stimulus that may cause the bladder to contract in an expulsive way in response to dreams that might be funny or frightening. The possibility of nocturnal molestation has to be another consideration with female children who wet the bed.

Therefore, parents should be aware that the problem may not be entirely one of rebellion or hostility as enuresis often seems to be. A continued problem calls for a medical consultation and gentle questioning by the consultant.

Somnambulism

Sleepwalking occurs predominantly in boys during the first third of the night and, like the other two complaints, occurs during deep, NREM sleep, suggesting that it is a form of spontaneously occurring hypnosis. Sleepwalking probably occurs at some time in every child's early life. Several children that I have seen with this problem have associated it with family unrest about money, jobs, or threatened divorce. It usually is self limiting and is not dangerous. The sleep walker avoids objects that stand in the way. He can respond to directions but his eyes seem not to see. The entire experience is forgotten by the time the child awakens.

When sleepwalking occurs with an adult, it is a reflection of a serious emotional problem or of organic brain disease and can be dangerous. It requires immediate consultation with a neurologist who is also aware of possible emotional origins of this problem.

Sleep Disorders in Adults

Insomnia

Insomnia probably occurs at some time in everyone's experience. We treat it when it is a continuing problem. There are two types. It may be difficult to get to sleep, or sleep is interrupted and the sufferer cannot get back to sleep. Insomnia is one of the first indicators of depression. Drugs that force a troubled patient into sleep may be dangerous and should not be prescribed by doctors. Keep in mind the possibility of the patient needing treatment for depression.

Treatment steps for insomnia are as follows:

1. Orient the patients in hypnosis to the first moment when "sleep or the lack of it became important." Have a "yes" finger lift at that point. Ask if there could have been an earlier experience that made this experience significant. Follow with the question "Now that you know this, will you agree that you have a right to sleep deeply and restfully at night?"

2. If these questions are optimistically answered, you can then have the patients remember a night of sleep that was pleasant and restful. A "yes" finger is to lift when they are falling asleep. Their "no" finger is to lift each time they are dreaming something enjoyable and the "I don't want to answer" finger is to lift when they know they are awakening the next morning feeling good.

3. The final step is to teach the patients self-hypnosis and have them rehearse going in and coming out of hypnosis with specific signals. I use the touching of the left index finger and thumb for entering hypnosis and the opposite fingers for coming out "feeling good." This skill can then be used prior to getting ready for sleep until such time as the patients are confident of sleeping well again.

Narcolepsy

Narcolepsy, or undesired falling asleep, may be an indicator of an underlying serious illness requiring specific medical attention. Diabetes, brain tumor, or liver or kidney failure are some of the possibilities.

Far more common is a habit pattern that started much earlier in life than the time the patient comes to you. Here is a case example that responded well to hypnosis intervention.

A nurse at a Symposium in Columbus, Ohio, asked me to talk with the resident in physical medicine who was preparing for the American Board Certification in his field. She said, "Every time I have seen him in the library he has fallen asleep. He needs to study but I am afraid he will flunk unless he can stay awake. Could you please talk to him. He is here at these meetings.

At a coffee break I approached him and asked if he was having trouble falling asleep when he wants to be studying. He was enthusiastic when I asked if he would be a volunteer for a demonstration. He said, "Every time I sit down to study I get so sleepy that I just can't keep my eyes open."

He went on to say that this had not been a problem for him in school or in college. He had always been a good student.

Instructor: Let me ask this right index finger to lift unconsciously when you think the word "yes," . . . (He selected the three signals.) Now please orient your thoughts back through the years to the first time in your life when sleep became too important in some way, some time when sleeping or not sleeping was very important to you. When you are there, your "yes" finger will lift, and, as it lifts, please bring that experience up to a level where you can talk about it.

Doctor: (After a lag of 70 seconds, the finger slowly lifts. This is followed by an amused change of expression and this, in turn, brings out a description of an incident.) My brother and I have just finished scrawling with crayons all over the wall in the dining room and Mother is pretty mad. She says for us to go right to bed without any supper. She doesn't punish us. She says that Dad will punish us when he gets home.

Instructor: How old are you at the time?

Doctor: Four, four-and-a-half. We're twins.

Instructor: Go on.

Doctor: Well, my brother and I talked it over and we decided it would be a good idea if we were asleep when Dad came home. (He chuckles.) Dad didn't punish us.

Instructor: Is that what makes sleep so important?

Doctor: (finger signal) Yes. (His "no" finger lifted to the question "Are there any other possible factors?") I guess I must be afraid about that exam. That's crazy, isn't it?

The doctor was then asked to feel all the sensations associated with being very wide awake and interested in all the things he will be relearning and fixing in his mind. He was asked to develop the feeling that the examination is just a way for him to show how much he has learned and how very qualified he is to treat human beings who need his help. His "yes" finger lifted to indicate acceptance of these feelings at a subconscious level, and he nodded to indicate that he could sense this feeling consciously as well. He was asked to have his "yes" finger lift when his unconscious mind knew that he could have these feelings of alertness and readiness to learn any time he was in a library or studying at home.

He was asked to rehearse subconsciously all the feelings of his next study period and to have an arm levitation indicate the moment he *knew* he would never have to worry about being sleepy or going to sleep at times when he wanted to be wide awake and alert. He was allowed to take three minutes for this while the therapist reviewed the steps of the session with the other members of the class. The steps here were simple:

1. Set up ideomotor responses.
2. Induce hypnosis by asking for a review of an important experience relating to sleep.
3. Orient to the first experience making sleep too important (as an escape from danger).
4. Allow the doctor to resolve the problem by exposing it to reasoning processes.
5. Obtain a commitment of optimistic outcome by pseudo-orientation in time to a successful experience studying.

This resident in physical medicine was seen ten years later at a conference at the University of Utah. He had passed his examinations and was practicing his specialty.

Narcolepsy While Driving an Automobile

This is a frequent problem because of good roads and quiet engines. It is very important for a sleepy driver to pull off the highway, get out of the driver's seat and walk, or just lean back and take a nap for a few minutes. Either of these strategies will permit a shift away from the mental fatigue that causes this type of sleepiness. The worst reaction is to try fighting sleep. It is a losing battle because the effort intensifies the driver's awareness of sleepiness and can result in a life-threatening accident.

Hypersomnia

In hypersomnia there is a continued need for an abnormal number of hours of sleep. It can be as much as 20 hours in a day. This condition may be a symptom of an important medical illness, and it requires a medical consultation before going ahead with a hypnotherapeutic approach.
Questions should be asked:

1. Does the problem serve any valuable purpose? If so, what purpose does it serve? Let a thought come as the "yes" finger lifts.
2. Is prolonged sleep being used as a sort of self-punishment? If so, is it possible that there has been enough punishment now? If the answer is "yes," the problem can be easily worked out. If the answer is "no," ask the subject's unconscious mind to go back to the first moment something happened

to make him or her feel guilty. The solution then will have to be an individual one and will tax the therapist's intuitions.

Consciously Unrecognized Stressful Ideation

This is a very broad area that will be considered in relation to any maladjustment that has not been improved by previous treatments. Basically, whatever may be the problem, ask if there has been a beginning, before whatever is reported. Could there have been a sensitizing experience prior to the incident reported? (Refer to Chapter 12.)

Comment

There are many avenues of study open to anyone using hypnosis for investigating nighttime sleep. It is my hope that those reading this book will work out a protocol for use of hypnotic methods in their investigations of human dis-ease.

The interested reader may want to read comprehensive books about sleep by Wolstenholme and O'Connor (1960), Nathaniel Kleitman (1965), David Foulkes (1966), Luce and Segal (1966).

17

Sexual Learning, Problems, and Abuse

I would like to present here the information given me by gynecological and obstetrical patients during 5 years of my hospital training and the following 47 years of my practice, first as a specialist in gynecology and obstetrics and, since 1985 working with psychosomatic medical problems with men as well as women. It has been my impression, shared with LeCron, that the sexual learning and problems of males are very similar to those of females. Treatment modalities, however, will differ.

Teaching institutions of the 1930s and 1940s gave very little, if any, attention to the possibility that sexual self-image might have something to do with endocrine development and interaction with tissues and organs as a child matures. The major research and clinical interest in medicine was, and generally continues to be, centered on what could be seen under the microscope, learned in the biochemical laboratory, and treated with surgery or with measurable quantities of hormones.

McGaugh (1984) and others during the 1980s drew attention to the role of endocrines, especially epinephrine, in the storage and retrieval of memory. In obstetrics we have known the role of epinephrine and emotion during pregnancy. Epinephrine may cause abortion during the first trimester or the return of concentric (nonlabor) uterine contractions with cessation of cervical dilatation at the final end of pregnancy. Fearful reaction in frightening hospitals may lead to caesarean delivery.

The connection has been repeatedly shown by regression studies of obstetrical patients who have had spontaneous abortions or others who have had caesarean sections for the wastebasket diagnosis of "cephalo-pelvic disproportion." As might be expected in these cases, the physiological response is determined by the background experience of each patient and her filtered response to her dreams or circumstances in the hospital (see Chapter 20).

Sensory stimuli seem to be modulated through the reticular activating system, which relays messages to influence the release of hormones and neuropeptides. Candace Pert and her associates at the National Institute of Mental Health (1974, 1981, 1985a,b) have been demonstrating that very important information substances are released by individual cells throughout the brain as well as by cells throughout the body. She points out that these peptide substances move in the circulation to bring about significant changes in the way tissues and organs behave. Under one set of circumstances the receptor areas of tissue cells are open for advice from these "messenger molecules." With different circumstances the receptors slap shut and will not accept advice.

What is rapidly evident in the case of epinephrine can also be shown with much slower processes involving the hypothalamic-pituitary axis and the gonads.

Clinical evidence is apparent when a patient threatening abortion is helped to find and remove the effect of a frightening dream sequence during a 10 minute telephone call at 3 a.m. or a patient with arrested labor precipitates in bed after discovering and removing the unconscious source of her fear. Simple and rapid means of bringing about change are available because of ideomotor review techniques involving the reasoning processes of the individual patient, as exemplified in the following case of pseudopregnancy.

> A woman has wanted children and has looked pregnant, felt pregnant, and has had milk-like secretions from her breasts for 18 months. During this time she has not been releasing fertilizable eggs. Eight pregnancy tests have been negative.
>
> During a brief hypnotic interview involving her unconscious answers with a Chevreul pendulum, she discovers that she has been unconsciously afraid that her husband would die if she had a child. Her basis for this unconscious fear was that she was an only child. Her father died of pneumonia when she was 3 months of age. She identified her husband with her father. She did not need to do this. She selected the date of her next menstrual period and had it a day after the selected date. The physical expressions of wanting a pregnancy disappeared in a few days.

My medical school training for taking histories in 1939 and 1940, my junior and senior years, did not include advice about how to take a sexual history or to ask about childhood molestation. This would not have been enough anyway. We have since learned that gender awareness and misunderstandings about worthiness may start during intrauterine life and may affect adult thinking and behavior. Hospital residency training for me included marvelous experience with surgery and obstetrical work but almost nothing about the possible emotional factors in the problems we treated in gynecology or obstetrics. My training was "purely scientific" in the approaches to diagnosis and treatment of women. We did not recognize that hypogonadism, endometriosis, myomata of the uterus, sterility, menorrhagia, metrorrhagia, dyspareunia, anorgasmia, and premature menopause might have psychological roots that could be removed without surgery.

Psychologists are given a wealth of information on these matters, but they are given little chance to use their knowledge because my medical colleagues are only recently beginning to recognize the help available from psychologists and marriage, family and child counselors.

My Personal Learning Process as Taught by Patients

I began my practice in 1946 in a city with a population of 12,000. After a couple of years, I began having patients coming back for routine annual checkups. By then they were comfortable in my office and were better able to talk about sensitive subjects like sex.

About once a month one of these patients would muster enough courage to ask me a question about her sexual responsiveness. I had not been asking questions about sexual attitudes of my patients. This was new material to me.

One question was repeated, almost word for word, by each woman: "Doctor, I have multiple orgasms when I have intercourse and none of my friends do. Is there something wrong with me?" Some would add, "Am I a nymphomaniac?"

Ten years passed before I learned to use ideomotor review methods to discover why such lucky women were able to have multiple orgasms when they were in a relationship of mutual love and respect. Nothing was wrong with these women; their less fortunate women friends were the ones with a problem. The essential factors permitting them to be multiorgasmic were with them at birth and were not altered by parental interference. These factors seemed to be as follows:

1. They all felt welcome as girls at the time of their birth.

2. They all had been nursed lovingly by their mother. By this I mean that

their mother had come to them while they were in the early stage of awakening from sleep, a time when babies usually are happy and are cooing and looking around the room while they explore their toes or put them in their mouth.

Some women, during the age-regression to this time of being nursed, remembered feelings that are later recognized as orgasmic. The Creator may have arranged for nursing to be pleasurable as an incentive for mammalian mothers of all species to nurse their young and for their young to bond with and be obedient to their mother at times of danger. If all mothers were engaged in other interesting activities, their babies would die victims of carnivorous predators or would die of starvation.

3. Orgasmic women seemed to have escaped a scolding when they explored their clitoris or vaginal orifice with their fingers while being bathed. Their mothers did not pull their hand away with a comment about being "dirty down there."

4. The father is important also in the development of healthy, normal sexual learning. He is the first male they know. The women in this study of normalcy have repeatedly told me about the pleasurable weakness of their knees when their daddy hugged them or chucked them under the chin as he says something like, "How's my little girl?" This is not incestuous. It is a step in the direction of normal heterosexual awareness and it can commence during the first three years of life.

5. Multiorgasmic women have remembered dreams that were associated with feelings akin to what they later knew as an orgasm. They believed these dreams started around the age of 6 or 7 years. They were not sexual dreams involving stimulation of their vulva or clitoris. Nothing was touching them that was not an everynight occurrence. The secret, they felt, was that the person they were dreaming about was showing acceptance and appreciation for them. *Caring acceptance is the major factor in normal sexual learning.*

6. Normal children are curious about their body, particularly the body of a child of the opposite sex. The multiorgasmic women never were in a situation when mutual viewing experiences "behind the barn" or in the basement were interrupted by an angry parent or older sibling making them feel that what they were doing was evil.

7. The multiorgasmic women somehow did not get involved with strangers or sexually troubled relatives who take advantage of children who are friendly and affectionate. They avoided the feeling of guilt that molested children sense telepathically in the person who is molesting them. This is a matter of importance to be discussed in relation to sexual abuse. Children who have felt accepted and loved from the time of their birth do not feel they have to work hard to be pleasing to other people. They do not radiate "love me" emotional pheromones to all people around them.

8. By the time these multiorgasmic women were "necking" as teenagers, they were having orgasms in a nongenital way because they felt cared for and accepted by the boyfriend when he put his arm around them or kissed them on their mouth. They responded according to their interpretations of male behavior—correct or mistaken. They felt this, but the boy did not know what was happening.

9. By the time these women were in a trusting relationship with a meaningful male and were involved in having sexual intercourse, they had orgasms being kissed on their mouth, being caressed around their breasts, feeling his penis enter their vagina, and tightening and relaxing their vaginal muscles repeatedly around his penis. The intensity of response would be building and be at its highest when they felt his penis suddenly expand and pulsate with his orgasm. While he was still tumescent they could again reach a climax as they contracted and relaxed their vaginal muscles around his penis. Of course, this responsiveness was encouraging and good for the self-respect of their sexual partner.

10. The summation of this progressive learning process was that the bonding they had with their parents as infants was extended to the husband they eventually chose to be with. The strength of this bonding would be insurance against subsequent differences that could lead to divorce.

Taking a History: Some Points to Consider with Both Sexes

Start with a question such as, "If I can be helpful in some way, what would be the most important things for us to work on together?"

Some cultures still insist that the first-born child should be a male. Among others, these are: Turkish, Chinese, Japanese, Greek, orthodox Jewish, Arab, and Armenian. Females born first or following a first-born female child in these cultures may feel inadequate and unworthy of love at the time of their birth. This can influence body build, hormonal balance, self-confidence, and relationships to others as they mature.

Male children do not learn as quickly, grow as rapidly, or run as speedily as a female sibling during their early years. If a boy is followed, in a year or two, by a female infant, he may be embarrassed to find the little sister reading before he can read, spelling better, and so on. This not only can be a source of poor self-image and confidence but it can lead to stammering and learning difficulties in school. It may sow seeds of resentment toward the sister and can generalize this subconscious hostility and jealousy to all women as he grows up. Adult premature ejaculation, inability to maintain an erection, and inability to ejaculate may sometimes be traced to these beginnings.

It is important to ask for a conscious answer to the question "When you were a child, did you feel it was OK for you to be a boy (or girl, depending on your patient's sex)?" The answer to this question will be "no" if the child sensed being unwanted during intrauterine life or at the time of birth. The conclusion may have been drawn on the basis of incorrect understandings but it is an imprint type of impression that can shape a lifetime of negative expectations until corrected.

I need to know several things about parents: Is each alive? Did they get along well? Did they stay together? If divorced or deceased, what age was the patient at the time? I write the age of the parent at that time and circle the age of the patient on the same line, "Mother, died 42 (6), cancer." Children under the age of 10 generally assume some sort of feeling responsible for death or divorce of parents. This needs attention later during therapy. If marriage of either parent occurs after a death or divorce, circle the age of the patient at that time and find out his or her attitude toward the stepparent.

Also circle the patient's age or the date at the time of serious illness or surgeries where general anesthesia was used and note why the surgery was performed. Unconsciously perceived conversations in the operating room will need exploration if there were postoperative problems. Keep in mind the fact that hospitals are places where people die suddenly, just in case you run into unusual sources of resistance to therapy later (see Chapter 27).

Recognizing the damaging influence of inhibited parents and some religions, I ask about masturbation like this, "Did you ever dare masturbate as a kid?" I usually add, "Did you know that all mammals masturbate? It is a very important way for a young mammal to learn about its body." Although the answer may be, "No. I didn't even think about it until I was in high school," it is probable that a patient saying this was scolded for trying as a child. The influence of command statements at such a time can block the instructive sexual dreams such a child would have had around the age of 6 and later.

Molestation History Without Physical Trauma

Adults who have been molested during infancy or childhood will only rarely report this experience without help from their doctor or therapist. Questions about molestation are necessary because guilt-associated molestation trauma will be suppressed. I am writing here about molestation that is not physically abusive.

The molested child may be flattered and erotically stimulated by the act. At the same time, the child will sense, by facial expression or possibly telepathy, that the molesting person feels guilty about what he or she is doing.

Erotic feelings that are associated with the guilt, picked up from the molesting person, can harmfully influence genital and urinary tract physiology. Females may have delayed menses, dysmenorrhea, ovarian cysts, endometriosis, myomata and recurring vaginal or bladder infections that can be traced in hypnosis to guilt-associated molestation. I do not believe males are as vulnerable in this way, but it should be considered with fertility studies in which the man's sperm count is low. Unconscious guilt could be a factor in feeling unworthy of having children.

The child may have been threatened if he or she "ever tells." The mother sometimes refuses to believe a child who comes to her with an account of being molested. She may angrily accuse the child of lying. This can lead to an ongoing fear of talking to anyone about molestation.

Women can molest children of both sexes, and this should be kept in mind. Similarly, molestation can be instigated by older girls or women and can target either boys or girls.

Oral Molestation

Oral molestation can occur during infancy. Babies have an active sucking reflex that can stimulate a father, uncle, grandfather, or older male sibling into the idea of putting his erect penis into that mouth. There is no erotic pleasure in this for the infant. The experience can be terrifying because it is hard for the infant to breathe. Its normal sucking reflex may be eliminated by this act. The infant usually senses, and absorbs to itself, the guilt of the person doing this. This is where the trauma seems to occur.

Since conscious memory does not begin until the age of 2 or 3 years, there will be no conscious recollection for this infantile trauma. Some patients will recall that they have had dreams of this being done to them. Infants dream and the pattern of this dreaming can continue after the beginning of conscious memory.

Be alert to possibility of oral molestation when you learn that your patient was wall-eyed or cross-eyed during childhood. Their dominant eye may have centered in terrified attention on the penis or trying to avoid looking at it.

Be alert for oral molestation when your patient has a history of gagging or has had repeated throat infections as a child. Both are examples of hypersensitivity problems conditioned by emotional trauma from molestation or a tonsillectomy. The problem of tonsillitis that leads to tonsillectomy will be remembered but the preceding molestation will be hidden by conscious amnesia.

Genital Molestation

Be alert for genital molestation when there is a history of recurring urinary tract infection beginning in childhood. Such infections can stem from congenital urinary tract abnormalities, but they are commonly caused by either molestation or rough parental cleansing of the vulva.

Female Sexual Problems

There are many more women suffering from sexual problems than women who occasionally come in for an interview because they are worried over being multiorgasmic.

Since the problem has usually been aggravated by complaints of the husband or sexual partner, I usually invite him to sit in on the first interview in order that he have an idea of how hypnosis will be used. The hypnotic part of the session may be started at the time of the first interview, restricting the demonstration to an understanding of the Law of Reversed Effect. Just as insecure males "trying" to ejaculate during intercourse may fail to do so, dys- or anorgasmic women are "trying" to respond in the way that seems to be expected.

This demonstration with postural suggestion is followed by an induction for both to experience. I prefer to arrange the therapeutic work for about a week later. This gives the couple time to talk over the process and ask questions. I see the woman alone. I ask her to let her husband review the tape later.

There are several variants of orgasmic problems that can be treated through hypnosis:

1. The woman has never had an orgasm that she can remember.
2. She can climax during masturbation but not with intercourse.
3. She has orgasms during intercourse but requires clitoral stimulation.
4. She has vaginal orgasms "most of the time." Ask for her estimate of the percentage of the time as a base line for determining improvement with therapy.
5. She has had what she considers healthy responsiveness in the past with this or other partners but is not responding now.
6. She has pelvic pain or bladder problems after intercourse unexplained by physical findings.

These designations are mainly for the therapist to use in gauging success or failure with therapy. The treatment for all of them is the same. The direction of treatment is a progressive one.

Before beginning treatment, ask these questions:

1. Do you always reach a climax during intercourse when you feel good about having intercourse? (This means that she is not angry with her sexual partner.)
2. If not always, about what percentage of the time do you reach a climax?
3. Any way of reaching a climax is fine, but are you able to have orgasms without the need for clitoral stimulation? (If clitoral stimulation is necessary, it is likely that the patient has grown up in a sexually inhibited or troubled family. Parental commands can cause vaginal anesthesia.)
4. Is your inner mind willing to let you have more pleasure than you have permitted in the past?

Record the interview. I believe it is very important in this type of therapy to record the session on audiotape for the woman to review in hypnosis when she is home in her bed. This also serves as a protection for you against being accused of making advances to her in the office. There is a potential for this problem to occur with women who have been criminally raped or physically abused during childhood. The danger of this relates to a flashback, state-dependent phenomenon relative to primary resistance during the induction of hypnosis (Cheek 1960c).

The patient should remain in a light hypnotic state. It is not necessary for a patient to be in a deep trance when ideomotor techniques are used. Rather, you want her in a light state but being aware of the ideomotor signals her fingers are making to reflect acceptance or rejection of suggestions. She is to make a mental note of anything suggested or any thought that occurs spontaneously that might be helpful. Feelings of discomfort or resistance to ideas need exploring before continuing treatment. It is made clear that she can come out of hypnosis at any time by merely opening her eyes to "break the circuits" and become totally alert.

Steps of Therapy

1. Discover why the patient feels she has had problems. "Please let your inner mind go back to the most important experience that seems to have interfered with your right to respond enjoyably with intercourse. When you are there, your 'yes' finger will lift. As it lifts, please bring that thought up to where you can talk about it. The method of helping correct the original problem will probably present itself to you. Usually the patient will resolve it by recognizing what it was.

2. Help her select an experience that she felt could have been very wonderful. When there, her "yes" finger will lift when she is starting the experience. Ask her then if her subconscious mind is willing to let her know what it could have been like if she had all the advantages listed by women who were worried because they had multiple vaginal orgasms.

3. If the answer is "yes," ask that she review the experience subconsciously without trying to feel anything consciously. The purpose here is to free the subconscious associative patterns at a physiological, "blueprint" level.

4. Her "yes" finger will lift when the experience is starting. Her "no" finger is to lift each time her inner mind knows she *could have had an orgasm* if she had never had any learning problems about sex. I say, "Each time that finger lifts, please think to yourself, 'It is all right to let go.' When you are totally relaxed, satisfied, and feeling very close to him, emotionally as well as physically, your 'I don't want to answer' finger will lift.'" (These statements are telling the patient of my confidence that her thoughts will be effective when she gives herself permission.)

5. The next step is to go over the experience again and let her body be twice as sensitive—her lips, her breasts, her vulva, and her vagina. I tell my patient that an office is not an appropriate place for orgasms. She is to keep the feelings at a subconscious, physiological level as though she were dreaming. The conscious feelings will all be there when the situation and the location are appropriate.

6. Ask the patient to review these thoughts in perhaps some other experience during her sleep tonight, to have her "yes" finger lift when she knows she will allow this to happen. She is to ask her "yes" finger to lift to lock into the thought just as she is drifting off to sleep.

Comment

In my beginning work I did a lot of exploring and reframing impressions during intrauterine life and at the time of birth. Unless there are strong reasons to do psychotherapy with the dysorgasmic or anorgasmic woman, I have found it unnecessary to do this any more. Clearly, sexual responsiveness of the multiorgasmic type is normal. My job is to help the patient rid herself of the factors that have superimposed difficulties on the responsiveness that the Creator gave her at birth.

At the close of the second interview I ask, "Have you thought of anything or learned anything today that could be helpful for you and your husband?" This question requires a review of matters that could be positive and often reveals information that can be used at the third, final visit.

Another appointment is set up for approximately a week following this second visit. I do not ask questions about whether or not there have been improvements. These will be spontaneously offered if the difficulties have been removed. If there is no offering of information, I ask the patient to orient her memory back to the beginning of last night's sleep, to have a "yes" finger lift then, a "no" finger to lift each time a dream is occurring, and her "I don't want to answer" finger to lift when she is awakening finally this morning.

This subconscious review induces an adequate hypnotic state to allow an answer to the question "Have you had any dreams or thoughts at night since you were here that have permitted you to experience one or more orgasms?" If the "yes" finger lifts, I usually add that the subconscious mind does not always offer a husband for the dream. It often is someone a woman would never choose as a sexual partner because such dreams occurring in childhood do not involve intercourse. It can be a postman, a teacher, etcetera. If the "no" finger lifted, I ask if her inner mind would permit her to have such dreams in the future. The "yes" finger will usually lift.

The next step is to have the patient select a target date for when she knows she is able to have as many or as few orgasms as she wishes. Her "yes" finger is to lift and, when it does, she will see a date as though written on a chalkboard.

The interview is ended with a suggestion that she go over an experience at that time as it is going to be and that she can feel subconsciously more than she had ever dreamed it could be. The same signals are used for the review.

The tape of this session is given her and she is asked to call in about two weeks from this time to report on progress.

Results are the best and the most rapid, in my experience, with women who have never been able to have a vaginal or clitoral orgasm during intercourse. They are worst when intercourse has once been orgasmic with the same partner but is no longer satisfactory. Here there often have accumulated unconscious emotional factors that have grown out of one of them having an extramarital affair or having done something that was a breech of faith.

The effectiveness of treatment is hard to judge because some patients can accept treatment immediately and others require a period of readjusting old patterns of thought.

Male Sexual Problems

Males' sexual problems seem usually related to maternal influences or to a past experience of relating to a castrating type of sexual partner. An overwhelming, manipulative mother can be jealous of her son's wife. There can be childhood imprints at emotional times when a mother has made statements implying permanency of their effect, such as, "Don't you *ever* do that again." Manifestations of difficulty are:

1. Premature ejaculation
2. Inability to ejaculate while the penis is in the vagina
3. Inability to maintain an erection
4. Total impotence, being unable to have an erection and never having an erection during sleep

The first three of these are totally psychological, in my opinion, and are treatable with hypnosis using first an exploration for causal imprinting with reframing of the experiences. The next step is to use the same sort of subconscious review sequences as discussed here with female problems, followed by a request for instructive dreams and choice of a target date for complete freedom from the past difficulty.

The fourth situation, total impotence, may also be psychological, but it requires an adequate consultation and evaluation by a urologist to rule out arteriosclerotic changes in the circulation to the penis or prostatic abnormality. A consultation with a neurologist is indicated if there are peripheral sensation changes in the leg or muscular weakness that could relate to spinal cord problems. If the physical findings are clear of trouble, hypnosis can be used as with the other cases. The results, however, may be disappointing. The urologist should again be consulted if hypnosis fails. The urologist may suggest medication and injections of a drug into the penis just before having intercourse.

Working with Child Molestation

The goals for me when I learn that a girl has been molested but not physically abused are to help the victim recognize that the problem is with the person who molested her; she was a victim who may have been flattered or even sexually stimulated by the experience. The person who molested her was selfish. He did not have respect for a little girl and deserved to be punished.

The next step is to discover who the person was who molested her. The patient is placed in hypnosis and asked to look at the most important parts of the sexual experience as though she were in a theater with a lot of other people in the audience. One finger is to lift at the start, another for each important moment and a third to indicate the experience has ended.

She is then asked to review the experience as it might have been if she had known then what she knows now about this kind of person. Have her notice the reaction of the molester when she has taken control of the situation.

Temporo-Mandibular Syndrome as a Possible Flag of Molestation

An adult who had been suffering from severe temporo-mandibular syndrome and almost constant pain in her tense jaws knew consciously that she had been victimized for several years by her very large, tyrannical father. He would place her on his lap and play with her clitoris in exciting ways but would frighten her by ordering her to hold his penis in her mouth. She was flattered by his attention but also emotionally disturbed because she felt his guilt. She wanted to tell her mother but was afraid of her father's rage if he found out.

We discussed the home situation and learned that her mother was afraid of becoming pregnant and had shut off all sexual relations with the father. As an adult she could understand her father's frustration but also that he had no right to include her in his problem. I wondered what would have happened if a little child with good sharp teeth had clamped them down hard on her father's penis after he had insisted that she hold it in his mouth. Could it have taught that selfish father a memorable lesson about respect for his daughter? How would he have treated her after she had recovered the power he had taken from her only because he was powerful and bigger than his little daughter? It appears to me, I said, that he might have been horrified at first but might have suddenly developed a respect for her. He certainly would not have been able to tell her mother about the damage done to his penis but his daughter could have done so if necessary. In that case he would have had real problems trying to explain.

The patient at first looked frightened to think of her father being angry. Then she realized that she would have held all the cards and her father would have been put on the defensive. She roared with laughter. In a few moments she was able to hallucinate the scene. She saw her father's shocked expression and then that he burst into laughter. Sharing the laughter with him, she realized that he would have treated her with genuine respect and would not have needed any more lessons from her. After this it was possible for her to remove the patterned response of clenching her jaws during sleep and at times of daytime stress.

I was able to present this scenario because it was clear from her recollection of her father that he only appeared frightening at times but had never physically injured her or her mother. He loved them both. If her father had been alcoholic and violent, I would have had to present a different methodology.

Regression to a Time of Trauma

It is helpful to know how inventive adults can be when they are regressed back to some time when they were troubled about being molested at a young age. They can use mature judgment and understanding in hallucinating different strategies and deciding what would have been the best solution. They can also recognize in most cases with adult understanding that the molester was the one with problems. The molested child might have had some sexual stimulation but this only meant that he or she had normal genital awareness and should not feel guilty just because the molester felt guilty. Child molesters often are under the influence of alcohol at the time. A child can quickly recognize on reviewing an experience that the person doing this was really not the father, grandfather or uncle (the most common molesters) that they usually had known. While drinking, he is a completely different person. It might not be possible to stop such a person from drinking, but she can hallucinate ways in which she could have avoided the molester when he has been drinking.

The trauma of molestation seems more frequently to be caused by sensing the guilt of the molester than because of physical pain or injury. Physical injury associated with sexual assault is a very different thing. It can be very difficult to deal with and may require a group type of therapy.

I have been impressed by the heightened perceptions of people who have been physically assaulted in a situation where they fear for their life. Whether robbery or rape, whether the victims are male or female, they develop a lasting sixth sense that can have great protective value in the future. Make this clear to the victim. He or she will have adequate warning when anywhere near someone dangerous and can, either consciously or unconsciously, move away from the danger. Have them rehearse in hypnosis the protective conversational ploy that could turn the threat away if suddenly confronted. Of utmost importance is the protection you can give victims of assault or rape by teaching them to awaken instantly when they start to relive the assault and recognize consciously that the event is long past and the dream was just a dream. This is can help the victim avoid the posttraumatic stress disorder that can occur after repeated nights of reliving the experience and having amnesia for the fact on awakening.

Some Speculative Comments about Homosexuality

Homosexuality, either male or female, is a complex subject that will not be discussed here, partly because I have never been asked by a lesbian for help in becoming heterosexual and have only once been asked for help by a male homosexual. He felt abandoned by his older partner, who had shifted his attention to another young man. This patient was basically unwilling to change to heterosexuality, as shown by ideomotor responses. He quickly resumed the anxious state that brought him in for help. His only benefit was in learning that he could use hypnosis for stress reduction. My qualifications for altering the sexual drives of lesbians or male homosexuals are, therefore, less than adequate, and I have never felt there was a need to do so. My work with both has been no different from anyone else when there is an emotional or physical problem.

I have dealt as a physician and as a psychotherapist with many lesbian women over the years. Many of them have started with disappointments in their male relationships and have evolved into a relationship that feels safe and satisfying. Women homosexuals do not share the sometimes cataclysmic anxieties that I have seen in gay males.

Some considerations I would like advice on are perhaps best expressed as questions needing answers from gay males regressed in hypnosis to the dawning of sexual feelings. I have had no chance to search for the answers. It was only in 1985 that I shed my bias and opened myself to what the fetus can tell us. Clearly, the fetus can make terrible mistakes in interpreting its mother's reactions to external problems (Cheek 1992). What feels like rejection will be imprinted and permanent. Subsequent love and nurturing by the mother will not alter the earlier assumption. It is my hope that other therapists will extend our knowledge about the roots of homosexuality when they are comfortable exploring conception and the world of the fetus before birth. These questions would be worth exploring:

1. Does male homosexuality evolve before birth?
2. If so, what are the factors—maternal or paternal influences?
3. Is male homosexuality a product of persuasion by older males during early childhood?
4. If so, does feeling unwanted by the mother make a child more susceptible to external sexual advances by a male?
5. Does divorce really initiate a "lost father" yearning that generalizes to other men and solidifies male homosexuality?
6. Is there room for these factors in considering homosexuality?
   a. Was the individual homosexual in a previous life?
   b. Has the individual been joined by the spirit of a homosexual male who died suddenly and carried his yearnings to the person who is now his host?

Another question relates to twinning. We have learned that about 17 percent of pregnancies start with twins. One twin dies and is resorbed before its mother is aware of the twinning. Only 1 in 80 pregnancies continues to delivery of two viable twins (1.25%). Could there be an innate loving bond between uniovular twins that would influence sexual tendencies? Surviving twins of both sexes have reported communication between them prior to birth. The survivor seems to come into the world unconsciously feeling guilty for surviving at the expense of the twin. The "lost twin" syndrome I have witnessed has resulted in a continuing, unconscious search for a vague "other self." Could this be factor in subsequent homosexual tendencies?

18

Gynecology and
Female Urology

Howard Atwood Kelly, the first professor of gynecology at the newly opened
Johns Hopkins Medical School in 1889, believed that urological problems
of women should be within the province of a gynecologist and that
gynecologists should be as capable of performing surgery on the kidneys
and ureters as they are in repairing the lower urinary tract. It was also Kelly's
belief that gynecologists should have a thorough training in gross and
microscopic gynecological pathology. In 1941 it was decided by the direc-
tors of the American Board of Specialties that female urology belonged with
male urology and that to qualify as a Diplomate of the new American Board
of Obstetrics and Gynecology a physician must combine adequate training
in obstetrics and gynecology. As knowledge about the physiology and
biochemistry of the urinary system evolved, the shift of thinking was a logical
one. I was fortunate in having urology included in my residency training
at Johns Hopkins during the transition period.

Urinary Tract Infections

Female cystitis (bladder infection) and pyelitis (infection of the kidney
tubules) can occur as a result of congenital anomalies that interfere with
drainage, but for the most part they are psychogenic in origin. Even without
hypnosis, patients are able to recognize that they have been under stress
just before the onset of infection. Childhood molestation and painful cleansing of the infant's vulva by a parent who is afraid of "giving a child ideas"

are both possible sources of a hypersensitive urethra and lower urinary tract, but it will take hypnosis and ideomotor techniques to reveal the fact. Problems of recurring urinary tract infections, which are predominantly due to *E. Coli* bacteria originating in the bowel, can easily be treated with antibiotics, but hypnosis can be very helpful in discovering and removing the factors responsible for recurring infections.

Some women from inhibited families develop recurring urinary tract infections that follow intercourse. "Honeymoon cystitis" has been thought to occur because of repeated sexual trauma during a honeymoon, but constipation also can be a contributing factor. Some gynecologists have believed that a displaced urethral opening and a shorter than normal urethra are responsible for urethritis and cystitis and have invented plastic procedures to elongate the urethra and keep the meatus from trauma during intercourse. The value of this is questionable. Adequate history taking suggests that emotional, rather than anatomical, factors are the cause. Patients who can be helped to rid themselves of sexual misunderstandings and to enjoy intercourse without suffering from fear or guilt have freed themselves from the urinary problem. Anything that can be done to diminish the need for repeated cycles of antibacterial drugs is worth trying.

The method of exploring here is the same as can be used with any physical or emotional disturbance. Look for the first infection. Help the patient recognize what was contributing to the onset and help her to reframe sexual misunderstandings in the light of mature knowledge.

Case Example: A 21-year-old obstetrical patient came to me for prenatal care in her third month. Her health was excellent, but she reported that she had been treated for pyelitis when she was a child. There had been no subsequent problems. In her fifth month she came to the office complaining of painful and frequent urination. She had a temperature of 103 degrees and tenderness over her left kidney. Her centrifuged urine showed 4+ protein and visible blood cells as well as pus cells. She had pyelitis that cleared quickly with a sulfonamide. She said that she had just visited relatives in Chico, California, where the temperature had been 105 degrees. She had been constipated. I thought, "This is just a summertime urinary tract infection." Two months later it was still summertime when she came to my office with the same symptoms and a temperature of 104 degrees. She responded immediately to tetracycline treatment. She had gone with her husband, she said, to visit his parents in Chico. This was too much. I had to know what was going on. It did not require hypnosis to find out.

She said, "I gave you the wrong date for our marriage. We did not get married until I was two months along. Bill's parents are very religious. Both times that we went up to Chico I was terribly worried for fear that they would discover we were having sex before we got married.

I said, "Can you guess how many people in the world who love each other have started a family before they made a commitment in marriage? It is about 10 percent, I believe. God does not look for marriage certificates on the wall. Now I don't want you to have any more kidney infections and I will not rat on you to Bill's folks."

She laughed. There were no more urinary tract infections after several more trips to Chico. Urological studies were done after her beautiful baby was born. Nothing abnormal was found. Bill's parents were very proud to be grandparents. This was many years ago. I did not then know enough to ask this sweet young woman about possible molestation prior to her childhood pyelitis, but I am sure now that it might have been a sensitizing factor.

Vulvo-Vaginiti and Inflammation of Bartholin Glands

There are many sources of infection of the vagina and vulva including viral; candida, a fungus; trichomonas, an amoeba-like protozoa; chlamydia, the viral-intracellular bacteria responsible for trachoma; and several varieties of pathogenic streptococci that may be aerobic or anaerobic. Children are very vulnerable to gonorrheal vaginitis. A multiplicity of infections involving a part of the body normally very healthy and resistant to infection as well as being especially able to heal from surgical or traumatic injury should call for a search to find the reasons.

Reasons are not hard to find when we look for what the patient recognizes as sensitizing experiences, often starting in childhood but fulminating in maturity when emotional stresses combine with sexual ones.

The Bartholin glands, two glands that lubricate the vulva, are especially vulnerable to infection with anaerobic streptococci. There is a spiral duct leading from this mucus-secreting gland in the labia to the mucosal surface. One theory is that tight jeans or trauma from sexual activity kinks and inflames the duct so that increased secretory activity during sexual arousal will cause the proximal end of the duct to balloon up. The stretching combined with inflammation causes great pain. Various methods of draining the gland are usually tried before eventual excision. Once sensitized, however, this gland tends to be vulnerable to infection. Until culture techniques were improved it was a matter of wonder that the foul smelling pus was thought to be sterile because it was not possible to grow organisms with the usual culture mediums. The organisms are usually streptocci that have learned to grow in the absence of oxygen.

One course of treatment that I have found helpful starts with discovering and offering help in removing sexual guilt and sources of self-punishment. This is followed by teaching the patient to first be able to anesthetize the area of infection with heterohypnosis and then learn to produce continuing analgesia with self-hypnosis. I usually have added an appropriate antibiotic to justify my position as a "regular doctor."

Just as is the case with genital herpes, however, it is not easy to clear the self-incrimination that so often accompanies these two problems. The intensity and prolongation of pain in both cases, herpes and Bartholin gland abscess, seem somehow to augment feelings that this is a sort of God's punishment for real or imagined sins.

Again, sexual molestation is frequently found as the cause of hypersensitivity and diminished resistance to infection but you will find it hard to obtain the information unless you approach it indirectly with ideomotor questioning or the "Christmas tree lights." Putting the causal experiences into the past and viewing them with adult understanding and perspective can allow the victim not only to be free of infections but free of the guilt that the child seems to pick up telepathically from the molesting person.

Herpes Genitalis Infections

Herpes genitalis infections can be a source of great concern to the victim. The virus causing the acute and recurring painful soft ulcers can live with us quite peacefully until we come under stress of fatigue or, much more commonly, following sexual contact in a relationship that makes either party feel used or angry.

The treatment of getting the affected skin to feel cool can be much more effective than any of the chemicals commonly prescribed. In light hypnosis, set up finger signals and ask for permission to get the tissues cool and to keep them cool for periods of two hours. Start with an unimportant area for coolness first. Sucking on a peppermint and breathing in is a familiar way to imagine coolness in your mouth. Ask the patient's "yes" finger to lift when her mouth feels cool and have her tell you verbally when she is consciously aware of the coolness. When she is confident about sensing this change, ask if it would be all right to experience that same coolness in the ulcer area. You may run into resistance, but keep looking for an emotional factor because there are very good reasons for helping your patient be permanently free of this problem.

Women in childbearing years now have been educated to feel terribly worried when they become pregnant after once having an acute herpetic lesion of the vulva. Obstetricians add to the weight of the fear by having their own fear of litigation in case their patient had an undiagnosed open lesion in the vagina and the baby was allowed to either suffer a malignant eye infection and encephalitis or a fatal pneumonia. Repeated cultures are taken. The patient is kept in a type of suspense that may trouble her sleep and lower her immune capabilities as she approaches term. She knows her doctor may feel safer (for the doctor's sake) performing a caesarean section. Caesarean costs a lot more money but it gives the parents a feeling that everything is being done. If something happens to the baby, at least the doctor has done his or her best to avoid the trouble. Caesarean section is not always a guarantee that the infant will be safe if the membranes have been ruptured for a few hours.

The situation here seems to be self actuating. We can be what we fear. Pregnant women need a lot of emotional support throughout their pregnancy. They need to fully understand that good nutrition, regular exercise, and healthy sleep are wonderful preventive forces and that delivery at home saves them from exposure to unusual organisms found in modern hospitals where people with impaired immune systems are being cared for in this very complicated period in history.

The herpes simplex virus can be transmitted sexually from a partner who has an open ulcer but once a herpetic lesion has been sensitized it can flare up because of having intercourse with an innocent male who does not have an infection. Healthy companionship can be broken up unfairly by one blaming another for his or her conditioned hypersensitivity. The virus has no preference for one sex or the other, but it can become alarmed and begin reproducing rapidly if its host is troubled about his or her world.

Just as with the cousin virus (Herpes simplex type I) of cold sores, the genital herpes simplex type II virus remains with us and in most cases has been transmitted to us vertically from our mother, according to Sir Macfarlane Burnett (1968) of Australia.

Condyloma Acuminata

Condyloma acuminata are the so-called "venereal warts," caused by a virus. They can be embarrassing, and their treatment by freezing, cautery, or applications of podophyllin in benzoin solution can be painful and unsuccessful. The piled-up tissue or the flat forms can clear up with a little checking on what was going on before they appeared. The virus causing the problem is sexually transmitted but once in place it can continue until the victim learns why the tissue vulnerability continues. Look for childhood molestation to begin with. If you have permission from the patient to teach her the means to cure the problem, the way that has worked the best for my patients has been the "peppermint coolness." Coolness diminishes inflammation and permits the host to send in her own immune cells to bring back normal balance of the tissues.

In the early days of podophyllin I tried treating just one wart and in a joking way saying to the warts, "All right now, you are going to feel pretty uncomfortable there before you drop off. I want the rest of you to get out too or you will get the same treatment!" I was surprised to find it does work. Of course from Mark Twain's *Huck Finn* we have known how suggestible the virus of common warts on the hands can be. This is a suggestible relative.

There are going to be many more sources of vaginal infections as fears about AIDS increases. The best way we can help our patients is to help them choose sensibly in their relationships that lead to sexual intercourse and help them learn ways of using their own healing resources.

Dysmenorrhea (Painful Menstruation)

The common history for this very frequent gynecological complaint is that there are several painless menstrual periods before ovulation occurs. It has been surmised that ovulation is the cause of dysmenorrhea because of the progesterone that is secreted from the corpus luteum at the end of the intermenstrual period. It is thought that this hormone increases the contractility of the uterus. There is some justification for this conclusion because dysmenorrhea may stop when a woman with regular ovulation is shifted into anovulatory menstrual cycles with estrogen therapy.

Menstrual blood contains the proteolytic fibrinolysin, an enzyme that keeps the blood fluid and free of coagulation in the uterus. If some menstrual blood escapes through the uterine tubes into the abdominal cavity the fibrinolysin will cause pain when it touches the peritoneum. So-called retrograde menstruation is definitely one of the causes of dysmenorrhea but its presence seems to relate to increased contractility of the uterine musculature at the time of menstruation. The pain due to fibrinolytic enzymes is constant rather than intermittent.

Many theories have evolved regarding dysmenorrhea. Some have believed that narrowness of the cervical canal is the problem. Doctors dilate the cervix with results that essentially depend on the enthusiasm the doctor has for this treatment. Because about 30 percent of women lying on their back on an examining table will be found to have their uterus "tipped" backward, it was thought that dysmenorrhea was caused by the backward angulation of the uterus, but women with a forward-bending uterus also can have dysmenorrhea. Pessaries (plastic or rubber form placed in the vagina) of various types have been invented for the purpose of forcing the uterus forward so that it could drain better at the time of menstruation. Again, success depends on the enthusiasm of the doctor rather than the type of treatment.

In my experience the most common reason for dysmenorrhea is the history of a mother or older sibling suffering and preparing the younger woman for the curse that will be her fate. Another reason may be that a disabling menstrual pain at some time has saved the sufferer from a worse alternative.

Case Example

A nurse cured herself of dysmenorrhea so severe that she had to plan for a substitute to take her place at the expected time of her distress. She suffered from vomiting and often fainted because of the pain.

During a brief discussion and a demonstration of postural suggestion to show that she could pay attention to one arm and forget the other, she had a sudden insight. She said as she put her arms down, "I don't need to work with hypnosis. I know what's the matter."

She said that she had never had any trouble with her periods until she decided to fake dysmenorrhea while she was in training as a "probie" on a service she found was unpleasant—male urology. There was an examination she needed to study for. Her supervisor gave her a day off.

She got her studying done while other probation nurses had to work. She was still on the same disagreeable urological service when her next period was due. To be consistent, she asked for the day off and her supervisor allowed her to take it. Being basically an honest and very conscientious person, she felt a bit guilty. She had a few cramps. Pain became progressively worse with the following cycles. This nurse was totally cured by her revelation. I did not need to intervene.

Treatments in the Past

One very successful treatment for dysmenorrhea was the cocainization of the "Fliess spots" in the mucous membrane of the nose. A German doctor by the name of Fliess had identified them as having sexual meaning. Cocaine applied to the membranes of anyone's nose would make them feel better, regardless of gender. The treatment fell into disrepute with passage of the Harrison Act.

X-ray treatment with mild doses to the pituitary gland and to the ovaries was tried for a time before World War I, until it was learned that infertility might result.

Gynecologists have performed suspensions of the uterus by shortening the round ligaments in order to prevent so-called "retroversion of the uterus." This operation is presently out of style.

During World War II many women were working for the armed services or in factories. Someone had the idea of teaching working women to do stretching exercises to stretch the fascia in the pelvic area. Exercise of any sort is helpful for the well-being of working women—or men—but this mode of treating dysmenorrhea was soon forgotten.

Another operation that has been abandoned was promoted by a French surgeon (Cotte) who wrote about an 80 percent cure rate for dysmenorrhea. His idea was to excise sympathetic nerve fibers and ganglia that lie between the anterior surface of the sacrum and the peritoneum. He was probably very persuasive, because other surgeons were not as successful. "Presacral neurectomy" is no longer considered a valid treatment for dysmenorrhea. Wise medical and hospital insurance companies no longer pay for its use.

The discovery that estrogen tablets could diminish chances of a woman becoming pregnant led to recognition of a side effect. It relieved some women from suffering with menstrual cramping. These may have been women who worried too much about a possible pregnancy, because many women continued to have their dysmenorrhea in spite of taking birth control pills.

Dysmenorrhea that does not respond to use of birth control pills often leads to a presumptive diagnosis of endometriosis. Even when there are no pelvic findings to substantiate the diagnosis, many doctors will recommend a laparoscopy in order to look for possible endometriosis through fiberoptic instruments. Even minuscule patches of endometriosis or slightly pigmented bits of peritoneum behind the uterus will be itemized and treated with a cautery in the hope of relieving the cramps. Gynecologists are particularly interested in use of laparoscopy when a patient being treated for infertility also suffers from dysmenorrhea.

Laparoscopy is now very popular among gynecologists. It is invasive and expensive and generally nonproductive. The patient's self-respect can be injured, and she may become unconsciously alarmed at the thought of suffering without a prospect of relief because nothing was found to explain her trouble. Some gynecologists "save face" by telling patients that they have observed varicosities of the pelvic veins around the uterus. This explanation does not make sense. Pelvic veins can become engorged because of relaxation and immobility due to the general or spinal anesthetic. This does not mean these veins stay engorged in everyday circumstances. Engorged pelvic veins can cause low back pain but rarely dysmenorrhea (Taylor 1949).

Use of Hypnosis for Dysmenorrhea

As with any chronic or recurring pain state, we need to make sure the patient is willing to let someone help with the distress. The circumstances around the first painful menstrual period need to be explored. The patient needs to recognize that there have been variations in the degree of distress and to understand what circumstances have made it worse or better.

I use hypnosis to help the patient feel totally relaxed. This is followed by teaching her to use self-hypnosis four or five times a day (Chapter 8). The exercise involving diminished sensations in the abdomen is the same as for childbirth preparation. This will make sense for the young woman planning to have children. She may have been told, "If you think menstruating is bad, just wait till you have a baby." Low threshold for pain with menstruation and fear about a future labor often stem from knowing or hearing about a mother's "terrible experience." The child somehow feels a need to suffer to pay the mother back.

For this reason, I have found it very helpful to have the patient first relive her birth experience as it was and reframe the experience as it would have been if her mother had been shown how to become instantly numb from the chest down at the start of a labor contraction and learned how to turn off the analgesia at the end of a contraction. A point is made of the value of bonding with both mother and father in the delivery room. In this way the patient is learning to create the same analgesia of her abdomen while experiencing how her mother might have been coached by her doctor. She can see how easily she can make her own abdomen and legs numb and she is also gaining first-hand knowledge about how a fetus thinks and feels inside that uterus during labor.

The next step is to have her recall the sensations of menstrual discomfort, using her left index and thumb pressure to turn on discomfort. Her "yes" finger is to lift unconsciously as it is starting and her "no" finger to lift when it is just as strong as usual. When the signal is given, I ask her to press the tips of her right index finger and thumb together with the accompanying thought, "I am turning off the pain." This turning on and off of the pain is repeated until she is confident about her control.

The final step is to hallucinate the date of her first really comfortable menstruation. She is asked to visualize the chalkboard and to dictate what she "sees." This tends to fix the idea in her mind that there will be such a time.

The session ends with the question "Now that you know this, can you be comfortable having menstrual periods lasting a day or two with just enough bleeding to let you know you are a normal woman?" The answer is usually "yes" with her finger signals, but if it is "no" or "I don't want to answer," I know that there is more work has to be done.

Premenstrual Syndrome (PMS)

PMS is a condition involving depression, anxiety, fluid retention, headaches and general malaise. Some women become violent and break dishes just before the onset of menstruation. They can be hard on subordinates in the workplace and can be mean to their families. The diagnosis is made when these problems end shortly after menstruation has started. Many professional papers have been written about this problem. Several books have cried out against any idea that this could all be psychological. It has been thought that progesterone imbalance is a factor, but clinical use of estrogen suppositories has not proven helpful.

The symptoms and the fluid retention suggest that this problem relates to subconscious stress that reaches conscious awareness toward the end of the estrogen production and the rising level of progesterone from the corpus luteum that forms after ovulation. Subclinical depression may be in the background and needing attention. Many drugs have been used with variable results. Efforts to teach the patient to relax at frequent intervals during the last few days before the onset of menstruation have not been very helpful, possibly because there are subconscious forces that need release before the relaxation can work.

My results using the standard search of early life experience, recall of the onset of first trouble, and so on have been successful no more than 50 percent of the time. I am still looking for the missing links in this very troublesome condition. It is important to recognize that some women spontaneously lose their PMS without any specific treatment. Changing a job can do it. We need help from the women who cure themselves. What made it possible for them?

Heavy and Prolonged Menstruation (Menorrhagia)

Heavy vaginal bleeding lasting more than seven days is not normal, and possible organic causes should be ruled out if it has occurred more than once. Organic possibilities could include a polyp in the cervical canal, a muscle growth (myoma), or a potentially malignant growth of the uterine mucosa. It can occur also if there is a disturbance in ovarian function such as a follicle or corpus luteum cyst. It is a responsibility for the gynecologist to rule these things out.

Emotional causes far outnumber the organic ones. It seems that, biologically, human menstruation is a sort of physiological weeping because pregnancy has not occurred on that cycle of preparation for pregnancy. Such weeping can occur also without relation to the menstrual cycle if a woman loses her job, is abandoned by a husband or boy friend, grieves for the death of a friend or relative, or learns with great relief that her pregnancy test is negative after a longer than normal interval without menstruating.

The control of heavy or prolonged menstruation with hypnotic suggestion has been reported by many doctors after pathological conditions have been ruled out (Forel 1907,1927, 1949). Kroger and Freed 1951). Their "control" was effected by direct suggestion for diminished bleeding. Their successes are anecdotal and hard to evaluate.

It would be safe to say that menstruation is a human form of nuisance that really has no value in preserving health. No other animal is so troubled.

Blood has an odor. It is dangerous for menstruating women to swim in shark-infested waters. Nonhuman female mammals will give off volatile oil when ready for pregnancy, some primates menstruate, and some mammals in captivity will have some sort of vaginal discharge, but bleeding is not required and could be dangerous for those in the wild.

We continually replace the lining of all our glands, our mouth, stomach, intestines, gallbladder, and urinary bladder without bleeding. It makes no sense for women to bleed while replacing the lining of their uterus. It was my habit to congratulate daughters who were 15 or 16 and had not yet menstruated. I had to be sure, of course, that they had normal female organs and there was no obstruction in the vagina, cervix, or uterus that would prevent menstrual blood from escaping. The congratulation was needed because these youngsters can quickly absorb the alarm of their mother who is wondering what is wrong with her child.

Amenorrhea (Failure to Menstruate)

Amenorrhea is a condition that can occur with chronic illness. It can occur following any great physical or emotional stress. Ballerinas and long distance runners may stop menstruating for long periods. A premature menopause may occur after massive hemorrhage as with a major injury or a postpartum hemorrhage (Sheehan 1939). An adenoma of the anterior pituitary can cause amenorrhea.

Subconscious alarm mechanisms can prevent menstruation as outlined in Chapter 19.

Exploration may reveal an emotional cause, and psychotherapy with hypnosis can allow the distressed patient to menstruate again. This has been possible in my practice three times with women who have been 40 or younger and have not menstruated for one or more years. Hypnosis should be used first before subjecting a patient to extensive and expensive endocrine studies.

Endometriosis

Endometriosis is another disease that seems related to endocrine disturbances having emotional components. Endometriosis was once thought related to escape of endometrial epithelium through the uterine tubes during menstruation with the fragments becoming transplanted and viable. The incidence of endometriosis has had a curious relationship to education and socioeconomic level. For many years it was almost nonexistent in black American women, until opportunities opened for them due to the activity of Marshall, King, and others during the late 1950s and 1960s. Its incidence now is nearly equal in black and white women.

That endometriosis represents some sort of neuroendocrine drive to make much tissue available for implantation of fertilized ova seems a compelling thought. At caesarean section we will see patches of clearly decidual tissue (changes in the epithelium due to the hormones of pregnancy) on peritoneal surfaces of the uterus and the ligaments supporting the uterus. The patches of normally smooth, single-cell thickness peritoneum have metamorphosed temporarily into the same sort of tissue that lines the inside of the uterus during pregnancy. If the same patient is operated on during a nonpregnant time, we find no evidence of these patches.

My impression, garnered from many evaluations of women who have presented with clinically significant endometriosis, is that emotional conflict over feeling unwanted as a female child but also having normal feminine sexual needs has a part in the process we recognize as endometriosis. There are many variations of possible cause, but attention to the subjective reporting and therapeutic reframing of misunderstandings has saved many of my patients from undergoing surgery for symptomatic endometriosis.

This condition has the appearance of a cancer. It can invade the wall of bladder and intestines, yet it is benign. It will disappear if a woman becomes pregnant. It is curiously associated with infertility, and yet there is rarely any blockage of the uterine tubes. Why should this be? At surgery it is impossible to remove or cauterize all areas of endometrial involvement. I usually made an effort in this direction while explaining that this is often followed by regression of the involvement and subsequent pregnancy if desired. Anesthetized patients are highly suggestible and they are always listening.

Case example: Mary, a 34-year-old nurse, was found to have extensive endometriosis when she was operated on as an emergency in a neighboring town of Willows. She had suddenly suffered severe abdominal pain and bloating of her abdomen. Her doctor called me in consultation. A presumptive diagnosis was made of a ruptured tubal pregnancy or a ruptured corpus luteum cyst. I removed about 200 cubic centimeters of clotted blood and resected endometrial cysts from both ovaries and from the back of the uterus. There were patches of endometriosis throughout the abdomen. I cauterized as many as I could while telling the family doctor who was scrubbed with me that cauterization of implants has often permitted patients with this problem to clear themselves and be able to get pregnant. At that time I did not know how attentive seemingly somnolent anesthetized patients can be to the conversations of the surgical team.

Mary became pregnant three months later and delivered a healthy child at term. The doctor told me that she was totally free of symptoms and had no pelvic evidence of endometriosis on subsequent examinations.

Myomata (Fibroids) of the Uterus

It is not commonly recognized by gynecologists that there may be emotional factors responsible for the localized growth of muscle of the uterus. These growths sometimes reach huge proportions in parts of the country where women cannot obtain gynecological consultation. During childbearing years it is customary to excise such tumors. Hysterectomy is done when the patient either does not want children or is past the age of childbearing.

Surgery is not indicated in older women (40 or more years old) unless the tumor causes symptoms of pain or hemorrhage because myomata tend to grow smaller or disappear after the menopause. Care must be taken, however, to rule out ovarian tumors, which are often malignant when they occur in women 35 or older. Ruling out ovarian tumors can now be done with the help of ultrasound imaging or computerized tomography scan, but formerly there have been tragedies when a doctor thought nodules in the pelvis of a woman were only benign myomata of the uterus.

That poor self-image as a woman and troubled sexual attitudes can stimulate growth of these tumors was considered long ago by the German doctors Kehrer and Heyer. In this country, Howard Taylor (1949) attributed such growth to "pelvic congestion."

Example of myoma growth: A 50-year-old, married, childless woman who appeared to be near term with a baby had been a familiar sight in the town where I started my practice. She called on me one Sunday morning to come to her house to catheterize her because she had been unable to void for approximately 12 hours.

On my arrival she introduced herself as "Jimmie." Later, I learned that she had never had intercourse. Her husband had suffered a stroke but had refused to see a doctor. In the course of helping him walk, she had tripped on a carpet and fallen forward on this "baby," which weighed 29 pounds when removed.

Her bladder and part of her small bowel had been traumatized. By the time she called me, she had been vomiting fecal matter. This woman's strong religious beliefs turned out to be important for her survival. It was impossible for me to get a catheter into her bladder. It took very little persuasion to get her into the hospital for urgent surgery to remove her huge uterus, repair the bladder and small intestine and release her small bowel obstruction. Her hospital course was smooth.

Her sense of intense privacy prevented me from learning the cause of her total abstinence from sex during 30 years of marriage, but my impression was that something had happened long ago to disturb her endocrine system. At surgery it became clear that she also had cancer with skin ulceration in both breasts. When I asked permission to take a biopsy she told me that I should work "down there" and that she would take care of her breasts.

This she did for ten years, until her husband died and there was no further need for her services. The cancer then spread rapidly throughout her body and she died.

Ovarian Cysts and Stein-Levinthal Syndrome

Occasionally a normal woman will develop a cyst (collections of fluid) in an ovary. Such a cyst may become large enough to twist on its supporting ligament that carries its blood supply. This twisting (volvulus) will cause acute pain and usually requires surgery unless the woman can get down on her hands and knees to change the effect of gravity. Ovarian cysts form either in the follicle of the developing ovum or in the corpus luteum gland that evolves from the follicle after the ovum has been released. Cysts may be single or multiple, depending on stimulation from the anterior pituitary gland and the hypothalamus. In my experience, cyst formation is always psychogenic. A cyst may range in size from 5 to 20 centimeters in diameter and may spontaneously rupture without causing much discomfort, or it may resorb over a period of two to three weeks. A rupture of a corpus luteum cyst is associated with blood containing inflammatory enzymes, which will cause severe pain and may mimic a ruptured tubal pregnancy.

A gynecologist is moderately concerned upon finding a freely movable, smooth, ovarian cyst because potentially malignant cystadenomas can start like that. We have a sort of rule of thumb that we worry if a patient is over the age of 35, but we wait three weeks anyway before deciding what to do. A benign (functional) cyst will resorb in that time. In the meantime, with the over-35 patient we get a sonogram and/or a CT scan to learn more about the contents.

The way hypnosis can be valuable with cystic ovarian problems of any sort is to use the imagery of "Christmas tree lights" (Cheek 1989) or to simply orient back to the time she "knows" subconsciously that her pelvic organs are working well and normally. A "yes" finger will lift. Without asking questions about that time, move forward chronologically to the moment she feels something is changing. Have her signal and to check to see if there has been some emotional possibility for altering the circulation to her pelvic organs or making them overly sensitive to an emotional problem.

Keep in mind always that organic problems of importance can also be associated with emotional stressors. Gynecologists will probably not refer a patient with an ovarian cyst problem to a psychologist or a psychiatrist because they usually have had no exposure to psychosomatic lectures in medical school or hospital training. I am writing this for physicians who do general practice and are sensitive to the problems of the families they serve. I hope also that a woman who has had the diagnosis of an ovarian cyst will have the opportunity to know that a waiting period should intervene between diagnosis and suggested surgery. For her, I urge a consultation with a competent gynecologist either for peace of mind or for a second opinion if immediate surgery has been ordered.

Multiple Cysts Involving Both Ovaries

Multiple cysts on both ovaries may be diagnosed as Stein-Levinthal syndrome. This condition involves a number of physical and physiological findings. The patient may consult her doctor because she has been unable to get pregnant, she has been overweight, and is concerned about hair on her face and arms. Often she has also had a problem with pimples on her face and chest. On pelvic examination her ovaries are found to be enlarged and studded with small cysts. Her menstrual periods may be irregular and widely spaced apart. Her pituitary follicle stimulating hormone level is usually normal, but her adrenal glands are secreting more than normal amounts of 17-ketosteroids.

In the past, surgeons have had some success in reversing the process and permitting a woman to become pregnant. They have removed the thickened capsule of both ovaries. The working hypothesis has been that the capsule prevents follicles from releasing the eggs. Careful psychological evaluation of all the patients with this syndrome that I have seen has brought out the apparent fact that they had a low regard for themselves as female. They have usually been molested, which has further diminished their self-respect as women.

Case Example

A 28-year-old woman came to me for obstetrical care. She had suffered eight miscarriages at four months. She lost this pregnancy at the same period of gestation shortly after I had seen her. She had hair on her face, shoulders, and arms since reaching puberty. She had been overweight since the age of 4 years. She had married a pleasant man who was not very aggressive sexually. She had questions in her mind about his sexual orientation because he seemed to have a lot of male friends.

A psychological evaluation, made originally to understand factors leading to her miscarriages, brought out that she had thought she should have been a boy when she was born. At the age of 3 she was repeatedly molested by her grandfather while her parents were away from home. She had unconsciously craved carbohydrate food in order to put on weight and not be attractive to men such as her grandfather. It seemed reasonable that her mental set might have had something to do with her endocrine balance. Her ovaries were slightly enlarged. She had the Stein-Levinthal syndrome but I felt that surgery on her ovaries added to the other childhood assaults would be more damaging than helpful.

She had another miscarriage and eventually divorced her bisexual husband after meeting a fine, thoughtful, masculine man who treated her with great respect. She called me when she became pregnant after moving away from the San Francisco area. I referred her to a woman obstetrician in another city. This time she went to the seventh month before starting to hemorrhage and eventually losing the immature fetus.

I lost contact with this woman during the next ten years until she attended a lecture I was giving. She had adopted a child and had given up the idea of childbearing. At this time she reported that a surgeon had found a large, solid tumor of her left ovary. I knew this doctor. He and his anesthesiologist were very good psychologists and well aware of the powers of suggestion.

She said that Doctor "P," her anesthesiologist, had told her as she drifted off to sleep with pentothal, "You will lose that hair when that ovary comes out." She said that this came true within two months of the hysterectomy and removal of a benign fibroma of the one ovary. She did not lose weight, but her husband was enormously overweight also. I will never know if the ovary had caused all the trouble or the combination of suggestion and her improved status as a woman with a child were responsible.

I have been the gynecologist for four other women whose infantile history and negative self-image as females were associated with polycystic ovaries. Each has somehow been able to stop producing cysts, losing the unwanted hair and getting back to normal weight after reframing the troubled early life impressions and getting help with their inhibited sexual responsiveness.

Comment

From time to time the American College of Obstetrics and Gynecologists has initiated interest in the psychosomatic aspects of obstetrics and gynecology. Joseph de Lee, J. P. Greenhill, Frederick Zuspan, William S. Kroger, William Werner, Melvin M. Schwartz, Theodore Mandy, and Edward C. Mann are some of the names that stand out because of their interest in this matter.

I have witnessed a surge of enthusiasm for a time. Discussions of psychosomatic obstetrics and gynecology have been held during conventions. William Kroger organized and started the Academy of Psychosomatic Medicine. There were 90 doctors on the program but no additional guests. Excitement has always faded; the turn out for meetings has dwindled into nothingness. I believe it will take the driving force of thoughtful women to bring about constructive change. Attention must be given to the concept of a mind influencing physical behavior and endocrine balance.

Perhaps women can insist on increasing thought and action before the subspecialty of psychosomatic obstetrics and gynecology will be represented in our medical schools and teaching hospitals. Most of our specialists who treat women, particularly the specialists who limit their work to infertility, give only lip service to the power of the human, feminine mind in relation to gynecological and obstetrical problems.

19

Factors Influencing Fertility

Women are best prepared physiologically for pregnancy between the ages of 18 and 25. We do not have to worry much about these young women becoming pregnant when they are ready unless they have had pelvic infection or been battered, molested, or traumatized by parental illness or divorce. There is a growing threat now for children of alcoholic, cocaine-using adults. These children are now reaching the 18 to 25 year zone. We do not yet know what has been happening to their limbic and hypothalamic endocrine systems or what kind of parents they will be.

There are exceptions to all these conditions. Exposed just once to a high school boy who had gonorrhea, one young woman was able to have children after removal of bilateral tubo-ovarian abscesses! The uterus was preserved to allow for artificial menstruation with cyclical estrogen. To prevent a possible cornual pregnancy in case some ovarian tissue remained, the peritoneum and round ligaments were sutured over the excised cornual segment of the tube on both sides. This did not stop this youngster, 13 years old at the time, from having two children six and eight years later. The catgut sutures must have dissolved and an opening to the uterus formed.

I was the surgeon, and I verified this unbelievable account with her doctor. I wonder if her subconscious overheard my anguished comments about this tragedy? She was the spunky eldest of eight children of a favorite patient of mine.

Infertility in Women Who Have Postponed Childbearing

The matters in this chapter are concerned with women who have postponed their desires and needs for children past the age of 30 and who need help

163

to reprogram their endocrine system for accepting and nurturing a pregnancy. There may have been a long period of sexual abstinence or a long period of dedication to a business or professional career or many years in a stressful marriage when a pregnancy had to be avoided.

During those years of not wanting a pregnancy there are changes in a woman's neuroendocrine system that can interfere with ovulation and produce myomatous tumors of the uterus, endometriosis and a complex of physical changes that are recognized as the Stein-Levinthal syndrome.

All of these seemingly organic problems may be psychosomatic in origin and reversible with psychotherapy (Kroger 1962). Surgical intervention is commonly the automatic treatment of these conditions, and pregnancies can occur if the patient has faith in the surgeon's judgment and expectation that good things will follow. But surgical intervention would in most instances be unnecessary if women were permitted to use modern hypnotic methods of accessing the very early life roots of their problems.

My colleagues know that endometriosis is associated with infertility. They know that it sometimes quite mysteriously disappears without surgical intervention. They know that when pregnancy unexpectedly intervenes, endometriosis may disappear. There is no scientific explanation in the gynecological literature to explain why endometriosis occurs.

Surgical removal of masses of endometriosis and cautery of visible remaining implants within the abdomen is performed usually when a trial of estrogen suppression has failed to permit a woman to become pregnant. The surgery cannot possibly remove all traces of this condition, yet women may become pregnant after such surgery. When asked about why this occurs, the answer from the gynecologist will usually be a glance upward and a shrug of the shoulders.

Age-regression exploration of the inner world of women with endometriosis will reveal the psychological cause of the trouble and will clarify why pregnancy can occur spontaneously or after what, to me, seems punitive surgery. The emotional relationships to the cause of uterine myomas was surmised by Kehrer in 1922 (1929) and by Howard Taylor (1949) on the basis of simple conversational evidence supplied by women. Myomatous growths in the uterus and endometriosis are both closely associated with poor feminine self-image. The child may have imprinted on feeling she should have been a boy. She may have been molested sexually during infancy or childhood or she may have been overwhelmed by parental sexual inhibitions and rigidities during her infantile autoerotic explorations while being bathed or having her diapers changed.

Possible Reasons for Postponing Childbearing

Since the 1968 edition of *Clinical Hypnotherapy* there seem to have been more reasons for postponing childbearing than were previously recognized.

Many women have been avoiding close male relationships or are too busy with studies or career to permit them. There has been an increasing rate of divorce since the end of World War II that has resulted in a second generation of men and women having an unclear idea of what they could trust in terms of stability and loyalty in a marriage.

Because the father usually goes elsewhere after a divorce, daughters may unconsciously avoid potentially good male relationships because "something tells me he would leave me." This point comes out during age-regression scanning of their impressions of boys in high school and the men they later meet. There seems to be an imprinted unconscious fear of abandonment that develops during parental difficulties that ended in divorce.

Women growing up in troubled homes tend to allow themselves to be drawn to what they believe will be safer companionship with men who have not swept them off their feet emotionally and who often are mercurial, alcoholic or otherwise irresponsible. They use contraception for prolonged periods to avoid having an additional problem of raising a child in unhappy circumstances.

They may go through one or two such mistakes in judgment before finally recognizing their right to have a reliable male companion, but by then their endocrine system may have been so disturbed that efforts to have a child by a good husband may fail. She may develop antibodies that can inactivate or destroy the sperm of her husband.

Men also can contribute to the problems a wife my have when she is ready to start a family. The child of an unhappy or angry mother may carry over his personal resentments to his innocent and loving wife. He may be so afraid a divorce would follow arrival of a child that he makes his wife feel rejected. A complaint that often surfaces with patients who have failed to become pregnant or who have had multiple fetal losses is the mistaken interpretation that "if he does not want my baby, he does not love or want me." This imprint may continue to influence her endocrine system in spite of her husband's later desire to have children and experiential proof that the marriage is stable.

Biological Readiness May Not Mean Conscious Readiness

Pregnancy will occur when a woman is biologically ready for pregnancy. External circumstances may, however, be totally incompatible with becoming pregnant at the time. She may be horrified to learn that she is pregnant. Worry and concern about conscious problems may lead to a spontaneous abortion or failure of the fetus to develop. Although consciously relieved at this, many women in this situation may feel subconsciously guilty enough to become sterile or fall into the unfortunate habit of aborting successive pregnancies without ever having a living child (Cheek 1965c).

The reason for this is psychological in most cases, although authorities on genetics will usually explain the losses in terms of a "lethal gene." I have had the opportunity of working with five women who had successive losses of six or more pregnancies. One woman who had a masculinizing tumor of an ovary was transiently under my care. She had nine miscarriages while married to a homosexual, rather difficult man. As a child she had been so frequently molested sexually by her grandfather that she had hoped she could turn into a boy in order to be free of this attention. She divorced the homosexual husband and married a very masculine and reliable man. She lost two more pregnancies under the care of other doctors after moving from San Francisco. Her total losses were 11 before having a hysterectomy and removal of the abnormal ovary. Three women lost the first pregnancy after coming under my care. One luckily went to term after six successive losses.

TABLE 19-1   Case Histories Summary

Cases	Age	Abortions	Living Babies
WC	26	11	0
SC	32	9	3
VF	37	6	1
GF	28	6	2
GS	37	9	1

Even under the best of circumstances in a community where abortion is freely available in a friendly environment, a woman can build unconscious feelings of guilt that can keep her from ovulating or may keep her uterine mucous membranes from developing well enough to nurture a fertilized ovum. This deeply organized physiological imbalance may continue in spite of external hormonal stimulation. It may continue in spite of the implanting of a fertilized ovum. Conscious reasoning in cases like this is too superficial; the intellect cannot remove primitive physiological patterns of behavior that have been frozen by emotional stress. This is comparable to other forms of post-hypnotic-like neurosis caused by trauma.

Fertility Specialists Seem Disinterested in the Feminine Mind

The problem can be solved if the specialists who are consulted by an infertile couple are willing to ask about possible emotional factors and are willing to listen to the women who consult them. Unfortunately, at present, this is not the case. The growing subspecialty of gynecology that is devoted to caring for infertile women attracts male and female doctors who are basically more interested in the endocrine and anatomical imbalances they encounter than they are in the emotional causes of infertility.

It seems clear that pregnancy will not occur or will occur and then be aborted if a woman is unconsciously afraid or is otherwise unconsciously avoiding pregnancy. It does not seem to matter that she is consciously willing or even anxious to get pregnant. Her subconscious mind governs the discharge of messenger molecules and it governs the cell receptors for the messages. External bombardment with hormones that seem to be lacking in the woman will do no good if the receptors in the ovary and endometrium are closed up.

Present-day specialists who are unwilling or unable to communicate subconsciously with their infertile patients will succeed with some women by virtue of implanting confidence that what they do will succeed. A large percentage of women, however, will not be helped in this way and will become a statistic to show that women who wait too long will remain sterile. "You can't win them all" is a common response when I talk about these matters with colleagues who are fertility experts.

Fertility work is expensive. It costs in excess of $1,000 a month, and insurance companies do not often pay for continuing fruitless treatments for infertility. Accumulating charges may total in excess of $30,000 before letters go out from the couple asking for help in obtaining a child for adoption.

Fertility experts who work organically are abundant, at least in the United States. A listing of names and addresses of U.S. fertility specialists runs to almost 60 pages and contains more than 600 names, as compared with 4 pages and 40 similar specialists in Canada (Berger et al. 1989).

There is general agreement among psychiatrists and psychiatrically oriented physicians (Dunbar 1954, Taylor 1949, Kroger 1951) that emotional factors are significantly related to infertility, but this view has been based on relatively superficial observations derived from psychoanalysis and conversational interviews. Conversational methods do not access physiological zones of interaction between environmental stimuli and physiological responses. The opinions of psychologically oriented physicians are therefore derived intuitively rather than scientifically. Gynecologists are scientists. They want "hard data."

We have the tools now that permit us to tap the unconscious knowledge of fertile and infertile women, but those best equipped to investigate and be therapeutically helpful with infertile women are not given the opportunity to work with them. They are not consulted by my colleagues.

It is now time for the situation to change and for women to insist on having professional consultants listen to what they know may be the factors keeping them from having children. The consultants need to know how to check such knowledge and bring about positive physiological changes with hypnotic techniques.

Considerations and Case Examples

There often are contradictions of consciously expressed ideas and those residing at unconscious horizons of thought. The difference is not a sign of dishonesty or rebellion. An investigator needs to recognize this and search for the source of conflicting attitudes.

It has been my experience that, under ordinary conditions, pregnancy will occur only when there is an unconscious, biological need for pregnancy. A woman can have an unconscious yearning to be pregnant even though external circumstances make a pregnancy undesirable. Conversely, pregnancy will not occur or continue if doctors drive a subconsciously frightened woman to ovulate with hormones or assault her with scientifically arranged artificial insemination.

An apparent contradiction to these statements occurs with rape victims. Approximately 70 percent of rape victims will become pregnant unless protected immediately with administration of contraceptive hormones. These women certainly would not want to have a baby. There would be agreement on this from all levels of their perception, but great fear and emotional pain seem to drive their thalamic-limbic system into releasing eggs that can be fertilized by the rapist's semen. This is a survival-of-the-species phenomenon. It has nothing to do with an act of conscious will or unconscious yearnings for pregnancy. It is comparable to the hypothalamic ejaculation a male may have when hanged by the neck in an execution.

Strange and interesting factors responsible for ambivalence about pregnancy will show up during investigation of women whose treatments have failed to produce a living child. More than half of the infertile women I have seen have had one or more miscarriages of an embryo without being consciously aware of this fact. There is a very clear impression about the presence of a viable embryo and a clear subconscious knowledge of when the embryo ceases to develop. Knowledge about such unrecognized false starts can, however, be psychologically helpful in therapy. The woman can realize that she is able to conceive. She can learn to prolong the pregnancy.

When my office practice load eventually made it necessary to keep infertile women waiting for three or more weeks, I began seeing patients who were already pregnant by the time they came in for a sterility workup. I recall six such women who had been trying unsuccessfully for two or more years to become pregnant.

One woman was six months along when she came in to see if she had gallbladder trouble because bacon gave her indigestion. She was 42 years old and could not believe that she could be pregnant. She had been trying for a pregnancy for 20 years! In hypnosis she discovered that pregnancy occurred when she decided, "Oh, to hell with that." The younger women became pregnant when they stopped trying and put the responsibility on my shoulders. The effect was the same. They just stopped feeling responsible for failure.

False Pregnancy, or "Pseudocyesis"

Occasionally a woman comes for help when she has all the symptoms of pregnancy associated with a failure to menstruate but is not pregnant because of intensely real fears. One was an intelligent clinic patient who was referred to me by the resident in obstetrics at my hospital. She had not menstruated for 18 months. She felt pregnant, was nauseated and looked pregnant. There was milk-like secretion from her engorged breasts. There had been a progressive weight gain. In spite of these signs of pregnancy there had been eight negative pregnancy tests.

I took a Chevreul pendulum with me because I was not sure she would expect me to use hypnosis with her. The investigation and resolution of her unconscious conflict took approximately five minutes after my taking her history and explaining that the unconscious part of her mind might explain why she had produced these physiological changes in her body without being pregnant. These were the questions I asked:

Q: Does your inner mind know you can have babies like anyone else?

A: (Pendulum swing) "No."

Q: Would it be all right for us to know why you feel this way?

A: (P) "I don't want to answer."

Q: Well, would it be helpful if your husband knew about your feeling that you could not have a baby? (This was a lucky guess because her problem related to him).

A: (P) "Yes."

I asked when an important event responsible for her feeling she could not have a baby had occurred. By this time she was so interested that she had entered a light hypnotic state. I gently pulled the chain of her pendulum through her fingers and had her select finger signals for answers. The problem started before she was 25-20-15 etcetera. Finally, after repetitive scanning for information, she was able to recognize the event consciously. Her first conscious recognition evoked, "My God, how could I be so stupid?" Then she added, "When I was 3 months old, my father died of pneumonia and I guess I have been afraid that my husband would die if I had a baby."

She was then able in hypnosis to see the date of her next menstrual period, a valuable unconscious commitment. She menstruated the day after the one she saw on a chalkboard. Now the hormones that had kept her from ovulating for 18 months were shifting back into a normal rhythm. Her next period came on schedule. I heard no more from her, but I am sure she became pregnant after that restraining identification of her husband with her father was recognized and removed.

Infertility of Seven Years Because of "Being Born Too Soon"

A patient who had been trying unsuccessfully to become pregnant during five years since discontinuing contraception shook her head slowly from side to side as she told me, "Oh, I've always wanted children" when I asked, "Did you want to have children when you were first married?"

I noted this contradiction in her record and asked the same question two years later when I gave her some pentothal in order to curet her uterus to look for intrauterine polyps or fibroid tumors that might have been keeping her from being pregnant. All the tests on her and her husband were normal but she had not become pregnant. She sleepily answered my question with, "No, because I was born too soon."

Her younger sister had shown her on their mother's Bible that Grace was born three months after the date for their parents' marriage. I laughed when she tearfully told me about this because it did not seem likely that her mother had put those dates down on the front page of her Bible. Later we discovered that the handwriting was that of her sister.

Within a month the woman was pregnant, and she had two more children after that. She no longer was imprinted with the fear that neighbors would "know" that her parents had to get married because of her. I said, "You know it's been seven years now since you were married. There is no animal that would need to be afraid of what the neighbors would think after that many years—not even an elephant." We laughed about this. She said, "I was bothered by that Bible thing all through high school. I thought everybody knew about me, that I was an accident."

Superstitious Identification of Husband with Alcoholic Father

A 26 year-old eldest child whose parents were both alcoholic and divorced when the patient was 10 years of age was unable to become pregnant during two years of intercourse without protection. There had been a long period of financial worries for her mother, who had four children and no help from her divorced, severely handicapped father.

During an interview in hypnosis she was asked to review her sleep ideation of the night before coming for the interview. There was something she was not ready to handle at first. Then she recognized a dream in which her husband was with her but suddenly disappeared. She interpreted this as an indication that he was dead. There had been many such dreams since her marriage to him. It became clear that she was identifying him with her father. Subconscious questioning revealed that she knew her husband was in no way like her father. He did not drink, worked at a good job and was very attentive to her. He wanted very much to have children with her.

A search was made of her birth. Her mother was unconscious and her father was not there. She felt abandoned. Shifting back from birth to intrauterine memory, she suddenly began to weep. When she was able to talk, she said, "He doesn't care" (meaning he does not care about her being there). Shifted to the moment her mother knew she was pregnant, she felt that her mother was not happy. When her mother was telling her father that she was pregnant, he felt "he was not ready." Again she started to weep. Then she added, "He only cares about himself."

Clearly she had imprinted on the expectation that a pregnancy would not be welcomed by her husband and that he would either die or leave after she had a baby.

We talked about this and the unfairness of this attitude both to her husband, who wanted a child, and to a "little spirit out there wanting to come to her." Then I asked her fingers to answer this question:

Q: Does your inner mind feel that you have been pregnant at any time since you were married?

A: (finger signal) "Yes."

Q: More than once?

A: (f.s.) "Yes."

Q: More than three times?

A: (f.s.) "Yes."

Dr.: You see, you have not been infertile at all. You have been pregnant at least three times, but your thinking may not have seemed friendly and a little spirit may have moved on or your uterus was just not able to offer enough food because of your fears.

Q: Now that you know you can get pregnant, I wish you would tune in to your psychic ability. Go forward to when you will be delivering your first baby. When you are there, your "yes" finger will lift. Tell me when this will be.

A: June 1991. (With some further questioning:) May 15, 1991.

This interview took place on August 10, 1989. I had asked to talk to her about the reasons for infertility a year earlier on a visit, but she had been unwilling to do it. Now she appeared very open and really ready to search for and clear up possible emotional reasons for her inability to become pregnant.

On October 20, 1989, she called to say that her last menstrual period had occurred on August 8, starting two days before our interview. By dates she would expect to deliver on May 15, pretty close to the hallucinated date she had seen on the imaginary chalkboard.

A sonogram had just been done and the doctor estimated that the embryo was now about 9 weeks gestation size. It would be difficult to say whether she became pregnant before or after our interview. Since she had felt optimistic for the first time just prior to seeing me, I am inclined to believe that her change in attitude rather than what we did was responsible for her shift to readiness for pregnancy. She delivered a normal male child at the time of her expected date of confinement!

Comment: I do not want to create the idea that positive results occur instantly after one interview. Sometimes it will take more than six months, and reinforcement of positive expectation may be necessary to overcome the previous negative conditioning. In this case there were two major factors responsible, I believe, for her infertility. She had felt unwanted before she was born and did not want a baby of hers to feel the way she felt during her childhood when there were many arguments between her parents. The second factor was a superstitious fear that if she had a baby her marriage would be destroyed in some way. Her fear was that her husband would die.

20

Hypnosis in Obstetrics

Before 1962 a baby was what the neurophysiologists said they were—nonthinking, nonsensitive, nonremembering blobs of fat, protein, carbohydrate, minerals, water and unmyelinated nerve fibers. They could not possibly know or remember how badly we treated them in the delivery room or when we circumcised the little males. Premature infants were even less likely to be traumatized because their nervous system was less developed than that of the term infant. How very unfair we have been to babies!

Much scientific information is now available to show that we must take a good look at the wonderful mind of infants. People like Joseph Chilton Pearce (1977/1992), Tom Bower (1974), T. Berry Brazelton (1961), David Chamberlain (1990), Anthony DeCasper and A. Fifer (1980), Vlademir Raikov (1980), Lester Sontag (1961), Ashley Montagu (1962), and Tom Verny and J. Kelly (1981) have given us a wealth of information to justify the idea that every normal infant is truly "an old one," meaning it comes into the world with much knowledge. But that entrance into the world may be just a progressive step into the gloom of anxiety, and depression. (Please refer to Chapter 22.)

We can learn helpful points about obstetrical care by regressing adult men and women to the time of their birth and the months before they were born. So doing can also allow us to make positive changes in the world outlook of traumatized babies.

One of the first lessons I was given was that a baby needs an audible welcome from its mother as it emerges at birth and it needs contact with its mother's breast at that moment. Absence of these two stimuli makes a baby feel "alone," "abandoned," "as though everything is "dead." When I see searching eyeball movements under the closed lids of a hypnotized subject, I ask "What are you seeing?" The answer is, "I'm looking for my mother."

Adults during age regression in hypnosis can recognize key experiences that have disturbed their self-image and their trust of others. Regressed "babies," however, are wonderfully able to replay the scenario of imprinted negative memories and can hallucinate what could have made them less painful.

Klaus and Kennell (1976, 1982) and Marshall Klaus and Phyllis Klaus (1985) have documented the importance of this bonding that has been such an important omission in hospital deliveries.

Babies delivered by caesarean section without the stimulation of labor are denied the skin stimulation they would have had. They seem to be more vulnerable to skin, respiratory and gastrointestinal problems than are babies delivered in the time-honored way. They can use their built-in chromosomal knowledge to hallucinate all the sensory stimuli of a normal delivery.

Physicians and midwives are in a wonderful position to help pregnant women avoid mistakes in communications to their unborn child. They can clear up misunderstandings and help a baby enter the external world feeling loved and eager for life.

In the earlier days of my obstetrical practice I was motivated to talk unhappily pregnant women into carrying their pregnancy to term and placing their baby in adoption. My reason was mainly to keep them from risking their life in an illegal abortion. County hospitals were so full of women who were dying or would be hospitalized for long periods with infection. Some parents who adopted babies delivered by me have kept in touch with me and have given me a chance to know how the adopted child has progressed. I have welcomed interviews with students, patients, and physician friends who were adopted babies. Some had true mothers who wanted to keep them; others felt rejected throughout their prenatal course.

Some of my unmarried women wanted to keep their infant but could not because of financial difficulties or because the father had abandoned them. Their babies did very well with their adopted parents. They somehow imprinted on loving acceptance before entering the new family. I still get rave letters from such parents. It was not necessary to coach the real mothers of those babies. They intuitively sang and talked to their enlarging abdomen throughout their pregnancy.

This did not happen with the women who resented their pregnancy and felt bitter about their abandonment and bad luck. I tried to encourage them to talk to their baby during their pregnancy in order to help make the baby feel happy about being there. I coached them to say hello to the baby in the delivery room as soon as it was born and hold it for a few minutes before it was taken to the nursery.

Sometimes they would do it but I remember one patient who said, "Hell no!" That infant had been quiet until she spoke vehemently. It instantly began violent crying that lasted 20 minutes. The husband of this woman had abandoned her and their first child during the pregnancy. I have not heard about its progress from its adopting parents in Utah.

In age-regression studies of adult adopted children I have attempted to learn how much their intrauterine impressions had influenced their life. The ones who felt accepted by a potentially good mother made healthy transitions to their adopting parents. The others, conceived by accident and feeling unwanted throughout the pregnancy, were indelibly imprinted with anger, rebellion and hostility that had not been softened by contact with devoted and loving adopted parents. They transferred their intrauterine feeling about their mother to the woman who adopted them and generalized their feelings to all women. I no longer try to make a woman think about placing a baby that she did not initially want to have. It would not be fair to the baby. It would not be fair to the parents who would adopt it. Such women should have the legal right and financial help to have an abortion. Authorities say that most murderers, robbers, muggers and rapists were unwanted babies.

The Dismal State of Obstetrics

During the years since the first edition of *Clinical Hypnotherapy* was published I have realized that we obstetricians have been working in intellectual darkness. Veterinarians eventually develop a combination of experience and intuition with their speechless animal patients but we have not done that, mainly because we have been too concerned with conducting a "tight ship" in our practice. Our ideals about obstetrics must not be rocked by the whims of our pregnant patients. I hope the time has come for us to sit up and pay attention to the women who are the source of our livelihood and can give us such sage advice about what they need in prenatal and delivery humanistic care.

Now we have access to the subconscious factors that can either damage or helpfully contribute to the well-being of mothers and their babies. There have been great scientific advances in the United States since World War II. We have blood banks, antibiotics, and RhoGam to protect infants from erythroblastosis; our nurses are well trained; and doctors specializing in obstetrics are highly trained and carefully examined before they qualify as American Board Diplomates. Highly trained anesthesiologists are available in our hospitals to relieve pain safely. Why then are we still in 21st place in the world in terms of fetal mortality, far behind Denmark, Sweden, Norway and Germany?

One of the problems might be the adversary relationship that exists between doctors and their patients. Doctors are constantly afraid of being sued. A baby may be abnormal; a recognized test may not have been made. The problem could relate to the legal profession's insistence that all physicians explain in detail all the possible things that might go wrong with surgery or even with the delivery of a normal healthy woman.

Obtaining informed consent suggests that we expect patients to have the problems we have outlined. That is just the way an unconscious mind works. Before the upsurge of medical malpractice suits started in 1974, the incidence of caesarean section was approximately 6 percent of deliveries. Now the national figure of 22 percent with a range of 6 percent to 40 percent is outrageous. The new order has been forced on us by the legal profession combining with naturally occurring human greed. In a modern textbook on obstetrics (Pauerstein 1987), the final chapter contains seven pages of small print relating to litigation against obstetricians.

Changing View about Repeat Caesarean Section

We are taking a newer look at caesarean section since instances of severe hemorrhage are occurring with women who have had several caesarean sections. Placental tissue may adhere to a scar in the uterus and extend into surrounding tissues. The old rule of "once a caesarean, always a caesarean" is changing. Women are now encouraged to deliver in the old way, through the vagina. This "V.B.A.C." (vaginal birth after caesarean) is advocated because the risk of uterine rupture is less than the risk of hemorrhage and the dangers of hepatitis B and HIV in blood units to replace the blood that could be lost.

Dissatisfaction with Obstetrical Care in America

Obstetricians continue generally to treat pregnant women impersonally rather than as colleagues in the birth process. Women who ask to be allowed to deliver on the floor may find themselves on their back on a delivery table with their legs and arms strapped down. Women who have been assured that an episiotomy will not be done have had it done anyway. Women who have wanted to use their Lamaze methods and deliver without sedation have been shocked to find that the doctor has decided they are too tense or too uncomfortable and has ordered drugs they neither need or want. Some have told me they had amnesia for the delivery and felt they had to check the wrist band to make sure the baby they eventually saw was really theirs.

Disappointed women who have wanted to participate fully in their labor frequently feel betrayed, as was Suzanne Arms (1975) when she was inspired to write *Immaculate Deception*, a book that should be read by all obstetricians.

The Tragedy of Premature Labor

A careful review of the prenatal history of women who have given birth to infants weighing less than 2500 grams (5 and 1/2 pounds) will convince anyone that this is a preventable disease. Uterine contractions have been going on long before the pregnancy but are especially needed during pregnancy to permit evacuation of used up blood and its replacement by fresh, arterial blood. This supplies nutrition and oxygen to the fetus.

Women during the third trimester of their pregnancy are vulnerable to alarm about themselves or their unborn child. A careless remark by their obstetrician, a question by a relative or a critical remark from a husband or a boss at work are among the source stimuli that can be revealed during a chronological search from the time of conception to the moment there is an unconscious hyperawareness of these normal uterine contractions.

There are three major times when a woman may feel intermittent pain during her pregnancy and believe that she is in danger of losing her baby. The first of these is around 16 weeks from the time of conception, when muscle fibers in the round ligament begin to contract as the uterus rises from her pelvis into the lower abdominal space. These ligaments run from the vulva on each side, through the inguinal canal, and attach to the cornu, or "horn" of the uterus. Unusual exercise or an emotional distress of some kind can draw the woman's attention to the contractions; usually they are felt more strongly on the right side and may alarm her about a possible appendicitis. A simple explanation of the physiology involved will usually remove her concern.

The second critical time occurs around the seventh month when a baby has decided to move into a more comfortable position with its head down in the deep pelvic area. The shifting from a sitting up to a so-called "vertex presentation" is aided when the fetus pushes with frog-like or walking motions of its legs. The Braxton-Hicks contractions may be uncomfortable for a short time during this fetal acrobatics but will stop when the mother recognizes what she has been told to expect.

The third period is the dangerous one. It may occur any time from the fifth month (20 weeks from conception) until the moment when there is a normal physiological change in the uterine contractility that begins true labor at term. With labor, the contracting uterine muscle fibers take on a peristaltic-like action, starting at the upper end of the uterus and pushing the fetus downward toward the outlet of the pelvis.

Adults during an age-regression in hypnosis are aware of this change from concentric to expulsive contractions. When asked what starts the delivery, most "babies" will say either "I do" or "It's just time." They seem to feel they are the ones who start this process. Recent research with sheep seems to substantiate this subjective impression of the human fetuses who have shared their feelings with me for the last five years. There are centers on each side of the midline in the mid–brain in pregnant sheep that are responsive to hormones secreted by the fetus. When these centers are destroyed bilaterally with electrical energy, the onset of labor is delayed. Adults recalling their delivery after artificial induction with oxytocin, rupture of the membranes, or an interval caesarean section will complain about this usurpation of their power. This has prompted me to impress pregnant women with the importance of refusing to have labor artificially started under normal circumstances. It may be necessary if one of the preventable complications like severe preeclampsia has occurred.

Premature labor follows repeated subconscious alarming experiences after the 20th week of gestation. Delivery before that time is called an abortion. There is usually an initial single disturbing stimulus that starts a repetitive train of alarming ideas. These usually have their greatest physiological impact during sleep. They are not dreams as dreams are usually understood. They seem to occur at deeper than dreaming levels of sleep and, for this reason, are forgotten on awakening. The change from concentric to expulsive contractions may, for this reason, escape conscious awareness and probably accounts for what is diagnosed as "incompetent cervix."

There cannot be a resolution or removal of the first troubled experience because it is not consciously recalled and its recapitulation is also not consciously remembered. There is an increase in the physiological reactions to reverberating repetitions of the original trauma. The pregnant woman will first become aware of painful concentric and normal Braxton-Hicks contractions. She usually will try to postpone calling her doctor in order to see if the discomfort will go away, but her concern will intensify during this waiting interval. Her attention will be increasingly centered on her uterus. The pains will not go away. Her alarm grows until she decides to call her doctor.

This is when the pyramiding of alarming stimuli begins. The doctor may sound alarmed. He or she may see the patient in the office and, depending on the doctor's cultural background, will put her on oral tocolytic medication and bed rest at home or will admit her to the hospital for more active, monitored intravenous treatment. (There are a number of tocolytic drugs that are beta-adrenergic derivatives of epinephrine that will tend to diminish the contractility of the uterus. Epinephrine in early pregnancy increases expulsive contractions but blocks it in the third trimester.)

The real trouble begins at this point. The contractions can change from concentric to expulsive before or after the usual forms of treatment begin. The optimum time to use hypnosis is when the patient first becomes consciously aware of painful uterine contractions, at the moment she wonders if she should call someone. The most effective instrument for com-munication between therapist and patient is the telephone. Ideas are transmitted directly into one ear at a moment when a pregnant woman is already in a hypnotic-like state of increased responsiveness to suggestions because of her alarm.

Comforting conscious reassurance will not help because the problem is working at a subconscious level of perception. It is difficult, however, to evaluate any treatment of problems during pregnancy because of the role of personal determination and/or the confidence projected by the physician or psychotherapist.

Sixty percent of women thought to be in premature labor will progress to delivery in spite of standard treatment. Forty percent will stop the threat, no matter what type of treatment, or even no treatment is offered. Any anec-dote about therapy, therefore, has to be considered, I believe, from the stand-point of what the patient feels in retrospect allowed contractions to return to normal.

In my obstetrical practice prior to using ideomotor search methods, my premature rate was 6.5 percent with 15 percent mortality. In the later group there were six premature infants, or 2.3 percent. All were over 4 pounds, 2 ounces, and all survived.

Case Example of Use of Hypnosis in Premature Labor
This 28- year-old patient had no problems with her first pregnancy and was in her 32nd week of her second pregnancy when she called a few minutes after 11 p.m. to say she had awakened from sleep with strong 2-minute con-tractions lasting about 40 seconds. She was excited and frightened. I wanted to get her mind shifted from the contractions.

Q: When did you go to bed?

A: About 10 o'clock. I was feeling fine.

Q: Let me see, tell me which is your "yes" finger. Do you remember? Just close your eyes and think "yes, yes, yes."

A: (after 15 seconds) It's my index finger on my right hand.

Q: Then hold the receiver in your left hand. . . . Let your inner mind go back to the moment you are falling asleep. Say "Now" when you are there.

A: (10 seconds later) Now.

Q: Go to the moment some thought or some dream is going on just before you start to feel the pain. When you are there your "yes" finger will lift again. As it lifts, just say whatever comes to your mind.

A: (25 seconds later). Oh my! I am dreaming that I am having a baby that is mentally retarded like the little girl my best friend had last year. It was her second child and the pregnancy was not planned because her first baby, a boy, was only 9 months old, just like my son was when I got pregnant this time. I guess I have been identifying myself with her.

Q: Let me ask your fingers a question. Does your inner mind know that this baby is all right now? It certainly has been developing normally since you first came in.

A: My finger is saying "yes" and I have been feeling good about it all this time. (She stops talking for a few seconds and adds, I'm having another contraction now but it isn't strong.

D.C.: You are eight weeks from term. I'm coming out to see you right now to make sure you really stop pushing on this innocent little baby.

The patient lived about 10 minutes away from my house in the San Francisco Marina. When I arrived, "J" announced that she had stopped having the painful contractions but was having the same sort of tightening that she knew was normal.

I asked her to let herself go into hypnosis and understand what sort of triggering experience had started the dream she had. Her "yes" finger lifted a few seconds later to say that she had received a note from the friend asking how she is doing and telling her about the difficulties she was having with the little retarded daughter.

Q: Now that you know this, will you protect yourself and this little baby you are carrying from being superstitious? You are not related to your girlfriend. The only connection has been the fact that you both had not planned to be pregnant so soon after your first child.

A: Her "yes" finger lifted. I gave her some suggestions about pleasant dreams and thoughts and that she would think of calling my office around 2 p.m. the next day.

The remaining weeks were uncomplicated. She went into labor on schedule and delivered a healthy 7 pound, 3 ounce boy instead of a girl.

This onset was quick and easy to handle. The patient came from a well-adjusted set of parents. Her husband was happy to know she was pregnant for the second time. She had lots of emotional support.

Much more work is required when premature labor starts at 18 weeks after a worried obstetrician was trying to decide whether or not to do a cerclage of the cervix because she had a "bad history." He had told this conscientious Jewish woman that her earlier elective abortion in Israel was the reason she had gone into premature labor and lost twins two years ago. The doctor had been treating her for infertility of two years' duration since that tragedy and had been giving her perganol to stimulate ovulation.

Contractions returned to normal after the first telephone conversation until she went back for a checkup with her obstetrician. When she told the doctor about the hypnosis, the comment was, "Hypnosis doesn't work with premature labor."

There were five more episodes of painful contractions that stopped with telephone communications before she delivered a 6 pound, 2 ounce healthy female infant at 37 weeks. She had been trapped into the relationship to this doctor because of her insurance restrictions. She said she felt depressed after every office visit because he kept telling her how lucky she was to be responding to his treatment with oral tocolytic drugs because she was such a poor-risk patient.

Comment
About 40 percent of women being treated with bed rest, uterine monitoring and tocolytic drugs will continue on to a time when the doctor believes the fetus may be "viable." This is usually stated as 32 weeks when there is a higher chance of survival in centers equipped for premature infant care. The target has been made known to the pregnant woman and now occupies her thoughts day and night. This target for delivery is predicated on the concept that delivery is imminent rather than on a goal of a delivery at *a normal full-term date.* This is an important difference. All of us do better if we set a goal that is beyond what we may have been thinking possible. Athletes have known this for many years. Reaching that 32-week goal may be a relief for the mother but is no relief for the pitiful little infant that remains in an intensive care unit, traumatized by such things as needle punctures, tubes into the stomach, and absence of its mother.

Twins and the Threat of Premature Labor
A new complication has appeared for women with twin pregnancies. When the diagnosis is made, they are warned about the risks of premature labor and the danger that this would be for their babies. This is comparable to telling a plump child, "Don't you put your hands in that cookie jar!"

Our subconscious mind is unable to process negative thoughts. They come out positive. A mother of twins will subconsciously process a warning about premature labor as meaning that her doctor expects her to go into premature labor. Since this will endanger her twins she is being prepared to feel guilty.

Before the rise of malpractice litigation we obstetricians believed that most women with twins will go into labor a little while before the expected date would be if they were carrying only one baby. We did not worry about that. Twins seem to be more mature at birth anyway, even though usually weighing less than a single baby at term. Rarely were twins so small at birth that they were in trouble. This modern way of alarming the mother of twins in order to remain legally sanctimonious in obtaining "informed consent" is bad taste and harmful.

Women with twin pregnancies are troubled from the start with worries about whether or not they will be a good mother. By the time they know the diagnosis they are usually past the time when a second twin may have expired and either has been absorbed or aborted. Seventeen percent of pregnancies are twin pregnancies, but only 1 in 80 pregnancies go on to delivery of viable twins. This is about 1 percent.

They deserve some time and effort being coached on using self-hypnosis for rest periods and being helped to select finger signals to be used if they have concerns at any time during the pregnancy.

Breech Presentation and Caesarean Section

Obstetricians are no longer trained in the art of delivering a baby who refuses to rotate into a vertex (head down) position or insists on turning back again after attempted external manipulation. It is generally accepted that caesarean section is indicated in such cases because there is less risk for the baby and less risk of involving the doctor in a malpractice suit in case something goes wrong with the baby. There is, indeed, a risk in vaginal delivery of a breech presentation. The mother of such a baby has been emotionally troubled during the days before the onset of labor. This diminishes the immune capabilities of the fetus and shrinks its thymus gland.

Interviews with more than 30 adults who were "breech babies" has demonstrated that all of them were telepathically sensing the worries of their mother and did not feel it was safe to turn around. Such an infant will be fatigued by maternal stress. Worried or frightened mothers are liable to have long, painful labors that will make additional physical demands on the fetus. This added stress for the baby may be a cause of cerebral hemorrhage or physical injury if a vaginal delivery is poorly conducted.

Lewis Mehl (1980) and I have independently discovered that the breech baby may turn around and "dive" down into its mother's pelvis if we use hypnosis to help relax the mother. We have urged her to talk to her baby, saying something like, "I'm looking forward to seeing you. How about putting your head down so we can see each other soon?" It appears from our results that relaxation of the maternal pelvic muscles can allow a fetus to turn to a vertex presentation. Sometimes this occurs just because we have learned what the mother has been troubled about and have helped her resolve her fears.

Between 1946 and 1956, 3 percent of my babies were persistent breech presentation. They were all delivered vaginally without problems. Three percent is the expected rate in the United States. After learning how to ask about subconscious fear in 1956 I had no breech presentations in 235 deliveries. This is a small series but suggests that the peace of mind of the mother does something to motivate her fetus to do what evolution of the large human fetal head has demanded for safe delivery. The fetal head makes a better wedge for dilating the cervix than the buttocks or feet.

Midwives Deserve Consideration in Modern Obstetrical Care

Midwives have always had an excellent record of noninvasive and safe obstetrical care in England, Holland, Norway, Sweden, and Denmark, but their work has been blocked in Canada and the United States by the medical profession until it became clear recently that well trained midwives can work helpfully and economically with obstetricians. Their acceptance will, I believe, help reduce the incidence of caesarean sections in the future.

Home Deliveries, a Possibility for the Future?

There is now a grass-roots trend toward home delivery. Initially it evolved because the cost of obstetrical care and hospitalization has been accelerating yearly. It is becoming apparent that there are more advantages in home delivery than can be found in a hospital. The laboring patient is in a familiar environment among her familiar bacteria with which she is on biologically friendly terms. The setting is quiet and peaceful. She usually will have two midwives in attendance. She has come to know both of them during her prenatal care and does not have the shock of finding a stranger in charge when she goes into labor because her doctor is out of town on vacation or at a meeting.

There is less danger of arrested labor because there are fewer reasons for a patient to become alarmed toward the end of the first stage of labor at home. Friends and relatives have been the greatest threat for a woman who plans a home delivery. Because they are innocent of experience or knowledge they are free to voice their doomsday opinions about "something going wrong" and "bleeding to death." Pessimistic remarks by relatives will override explanations and assurances by midwives who know the safety of home delivery.

The risks of home delivery were considerable before World War II, when telephone service in city slums was unavailable and home deliveries were done by medical students attending tired, poor older women in their sixth to ninth pregnancy. Most medical schools terminated home deliveries before the end of 1938. Transportation was difficult, there was no "911" to call the police or fire department, and the streets were often clogged with horsedrawn wagons. Complications were due to previously undiagnosed abnormal presentation or postpartum hemorrhage from a uterus too tired to contract.

Fear and troubled expectation are the causes of eclampsia, premature labor, hemorrhage, shock, and uterine atony following delivery. Fear and troubled expectation are the enemy. They come from more possible sources in hospitals than at home. A woman who learns about her resources and has confidence in her power will be as safe at home as she would be in a hospital.

Women wondering where to have their baby should avoid the advice of inexperienced but opinionated people. They should talk to experienced midwives or women who have delivered in both places—hospital and home.

Who should be delivered in a hospital? Women who have had previous conditioning for fear and troubled expectation should be delivered in a hospital, where they know that immediate help is available in the unlikely event that something will not turn out as planned. Their number would include those who:

- Have had problems with prolonged infertility
- Have had fetal losses
- Have a baby that refuses to turn into a head-down posture
- Have had severe, disabling menstrual pain (low tolerance)
- Have relatives or friends with bad obstetric histories
- Have preexisting liver or kidney disease
- Have had persistent vomiting during their pregnancy
- Are diabetic
- Are being treated for epilepsy

Women with these problems, I believe, would benefit greatly if coached in the manner used for women who have no problems. They should learn as much as possible about their body in preparation for labor. In so doing they might also gain some insight about the cause of their physical problem and possibly find the emotional tools to assist in freeing themselves from its continuation (Dunbar 1954, Kroger 1962).

Nausea and Vomiting in Pregnancy

Some nausea is common during the first two weeks after conception, when there is a physiological adjustment to pregnancy. Initially it is probably hormonal and, therefore, not psychological. When it continues and vomiting occurs as well, the problem will combine both physiological and psychological elements but the treatment is wholly psychological. This is not meant to imply that vomiting women are consciously involved and that vomiting is "all in her head." The problems are subconscious. No one is to blame.

Not all women are troubled by nausea and vomiting, and those who have it usually find it clearing up without treatment during the first three months. It is still a nuisance and, since the drugs we formerly used for its treatment are now considered potentially dangerous for the fetus, we should use psychological means of treatment that are safe and truly helpful.

The ideomotor questioning techniques described in Chapter 12 will quickly reveal the unconscious fears, guilt feelings, and negative identifications that seem to underlie this problem. These sources of trouble are usually immediately eliminated by the patient when she can recognize them.

Patients who are truly unhappy about being pregnant and have subconscious forces that do not respond to reevaluation and the strategies to combat resistances (Chapter 27) should be permitted to have their pregnancy terminated. The problem may not occur in a planned subsequent pregnancy.

Physicians will sometimes continue reassurance and requests such as "Drink a lot of water and eat crackers until your nausea goes away." It may not go away. A shift from nausea to vomiting three or four times a day and a shift into a life-threatening "toxic vomiting of pregnancy" can occur almost overnight. There can be rapid loss of weight, dehydration, ketosis, and acute yellow atrophy of the liver that does not respond to hospitalization and fluid replacement. Immediate termination of the pregnancy under dangerous circumstances may save the unfortunate woman's life, but it should not have been endangered in the first place.

The time to work with this problem of early pregnancy is the moment a pregnant woman is troubled by nausea and before it causes vomiting. Nausea may be a form of body language for being frightened or unhappy at the realization that pregnancy has occurred. Children often use the word *upset* when disappointed or chastised. The process may be activated by that same childlike response of vomiting when pregnant women are subconsciously "upset." I urge those who work with ideomotor questioning to keep an open mind. Your patient may come out with a report about dying in childbirth in a previous lifetime. Work with it. You can ask for a finger response to the question "Could you just leave that lifetime and keep it from causing trouble up here in this life?" A finger may lift to say "yes" and that may be the end of the problem.

My suggestion for treatment of pregnancy nausea would be to ask for the patient's feelings about being pregnant and about having children during an initial conversation. She may have definite conscious feelings against pregnancy at this time and should have a right to terminate the pregnancy.

My next step of treatment with a woman who consciously wants to have a child but has had some subconscious negative forces causing her nausea is to teach her self-hypnosis and then have her practice feeling subconsciously hungry. When she experiences hunger consciously as well, she presses her left thumb and index finger tips together as a conditioned signal and asks the "yes" finger on the other hand to lift when she has "locked in the association between the signal and the feelings of hunger."

I point out that the sensation of hunger activates her digestive organs to be ready for work on food she will eat. She is stimulating her liver to put out bile and her pancreas to put out insulin to store carbohydrate, proteolytic enzymes to digest protein, and enzymes for converting starches into glycogen for storage in muscles and liver. The patient is encouraged to imagine sucking on a lemon in order to stimulate her salivary glands.

Each physiological sensation has a counterpart, so if she feels hungry she can also remember the feeling of being nauseated and miserable as well. I have her recapture that feeling of nausea, using the same left thumb and index finger as a start-up signal. When she has the nauseated feeling strong enough to want to remove it, she can do so by pressing the thumb and index finger tips of the right hand together and order her "yes" finger on her left hand to lift to let her know she is completing this job subconsciously. She is to nod when she feels hungry again.

I explain the reason for this exercise. Her subconscious mind will quickly learn that any symptom she turns on can also be turned off, and she is learning the tools to do that.

Women who are capable of being honest with their feelings, as most nauseated pregnant women are, are all wonderful hypnotic subjects as soon as they learn some skills and can be sure they want to continue with their pregnancy. They can easily understand that enjoying food and liquids in moderation will be giving their baby the nourishment it needs to develop happily and enter the outside world feeling welcome.

I would want to see this patient within a day or two for an hour appointment. This is an important time for her to gain respect for her abilities. This is when I would go through the review steps outlined below. I need to know her feelings at birth and how her mother feels when she learns she is pregnant. This is an emotional moment for the mother. The child's feelings then become fixed in the developing nervous system. If the patient is asked to let her subconscious mind show her with her hands how big she is, she will probably give a dimension with two fingers that is twice as big as it would actually be at the six- to eight-week stage.

Suggested Outline for Adding Hypnosis to Usual Obstetrical Diagnosis and Laboratory Work

1. Take a careful history that includes the health history of the patient's parents and relationship to siblings. Rather than my duplicating the

preliminary part of the history, please turn to the steps as discussed in Chapter 17 (Sexual Learning).

2. Explain that a women whose mother has had a difficult pregnancy and delivery tends to duplicate her mother's problems. For this reason, you want to explore your patient's subjective impressions of birth and earlier in order for her to know how to make the pregnancy and delivery of her baby easy. A baby who delivers quickly and easily will come into the world well prepared for life and is usually smiling. A baby whose mother has suffered because of fear and pain will come into the world shrieking in anger with its little fists clenched and its eyes closed tight and its soul filled with guilt. Babies should not be born feeling guilty. It affects their subsequent development.

You are appealing here for her to be free of fear and pain in labor for the benefit of her baby. This is strong motivation for an expectant mother.

3. Explain the principles of hypnosis and demonstrate postural suggestion with one arm heavy and the other feeling normal. This shows that attention can be centered on one arm while the other is relatively ignored and yet the centered arm will be feeling the pull of gravity more than the other arm. This test also allows a demonstration of the Coué Law of Reversed Effect when you ask the patient to "try" to lift the heavier arm. Resolve the conflict by having her "remove the weight" from the heavy arm and substitute balloons to pull the arm upward.

4. It is an easy step from this experience to helping your patient select finger signals. You can, with a little practice, get permission from the patient to review her birth from the time of your interview. Learn her impressions of how her mother feels when the contractions are changing from the concentric, previously ignored Braxton-Hicks contractions to the expulsive, downward pushing ones of labor.

5. At this time your patient's fingers will tell you whether her head is down in the pelvis or she is still sitting up in a breech position. All people regressed to intrauterine experience are aware of their position. They also have an amazing sense of their size at various key moments of stress, as when mother learns she is pregnant and when there is an argument going on.

6. Shift now to the moment of delivery. If this is a usual vertex presentation, she will know which way her head turns as it comes out (Cheek 1974) and which arm delivers first. Her muscle memory helps you to know how valid her report will be of how she feels and whether her mother is awake or asleep. Make notes about whether or not she feels it is all right for her to be there as a girl. Ask if her father is there in the delivery room. Ask if a baby thinks a father should be there. It might surprise you to learn how important the presence of the father is for the sense of acceptance and well-being of a little girl.

7. Having the patient reprocess the labor and delivery is very helpful in most cases. By having her imagine the process of teaching her mother how to walk into cold water, become used to the cold and developing analgesia (these steps are outlined in Chapter 21), the patient will be developing the analgesia second-hand with her mother. She can then imagine how that labor would have been if her mother had practiced enough times to be sure she could turn off discomfort any time a contraction was strong. Point out that freedom from pain during labor takes pressure off the baby and makes it easier for the baby to slide out rather than being pushed out. In redoing the delivery you can have your patient be born with her mother squatting on the floor. This is built-in knowledge imprinted during three million years, at least, of humanoid evolution. Women should never be tied down on a delivery table.

8. With this hallucinated delivery as it should have been conducted, the patient can feel what it would have been like if a nurse had eased her out and given her to her mother, who is now sitting with her back supported by her father. She can feel the warmth of her mother's bare skin and feel herself being held against her mother's breast.

9. This is enough to do the first time you work with hypnosis. It will have taken less than 30 minutes of time when you have had some practice. It is a valuable 30-minute period of building self-confidence for your patient. She has had a chance to compare ways of delivering and she has learned that she can develop sensation alterations along with the hallucinated training that her mother could have had. You have had a chance to recognize possible negative imprints that can be removed at the next visit. You may also find that your patient has become much more understanding and thoughtful of her mother.

This indirect method of teaching sensation control to her mother is not as threatening to a new patient as might be the case if you started off with a hypnotic induction and asked her to develop stages of analgesia. Her fear of failing might make her fail.

10. Before setting up the next appointment a month later, you can tell the patient that at the next visit you want her to learn how to put herself into hypnosis for brief periods of rest during the pregnancy. It will come in very handy after she is home with her baby.

Second Office Visit

Agenda
- Check experience and feelings since previous visit.
- Abdominal and pelvic examination, blood pressure, and urine check for sugar, protein.

- Move to consultation room: 15 minutes used for teaching self-hypnosis and the way of reviewing nighttime ideation.

Self-Hypnosis Rehearsal
(Details of my two-minute rehearsal are given at the end of Chapter 8.) I have my patients go through the steps two times with my help. Then they do it twice themselves without my intervening.

The practice usually takes about 15 minutes. The patient is then given an appointment for the next month and asked to practice the self-hypnosis at home when alone. She is given the audiotape of this session to have for reference.

Program for the Third Prenatal Checkup

The third prenatal checkup usually occurs after the patient is feeling fetal movements. I did not have sonography available during my clinical practice of obstetrics but would not have used it because I am not convinced of its safety during the early months of pregnancy. I would not use sonography today.

Checking Unconscious Belief about Sex of Baby

LeCron felt that women had knowledge of the sex of their baby and asked several of us to test our patients to see if this was true. My finding on a single test, either with a pendulum or with finger signals, was that mothers were right about 50 percent of the time. Later I checked patients repeatedly during the remainder of the pregnancy and found them giving different sex reports, pretty much depending on which relative had been discussing the matter with them.

A valuable observation came out of this study (Cheek 1961a). Women who were frightened, either for themselves or for their baby would answer "no" or "I don't want to answer" when asked, "Does your inner mind know the sex of your baby?" The next question was "Are you subconsciously afraid, either for yourself or your baby?" The answer was invariably "yes" when they did not feel they knew the sex. It was then important to learn which of the alternatives was involved and then to orient her memory back to the moment that fear started. The reason was usually recognizable as inconsequential when brought up to a talking level of awareness. Thereafter the same question could be posed to make sure the fear was no longer present.

I found that the optimum time to use this questioning with an otherwise normal patient was after she was feeling fetal movements. The reality of her pregnancy was then apparent and had a personal meaning to her.

A by-product of this testing was its value again as the time for delivery approached. This is a time when dreams can be troublesome. The repetition of troubled, often superstititious, dreams might be revealed by sudden fluid retention and elevation of blood pressure—precursors of preeclampsia, a definitely psychological complication of pregnancy that usually occurs in young women 20 years of age or less in their first pregnancy or women over 35 in their first pregnancy.

Since the advent of early testing for genetic abnormalities with amniocentesis, I have given up the question because the patient then knows what the sex is. If, however, the patient tells me that she did not want to know the sex of her baby, I have found, with a pendulum or finger signals, that she is subconsciously frightened in some way. She will at first deny this and give some reason like, "It really doesn't matter. We will be happy with either sex." The ideomotor response has, in my experience, always contradicted her. There has always been some vague fear that can be easily removed.

21

Surgery

Able, the best space monkey the Army ever had, is dead today because of a thousand-to-one anesthetic fluke. (Original news releases by the United Press in June 1959, quoted the Army as stressing that her death was not linked to the space trip.

This was Able's second exposure to an anesthetic agent. There had been another, and nobody had been communicating with Able to learn what subconscious effect had been produced by the first anesthetic. She had been strapped to her seat for 38 hours before takeoff. Pressure on her body had increased from 15 to 570 pounds per square inch after takeoff. A period of weightlessness followed during that 300 mile trip before her descent and sudden deceleration as the parachute opened.

Able made a great, involuntary contribution to our knowledge about travel in space. She might not have perished, however, if there had been someone in the Army conversant with monkey understanding to inform Able about what was to happen to her after that frightening experience. She needed to know that this experience would be different. There would be the same room, same smells and the same people as before but there would be nothing more to fear. She needed to know that the medicine she smells is to make it easy to remove the wires under her skin without hurting her, and that she would soon be back in her cage where she would have something good to eat.

Just as in the case of the monkey, Able, we must do our best to discover and resolve experiences that might influence the safety of a patient we schedule for an operation or refer to a surgeon for an operation. The patient needs to know in advance what is to be done, why it will be done and what is expected of him or her to ensure rapid recovery and return home from the hospital.

Present-day Hospital Care of Surgical Patients

There have been some changes in the way surgical patients are treated since the 1968 first edition of *Clinical Hypnotherapy*. Because of rapidly growing hospital costs, insurance companies have insisted that patients be admitted in the morning of the day of surgery instead of the more sensible preceding day that allows some accommodation to the hospital surroundings. Patients now go through the admission process two or three days before their surgery. They have seen their regular doctor for a physical examination and laboratory tests within a week of surgery. They have an interview with one of the anesthesiologists who is available at the time the patient comes in for the admission formalities. These include the various legal releases and promises not to sue anyone but rather to go through arbitration if things do not go well. They are further impressed with the need to pay their bills on time in case their insurance carrier refuses to pay for hospitalization.

They are not to take any food or fluids after 12 midnight and are to be in the hospital lobby by 7 a.m. This may mean that they must arise around 5 a.m. if they are scheduled for surgery to start before noon. They may understandably need to have a quiet time before surgery to quiet their anxieties and make up for lost sleep. Many of us have had fears that admission on the day of surgery would lead to anxiety for the patient. The old plan of having a patient spend an adjustment night in the hospital prior to surgery seemed right. To my knowledge, however, there have been no statistics to justify this fear. Furthermore, with each hospital day costing approximately $ 1,000, saving this day would diminish anxiety for the patient with inadequate insurance coverage.

The Surgeon's Goals

The competent surgeon exercises good judgment in deciding on an operation, carefully prepares the patient and gives meticulous attention to the details of surgical technique. He or she offers complete explanations of what has been done as soon as the patient is recovered from the anesthetic and sees to it that reports from the pathologist and clinical laboratory are given to the patient as soon as they are available. A delay in reporting will lead to a growing, potentially damaging, alarm. The pathology report often needs clarification because the terms can sound ominous to a patient. Finally, the surgeon needs to see the patient personally on the day of discharge, rather than leaving this task for an assistant or a resident.

Success with the outcome of surgery is not a one-man or one-woman job, however. Surgeons need assistance from relatives, nurses, house officers, laboratory technicians, the anesthesiologist, unseen helpers in the kitchen, and, especially, the patient. A good-risk surgical patient can be converted to a bad one by careless remarks of relatives and friends on the eve of surgery. The question "Why didn't you go to Doctor XYZ?" can have a devastating effect, even when the patient consciously knows the person talking is not an authority on surgeons. The admitting officer asking about the "nearest relative" or insisting on removal of a meaningful ring may initiate very troublesome thoughts, particularly if it is a wedding ring associated with "Till death do you part." Statements that could seem silly when a patient is normally conscious can take on a very different meaning when that patient is in an altered state of anxiety prior to surgery or while losing consciousness with a general anesthetic later on.

Any of the people just mentioned, including the patient, can be the cause of shock, cardiac arrest, or hemorrhage during the operation. Any of them can be responsible for postoperative paralysis of the small intestine (ileus), vomiting, distension, coagulation of blood in the pelvic and leg vessels, showers of clotted blood to the lungs (pulmonary emboli), renal shutdown and/or wound disruption with evisceration of the bowel.

Information on these matters has come from people who have survived these complications and have been able to report their impressions during age regression studies using ideomotor techniques.

These gloomy complications do not need to occur. They can be prevented. If they have already occurred, it is possible to help the troubled patient stop them and return to an optimum recovery. The surgeon, or a psychologist who uses ideomotor techniques, can help the patient discover and reframe the causal events. It takes very few minutes to do this because a surgical patient, during a critical time with complications, is already in a hypnoidal state of increased suggestibility. Finger signals are easily set up and the patient asked to go forward from the moment of losing consciousness to the moment something significant is happening during the operation. When this has been recognized and verbally reported, the surgeon or therapist can help the patient look at the experience with conscious understandings and eliminate the problem's harmful effect.

For example:

A patient awakened in pain, feeling frightened without apparent cause. At my morning visit to her I was disturbed by her swollen abdomen and absence of bowel sounds. I asked her to go into hypnosis and search for the cause of a problem that was totally unexpected.

She burst into tears as she said, "All my life I have been afraid I would have a cancer like my two grandmothers and an aunt." When asked what made her think about this, she said, "The nurse is saying, 'What is this lump I am feeling?'" The patient did not add my explanation I had thought would prevent an unconscious patient from worrying.

I had said, "Oh, that's just the lump of scarred omentum from the hernia sac that you saw me drop back into the abdomen." I had asked the nurse to feel the normal gall bladder that was visible through the incision but her hand contacted the "lump" instead. She was assisting me in the absence of the resident, who had been detained in the delivery room. I again explained that the lump had nothing to do with cancer.

I explained to the patient what had happened. She was relieved and within half an hour her abdomen was flat and peristalsis was audible. This is a prime example of an alarming impression taking priority over a nonthreatening one, my statement in the operating room. Her unconscious fears could have continued with a pyramiding harmful effect.

Complications can occur days or weeks after what seems to have been a routine operation. Repetitive dreams of reliving the surgical experience can build stress reactions that lead to the complication.

Prophylactic Preparation for Trouble-Free Surgery

The patient who knows what is to be done and has had time to think it over and perhaps obtain another opinion from a competent consultant is the one best prepared for an operation.

In addition, I believe, the surgeon or an associate should teach the patient how to use self-hypnosis; how to remember hunger, thirst, and hyperactive bowel peristalsis and how to develop analgesia for the surgical field. The patient should rehearse these changes until fully confident in these abilities.

Learning to Disassociate One's Self from the Operating Room

The value of separating from the environment of the surgical theater should be clarified and the patient instructed on how to go on a prolonged "vacation trip" during the time between a preoperative medication and return to his or her room following the operation. In this way the sounds of an operating room will blend in with background sounds of traffic or distant conversations of people in a restaurant. It is helpful to state the value of ignoring conversation in the operating room. Instruction should be given during the hypnotic session, however, that the patient will pay full attention to whatever direction is given when either the surgeon or the anesthesiologist addresses the patient by his or her first name.

I have never found a way to completely eliminate awareness of what is going on in the operating room. Part of the patient's attention is always right there.

For further protection, the surgeon should make it clear to the anesthesiologist, the operating room nurses, and the nurses in the recovery room to either refrain from talking or be as careful with conversation as they would be if surgery were being done under local or spinal anesthesia.

The primitive part of the brain is acutely aware of changes from ordinary circumstances to a stressful one that requires physiological and emotional adaptation. At an ideomotor level of awareness, reflected by finger signals, a hypnotized subject can discover and communicate recognition that a certain stimulus brought about a physiological response such as a drop in blood pressure followed by the beginning of a hemorrhage. This ability is present when a patient is awake, sleeping or unconscious from injury or a general anesthetic.

The subconscious mind is constantly monitoring sensory stimuli and recording physiological responses to threatening stimuli whether the conscious mind is awake or blocked out by natural sleep, injury, or general anesthesia. I compare the job of the reticular formation (reticular activating system or RAS) surrounding the brainstem to the work of an expert observing the changing patterns of a radar screen. He is alerted by disappearance of a blip that has been previously visible and he is alerted when a new blip appears. The rostral end of the RAS decides what information should be relayed to higher centers for action. It also suppresses nonmeaningful sensory stimuli (Magoun 1963, Hernandez-Peon et al. 1956).

People in hypnosis can shift subconscious memory back to an operation many years after the experience and can report their unconscious interpretation of an auditory stimulus and the physiological reaction to that stimulus. They can also report, with remarkable accuracy, what they believe resolved a problem, or they can teach us what they believe would have corrected the problem if the right things had been said or done. General anesthesia does not remove this subconscious alertness to conditions in the outside world.

Bernard Levinson (1965) did the first carefully controlled test of hearing under anesthesia. Ernest Werbel, (1965), a surgeon and David Scott (1974), an anesthesiologist, were the first to put information about hearing in a book. Bonke, Fitch, and Miller (1990) of Rotterdam assembled a number of papers from the First International Congress on Memory and Awareness in Anesthesia held in Glasgow, Scotland in November of 1989. Progress is now being made.

I want to stress the fact that an anesthetized patient will ignore "canned," nonmeaningful voices used in experiments to test whether or not a hearing sense persists during general anesthesia (Cheek 1981). My studies have shown that the patient pays selective attention to familiar voices during an operation. First it is the anesthesiologist; then it shifts to the surgeon and to the assistant as the surgeon makes the incision. Attention reverts to the anesthesiologist at the end of the surgical procedure. There is, however, global awareness throughout the unconscious period. Any sound of alarm from the anesthesiologist will immediately shift the attention back to him or her during the surgical work period.

Obtaining "Informed Consent" May Be Hazardous to Health

The tedious and subconsciously frightening outlining of possible untoward results of surgery while obtaining "informed consent" to have the operation may be the cause of some of the complications I have mentioned. To give informed consent the patient is supposed to have the knowledge that transfusions of blood may be necessary because of hemorrhage. The surgery might not do what is thought to be needed and new things might be found that could require more extensive work. This doomsday requirement by the legal advisors for physicians and hospitals is damaging unless it is countered by teaching the patient how the complications can be avoided. The subconscious interpretation of what is outlined is that "my surgeon expects these things to happen."

The subconscious mind pays attention to threats and ignores positive assurances on the eve of surgery. Ideas about danger outweigh nonthreatening bits of information. This is why the ordinary way of obtaining an educated understanding about operations is medically and psychologically inappropriate.

Generalized Anger

Furthermore, if a patient feels angry about treatment during a hospital stay, the anger is not limited to the person creating that anger. It becomes generalized and may influence the response of the patient to the anesthetic, to the surgeon, to what the surgeon does, and to the nursing staff during the recovery period. The patient will have no conscious knowledge about this generalization.

Case Example: Litigation Against the Wrong Source of Anger

An example of blaming the wrong person and generalizing of resentment was given by a woman I interviewed in Sacramento in 1979. She had been in the process of suing her very competent and innocent surgeon because of complications relating to an abdominal operation 18 months prior to my interview with her.

Her surgeon had been unable to see that the anesthesiologist inserted his penis into this woman's mouth during the operation. The usual drapes over supports around her head screened him from the surgeon and his assistants, but nurses had been aware of his actions and eventually brought about arrest and conviction of this disturbed person.

Her complications of continuing fever, wound infection, and disruption of the incision were strong evidence confirming my findings when this woman reviewed her operation during an age regression. Repeated, consciously unrecognized dreams of being assaulted sexually while being unable to move apparently lowered her immune capabilities to organisms in her skin. Her operation was a simple hysterectomy and should not have been complicated in any way.

Additional evidence of the anesthesiologist's involvement in using this woman and many others to satisfy his sexual drives was revealed by this patient and two other women that I interviewed. Each reported that he had not visited her preoperatively. He came into the operating room while she was drowsy from the medication. None of them heard his voice before, during, or after surgery. He did not intubate the three women to make the anesthetic safer. He did not visit them during their prolonged hospital stay. The other two women had also had wound infections and continuing fever postoperatively.

Example: Damaging Versus Constructive Influences by Surgeons
As a contrast to this was the information I obtained from a woman who had nearly died at the moment of losing consciousness during three failed attempts to repair a congenitally impaired hip socket.

Prior to each near tragedy in her first three operations, the communications had been between the surgeon and her parents. She was excluded as though she were a bystander. She was 10 months of age with the first operation, 11 and 13 years old with the near fatal second and third operations. She felt coerced and angry when she went into the operating room for each of the first three operations. She "did not want to be there" as she lost consciousness. Breathing stopped during the induction as she experienced a flashback to her sensations at birth.

A review of this woman's birth revealed that her mother had been heavily sedated and was unable to talk. The baby felt apathetic, unwanted, and unloved. She had to be resuscitated. The chemicals used for each subsequent surgery were the state-dependent connection with her birth experience.

During her cardiac arrest at age 11, she described the alarm of the anesthetist as he jumped up, moved to her left side, and began pushing on her chest. She demonstrated with her hands the rhythm of the pushing. Her spirit left her body at this point. Again she "did not want to be there." Her spirit visited her horse at the stable and her cocker spaniel at her home before going to the coffee shop in the hospital. She saw her mother and father appearing worried but somehow did not feel she could talk to them. Coffee the horse and Vicki the spaniel were both alarmed at seeing her floating in an unusual position. Next, her body felt the jolt of an electrical shock, followed by insertion of a "long needle" into her chest. She demonstrated with her finger that the needle went in just to the left of the sternum in the sixth space between her ribs. Of course, she might have known about these things being done to people when their heart stops, but this report was by the 11-year-old child talking in the present tense with absolute sureness about her perceptions.

There was a "sort of tingling, burning" sensation in her chest just before the needle was removed. This is when her body began breathing again and she felt her heart beating. Now her spirit got back into her body.

Following this graphic report, which is recorded on videotape, I asked her to go over that experience, hearing what could have been said to her that would have prevented her from nearly dying. This is her statement: The anesthesiologist would have leaned over her at the start and would have said, "You are going to be all right. We are going to help you get well and be able to do the things you want to do."

I have to report that the operation record and the notes by the anesthesiologist show no trace of this near tragedy in the operating room. The surgeon is dead and the anesthesiologist is retired and could not be found when I tried to learn more. Is it possible this intelligent woman could have fabricated the whole thing? Perhaps altering the record seemed legally safer for those involved, in case something should happen later.

Something did, in fact, happen. There was a hematoma and a wound infection. She remained in the hospital 16 days. The operation was a failure. These are suggestive facts, but the hospital records suggest that this patient invented her cardiac arrest on January 4, 1966.

The third failed attempt to repair the hip socket was when she was 13 years old. She felt that her doctor had no idea of what he might be able to do. This was her original orthopedic surgeon working in the hospital where her first disaster had occurred. Again she reacted badly during the induction of anesthesia.

Her fourth surgical experience at age 14 was uncomplicated and successful. This was a hip replacement, a major surgical procedure, at the Massachusetts General Hospital in Boston. Her orthopedic surgeon, Dr. Roderick Turner, told her that she would be the most important part of the repair process. He asked her to work with him to make it a success. He outlined what he expected of her when she came out of the anesthetic and for months to come. This had the effect of tacitly implying that she would live through the operation and do well in the future. It centered her mind on events of the future instead of the possible panic of the present at the time she would be unconscious again.

This woman, now in her thirties, attributed the success to the way her surgeon included her as a co-worker in the project of overcoming her handicap. Most valuable, she felt, was the intensity of his commitment to making the operation successful. Perhaps there was also some telepathic healing energy crossing from Dr. Turner to his little patient during the operation.

Telepathy and Fear

Telepathy

There is no question in my mind that people hear conversations in the operating room, but it appears that they are also capable of picking up the thoughts of their surgeon and anesthesiologist. Loss of consciousness is an alarming event. All the survival senses are at their highest pitch. It seems clear that more than the hearing sense is available to the patient.

David Dillahunt, a physician of Columbus, Ohio, in 1962 was the first to suggest to me that anesthetized patients are telepathically aware of thoughts of the surgeon and the anesthesiologist. I have learned that impressions I once thought were overheard have been picked up telepathically. The question "Do you hear the surgeon say what you have just told me?" may evoke a verbal "yes" and a nod of the head but these higher-level perceptions may be contradicted by a finger saying "no."

At this, I ask, "Let a thought come to you to explain how you know what you have just told me. Your 'yes' finger will lift at that moment. When your finger lifts, please tell me what comes to your mind."

As the finger lifts, the patient will say, "I just know it."

I then say, "Please tell me what part of your mind knows this." The patient will put a hand up to the right side of his or her head. It does not matter whether the patient is right- or left-handed when recognizing the location of this understanding.

Words, therefore, that are thought to be overheard in the operating room may be simply thoughts transmitted telepathically. If this assertion can be substantiated by the work of other independent observers, it will be very important for surgeons and their assistants to keep positive thoughts while they are working with their surgical patient.

Consciously Recognized Fear at the Time of Surgery

Many famous surgeons, including J. B. Murphy, J. M. T. Finney, and the senior George Crile, have pointed out the danger of going ahead with surgery after a patient has expressed a fear of dying. It is possible with hypnosis to discover the origin of such consciously expressed fear. The origins are usually ridiculous identifications or assumptions that now is the time to be punished for real or imagined sins. Sometimes fear stems from un-scientific assumption that the diagnosis will be cancer, and death during anesthesia is preferable to a slow and painful one with cancer.

A Way of Discovering and Working with Fear

It is possible for these fears and assumptions to be corrected in the hospital if the need for surgery is urgent, but there is seldom such an emergency. It is wiser to reschedule the operation, send the patient home, and make arrangements to have someone explore the unconscious reasons for fear with hypnosis and ideomotor questioning such as this:

Q: Is there some past event responsible for your feeling that you might die with this operation?

A: Will usually be a "yes" finger or "I don't want to answer" which really means "yes, but I don't want to know about it."

Q: Would this source of fear have occurred before you were −? (The completion of the search and resolution is carried out as described in Chapter 12.)

Before terminating the search, be sure to ask, "Is there anything else we need to know in order to ensure that your surgery and recovery will be safe and comfortable?"

If the answer is "no", you can ask the patient to hallucinate the *earliest* date that would be good for scheduling the surgery.

Variants of Fear

1. We can be afraid and feel free to talk of our fears. We do so usually because we understand that others have had similar fears. We are willing to listen and be reassured in return.

2. We can know our fear consciously but feel unwilling to talk about it because of the conviction that others might think us foolish.

3. We may have a consciously recognized fear and be unwilling to talk about it lest it be justified. We may not want to "hear the truth." This kind of fear causes people to put off visiting a doctor after recognizing suspicious symptoms. Older people with such fear may have suicidal thoughts that can lead to actual suicide.

4. We can experience fear subconsciously in tremendous reality and be totally oblivious to its presence in our conscious thinking. Recent studies have convinced me that such consciously unrecognized fears may be responsible for major complications like hypercoagulability of the blood. Thrombosis in pelvic veins may be followed by showers of clot fragments to the

lungs. Initial intravascular coagulation with shock may be followed by massive fibrinolytic hemorrhage.

Subconscious Fear

I believe the fear that cannot be recognized or expressed may be even more dangerous than the kind a patient is able to talk about. No careful study had been made, however, to see how many patients have survived when they thought they would die or dreamed that they would die during surgery. Whatever the statistics might be, it would be safe, I believe, to assume that there would be less chance of complications if patients were free of fear and were looking forward to a quick recovery from surgery. Surgeons should be capable of asking about the presence of subconscious fear. They or their assistants should be able to discover and resolve the fear before going ahead with surgery.

There is an easy way to discover subconscious fear without indicating a belief that such fear is present. It is revealed when, after coaching a patient about analgesia and control of physiological behavior, you say, "Most ordinary people with the surgery you will be having will go home from the hospital in five days. You are able to do things that the ordinary patient cannot do. Let me ask your subconscious mind this question, 'Does your inner mind know you can go home in five days, or even sooner?'"

A "yes" finger tells you that the patient is optimistic; a "no" signal indicates fear that going home may not be possible. In reaction to the "no" signal, you can ask, "Are you afraid either for yourself or the surgeon?" The answer will always be "yes" with a finger signal. The reason will often be so ridiculous that the patient will feel sheepish when telling you. You can follow up by repeating the initial question, "Now that you know this, does your inner mind know you can go home in five days or even sooner?" The finger signal will probably be "yes."

Fear and Uncertainty While Unconscious

Whatever the statistics might show in relation to fear, we can probably assume that surgical patients will do better and recover more rapidly when they have confidence in their surgeon, know what to expect, and are free of conscious and unconscious fear. Interviews in age-regression with adults who have undergone surgery in early childhood have revealed that primal fear is initiated and aggravated by uncertainty. There are new sights, new sounds, new smells in hospitals. Then there is loss of ability to talk, to move, and to feel.

Preparation for Trouble-free Surgery

What the Patient Needs to Know Before Surgery

A patient headed for surgery should feel comfortable with the surgeon scheduled to do the surgery. Patients are sometimes referred to a surgeon whom they do not know. You will know him or her better if you ask questions. Most surgeons are willing to take time to understand and to answer questions.

You also have a right to trust your instincts. Do not undergo surgery of any sort if you do not feel comfortable with the way your surgeon behaves toward you.

Surgery is a joint responsibility between you and your surgeon. If you are suspicious, if you identify your surgeon with some other person you have known and disliked in the past, you owe it to your surgeon and to yourself to go in some other direction. Complications of surgery that can lead to unhappy litigation are almost never because the surgeon is inept or careless. They occur because a troubled patient under general anesthesia may misinterpret conversations in the operating room and incorporate misunderstandings into the structure of sleep patterns during the recovery period.

Questions to ask your surgeon are:

1. What will you do in this operation?
2. How long should I expect to remain in the hospital?
3. How soon can I get out of bed after the surgery?
4. What should I do, or avoid doing, when I am home?
5. When do you think I will be able to return to work?

Above all, remember that it is your body you are caring for. You have every right to demand information about the drugs given you. You have a right to refuse "shots" offered you "for pain" when you are in the hospital. Pain medication tends to slow down action of your bowel and may interfere with your appetite. You are going to learn how to be free of pain so refuse pain medication that you have not ordered for yourself.

You may not win friends among the nurses and attendants while you are in that hospital, but this is not your goal anyway. Your goal is maintaining your power to make sensible decisions about yourself. Bernie Siegel (1986) has pointed out how important it is for cancer patients, for example, to be stubborn, rebellious and hated by the hospital attendants. His observation on this matter stems from long experience with patients who have performed miracles when they seemed to have no chance to survive with their problem.

What Bernie Siegel says of cancer patients really applies to all patients, medical and surgical. Nice, polite, and obedient people tend to incorporate the atmosphere of those around them and may unconsciously give up when things are not going well.

What the Surgeon Needs to Know

The surgeon needs to keep all communications with the patient in positive terms. It takes a lot of thought to avoid using negative words. This matter has been considered in "Principles of Suggestion" (Chapter 7).

It is important to know about any troublesome experience your patient has had at birth or with an early life operation under general anesthesia. The most frequently found stressful experience has been a tonsillectomy. You don't want your patient to flash back to a frightening tonsillectomy when the anesthetist is starting the anesthetic. Patients often repress the memory of a nasty tonsil operation. You need to ask specifically, "Have you had your tonsils removed surgically?" Just as with childhood sexual abuse, you must ask directly or you will miss a very important part of the patient's history. The remaining problems of allergies and sensitivities to drugs usually will be covered by the anesthesiologist.

A valuable means of relieving possible unconscious fears is to instruct the patient about postoperative care when you are seeing the patient before admission to the hospital. Also important is the appointment by your nurse for a postoperative checkup in your office. This tacitly suggests the certainty of the patient's survival in order to keep the appointment.

Preliminary Steps Prior to Scheduling Surgery

It is important, I believe, that the patient be given plenty of time to assimilate the reasons for an operation. The atmosphere for surgery is best for the patient who has thought it over, obtained another opinion regarding the need for surgery, and weighed the pros and cons for the operation. It is surgically unwise to hurry a decision for an operation.

Rarely are pain and increasing disability so urgent that surgery has to be immediately carried out. The general principles that have proven helpful in my personal experience with surgery have been as follows:

1. The reasons for doing the operation are outlined.
2. Questions are thoughtfully answered.
3. I have suggested that another opinion from a surgeon would be welcomed and I will share my findings if requested.

4. I explain that I will teach the patient how to use self-hypnosis in order to ensure a comfortable post operative period and the most rapid recovery.
5. An appointment is made for a final discussion of plans before scheduling the surgery.

Preparation for the Surgery

Admission is now required to be on the day of surgery. There is no time for preparation in a bustling morning holding area. If I were doing surgery now I would do this preparation at the time of the discussion prior to scheduling surgery, usually one to two weeks before the day of admission.

Summary of Steps of Surgical Preparation

1. Explain the value of prolonged freedom from pain.
2. Tell the patient about James Esdaile. In 1845–1886 he found that all signs of inflammation disappeared when pain was removed with deep hypnosis.
3. Demonstrate shifting of attention: postural test.
4. Give challenge: "Try to lift your heavy arm."
5. Get around negative effect of *trying* to lift the arm by imagining what would lift the arm.
6. Induce hypnosis with your choice of method.
7. Set up ideomotor symbol movements of fingers for "yes," "no" and "I don't want to answer."
8. Ask, "Are you willing for me to teach you how to turn off painful sensations after you awaken from surgery?"
9. Develop the means of doing this: (cold water).
10. Set up an "anchor" for instant subconscious numbness.
11. Have the patient rehearse turning it on and off twice. Stress the importance of practicing this ability.
12. Explain about being "away from an operating room" in order to ignore careless conversation.
13. Help the patient select a "vacation trip" to use.
14. Obtain a subconscious "promise" for restful sleep while in the hospital and when home.
15. Ask whether or not the patient feels it is possible to go home at least as soon as the average patient.

1. The Value of Prolonged Freedom from Subconscious Pain

I will quote my communications with a patient several days before surgery is scheduled:

You will be given an injection of a mild sedative about an hour before you go into the operating room. The anesthetic puts you to sleep comfortably with the fluid that has been running into your arm. The anesthesiologist will give you some medicine that totally relaxes your muscles for a few seconds while he tips your head back and inserts a tube down your windpipe. You will not be able to breathe for yourself during those few seconds. The machine will do that for you until you can breathe naturally again.

This tube is covered with lubrication that makes your throat feel cool and numb. The breathing tube allows you to have less anesthetic agent than would be needed otherwise and it makes sure that you are getting all the oxygen you need. It will come out as soon as the operation is over but your throat will feel cool probably for a couple of hours after that.

A general anesthetic keeps you relaxed and free from pain during the surgery but the average patient immediately tunes in to sensations from the surgical area and will begin feeling pain when anesthesia has been stopped. You will know how to avoid this. You will just press your left thumb and index finger tips together to remind you to become instantly cool and numb.

A nurse may offer you an injection for pain-relieving medicine when you get back to your room because the average patient will be complaining. When you tell her you do not need the injection you will feel even more comfortable and relaxed than before. You are free to use medicine any time but the less you use the better because pain medication only relieves conscious pain. It does not touch the subconscious awareness of painful stimuli. It does not prevent muscle spasm and swelling of the tissues in the surgical area.

I want to teach you how to use self-hypnosis so that you are in a different class from the average patient. I want you to feel hungry right away when you wake up so that you can eat and stimulate your stomach and intestines to behave as though nothing had happened. Does that sound reasonable to you?

You will be able to make any part of your body cool and numb. You will not be wondering when a nurse is going to give you an injection or a pill to relieve pain because you will have no pain. If something happens to remind you that you should be uncomfortable you will just pinch your left thumb and index finger tips together to get the instant result you can experience today and will be practicing before you come into the hospital.

2. James Esdaile's Contribution to Our Knowledge
I believe it is helpful to present some information to surgical patients that will motivate them to work with control of their reactions to surgery. I would

suggest telling a prospective surgical patient about the work of James Esdaile, a British surgeon in India in the mid-1840s.

Esdaile's surgical mortality was close to 50 percent in the days when patients had to be held down while a surgeon worked as quickly as possible. Anesthetic agents were not yet available in India, and there was no protection from infection. Then he learned how to mesmerize patients and lowered his mortality to 5 percent, the lowest figure in the world until the time of Joseph Lister and his introduction of so-called "antiseptic surgery" in 1865. Apparently Esdaile's secret was his observation that redness, swelling, and local heat disappeared when a patient turned off pain while in a deep level of hypnosis with his mesmerism. Something wonderful was happening with factors in blood coagulation, the resistance to trauma and the power of his patients' immune system against potentially dangerous bacteria that were always present.

3. Demonstrating Shift of Attention with Postural Suggestion
The next step is to start the process of improving self-confidence in the surgical patient. I ask him to hold his arms extended forward without contact between his hands. With his eyes closed, he is to focus attention on his right arm. I ask him to imagine a heavy telephone directory hanging from a strap around his wrist and pulling his arm down toward his lap.

4. Giving a Challenge
The arm will begin moving down. It will feel heavy while the same weight of gravity in the other arm is ignored. Before the "heavy" arm reaches his lap, the patient is asked to *try* to lift that arm. Usually he will recognize that it is difficult to lift that arm. *Try* involves the idea that the therapist does not believe the action is possible.

5. Getting Around the Negative Effect of "Trying"
The lifting becomes easy when the patient replaces the hallucinated heavy book with a bunch of helium-filled balloons tied to his wrist. It is always easier to add a new thought to accomplish a result rather than trying to oppose a challenge that suggests a difficulty.

(The value of this first step is that it demonstrates that a patient can pay attention to one part of his body and at the same time ignore another part. The pull of gravity downward is augmented by the idea of the heavy weight on one arm. The other arm does not feel heavy when attention is placed elsewhere. Recognition of this phenomenon can be helpful with the next steps.)

6. *Inducing Hypnosis by Your Choice of Methods*

I usually incorporate a selection of ideomotor symbol movements both as a means of communicating unconsciously and to permit a patient to enter a hypnotic state while wondering which finger will lift for each type of answer to a question. For a surgeon starting to use hypnosis, I would suggest a simple induction such as this:

> Please hold a pen between the thumb and index finger of your left hand. I am going to ask your subconscious mind to pull the fingers apart when you are relaxed enough to learn about turning off sensations in your body. It is easier to let your subconscious mind decide about that moment because you will probably be thinking that you are not being hypnotized. You are much more aware of everything around you when you are in a hypnotic state. You never become a zombie.
>
> In order to get into a readiness for turning off sensations, the easiest way is to close your eyes and get a picture of a lighted candle in your mind's eye, as though you had put one on a table across the room and could watch the way the flame moves, gets bigger and smaller with the movements of air in the room. Allow the muscles of your forehead, neck, and shoulders to relax progressively as you breathe out with each respiration.

7. *Setting up Finger Signals*

Suggestions about relaxing will continue until the pen slips from the patient's fingers. Usually the patient's arm will remain in the original position, indicating catalepsy, a sign of a medium hypnotic state. I ask for the index finger on the left hand to lift when the patient is "twice as deep as the moment the pen dropped." This finger then will be the "yes" finger. When it lifts, it is usually very easy to get a signal for "no" and another for "I don't want to answer." I tell the patient that we now have a way of communicating with very deep levels of perception where the mechanisms for turning off pain reside.

8. *"Are You Willing to Turn Off Subconscious Pain?"*

A "no" signal will tell you that your patient has some residual fear of losing sensations or losing control. Often you can get around this with some questions about the origin of this fear. It will help if you say that you do not want to eliminate all feeling as occurs with an anesthetic. You want your patient to feel touch and pressure but be free of any painful stimulus. This is usually very well accepted at a subconscious level.

9. *Develop the Means of Doing This*

If the answer to the initial question is a "yes," you can continue with suggestions about standing in cold water until the tissues become numb. The "yes" finger is to lift for the coldness and the "no" finger is to lift when everything beneath the wet skin is numb. This is to include the muscles and the bones. Make this a progressive staging, to the knees, then to the waist, and finally to a point a little higher than the place where an incision will be made.

Have your patient do the testing for sensation changes. A pinch is usually adequate. Some patients do not trust doctors. The numbness might not be there at all if you do the initial testing when the highest level of numbness has been reached. The degree of numbness can be augmented by asking the "yes" finger to lift when the tissues are "twice as numb," and so on.

Some patients are able to make their legs numb below their knees but fail to give a signal for coldness and numbness above this level, particularly for the abdomen. You will recognize this problem if you get a signal for feeling cold but no signal for the numbness. This usually reflects fear stemming from some dental experience or an earlier unpleasant anesthetic experience. It will usually be easy for the patient to decide to keep that experience from interfering here.

10. Set up an Anchor for Instant Subconscious Numbness

With naturally occurring enhanced motivations involved in a presurgical experience, it is very easy for a patient to learn about using a familiar experience from the past to develop mild analgesia. I explain that this will be useful during the recovery period when the anesthetic has worn off.

Removing subconscious perceptions of discomfort will prevent the inflammatory reactions that occur when an inexperienced patient's attention is focused on the surgical area as the anesthetic wears off. With aseptic surgery under sterile condition, there is now no need to have the muscle guarding, the leakage of fluid into tissues around the incision, the retention of fluid and salts, and the general unwillingness to move. These are reactions that have evolved for lower animal having injuries that could otherwise be associated with infection. Modern surgery does not require outmoded survival mechanisms needed when wild animals have to contend with their dirty wounds.

After making sure the patient is satisfied about his ability to diminish sensations, as directed, he is shown how to set up a signal to himself that will automatically call out the numbness instantly whenever he needs it. Pressure between the tips of thumb and index finger on the left hand will initiate this process from now on. The "yes" finger on the opposite hand will lift unconsciously to indicate when this response has been established for future use.

The finger pressure of the left hand will relax when the numbness has been activated at a subconscious level. Pressure between the tips of the right thumb and index fingers will remove the analgesia and bring sensations back to normal.

11. *Have the Patient Rehearse Turning the Numbness On and Off*

Having the patient rehearse turning the numbness on and off twice is usually enough to give the patient confidence in doing it in the future. A little reinforcement may be needed when you see the patient in the recovery room after the surgery is completed.

12. *The Value of "Being Away" from the Operating Room*

I explain now that it will be very helpful if the patient could take himself to some beautiful location where there are sensations of peacefulness, rest, and relaxation instead of remaining in an operating room listening to clashing steel instruments and pans. "Those noises will become distant sounds of traffic or conversations of people in a restaurant while you are eating during your vacation."

13. *Having the Patient Select a "Vacation Trip" to Use*

The explanation about the value of "being away" can be given during the initial induction of hypnosis (step 6), or you can have the patient come out of hypnosis during the explanation and reenter hypnosis now as you say something like "Please shut your eyes now and let your inner mind go back to the start of some pleasant vacation period in your life. When you are there, your yes finger will lift. It is not necessary to consciously remember the vacation trip. When your inner mind knows that you will go on this trip tonight at some time while you are asleep and again when you are given the preoperative sedative injection in the hospital, your yes finger will lift to let you know that this is now in your mental computer. You can select other vacations when you want to sleep while you are healing in the days or nights after the surgery is completed.

"Hypnotic sense of time is wonderful. You can contract a two-week vacation into the period of time between the hypo and the moment you are returning to your room, or you can stretch a one-hour moving picture you have seen so that it takes up a two or three hour interval that would include your operation and recovery room time.

"You can be right back in the operating room any time your anesthesiologist or your surgeon tells you how things are going or any time they want you to do something. They will use your first name to bring you back temporarily to keep you in touch with their work."

14. *Subconscious Promise of Restful Sleep*

A promise of restful sleep is obtained at the close of the interview or has already been included with step 13. Ask, "I would like you to sleep really deeply and restfully tonight. A good way to ensure that would be to press the tips of your left index finger and thumb together and say to yourself, 'When I know I will sleep deeply and restfully tonight and awaken feeling good in the morning, my yes finger will lift.' After the finger lifts, simply imagine staring at the flame of an imaginary candle until you drift off to sleep."

15. Questioning about When a Patient Thinks He Can Go Home

This question can reveal previously unrecognized subconscious fears. It reveals fear without suggesting that fears could be present. I will say something like this: "Most patients who have this kind of surgery will be leaving the hospital after five days, but you have been learning to turn off pain, to feel hungry, and to know that you can put yourself into hypnosis when you want to. Does your inner mind know that you can go home at least as soon as they do?"

The patient is saying "I am afraid" if the subconscious answer is "no" or "I don't want to answer." It is very important for such a patient to realize that his conscious desire to be optimistic is being contradicted by a powerful unconscious energy that will probably turn out to be ridiculous. Now you can ask for a finger signal when his subconscious mind has oriented to the moment he began feeling he might not be able to go home on schedule. Check on the validity of the recognition by repeating the original question and getting a subconscious "yes" response.

Comment about Telling Patients Not to Listen

It is probably helpful to urge the patient to "ignore" operating room conversation. After writing about this (Cheek 1960b), I learned that suggesting such a thing really alerts the patient to paying attention to such conversation. This is comparable to putting wet cotton in the patient's ears or putting headphones on and turning on music to drown out careless operating room talk. Patients treated in this way generally feel that there must be something important to hear or you would not be trying to shield them from it. I think it is helpful, however, to suggest that all the sounds be either ignored or translated to something else unless they hear their first name spoken. If a careless remark impinges on the patient under these circumstances its effect seems to be diminished or diluted.

What to Do When There Are Complications

I should point out here what most older surgeons discover for themselves before they retire. The number and seriousness of complications diminish as their experience with surgery grows. Part of this experience includes the surgeons' recognition of the fact that surgical patients have enormous resources for healing if their medical and surgical consultants give them a chance to use them.

The surgeon may not recognize that his or her respect for these resources is what does the work. This was demonstrated by the case example of the youngster with hip surgeries. If hypnosis is used to implement these patient resources, there will be fewer complications for a surgeon to face.

The following are examples of showing respect for patients' resources:

1. An inexperienced, young surgeon who had read about or been told about the healing potentials of acutely ill and/or unconscious patients ordered a hemorrhaging patient to stop bleeding and observed the abrupt termination of hemorrhage.

2. Another similar young surgeon asked a patient suffering from postoperative paralytic bowel to regress to the moment something is happening to produce this ileus and to understand that reframing of the cause can permit normal bowel activity to begin. Abdominal distension disappeared and peristalsis became active within an hour.

3. A seasoned but depressed urologist under general anesthesia heard his surgeon comment on the size of the ulcer in the stomach specimen and the possibility that it could be a malignant ulcer. At that moment he decided it would be more peaceful to die from renal shutdown and uremia than from cancer of the stomach. His kidneys put out only 30 cubic milliliters of urine during the first four postoperative days but released 500 milliliters of urine within four hours of hearing the resident talking with the surgeon in the hallway outside his room and saying that the sections were back and the ulcer was benign.

This doctor told me he would not have believed the good news if the surgeon and resident had reassured him in his presence. This complication probably would not have occurred if the surgeon, while examining the excised stomach specimen, had said, "This is a big ulcer. Even if it is malignant, we have removed the whole specimen."

4. An anesthesiologist in Honolulu, Carl Johnson, was able to help a surgeon out of a problem by appealing to the unconscious resources of his patient during a gastrectomy. Dr. Johnson told me that the woman began bleeding from small vessels just after removal of her stomach for a peptic ulcer. He put his head close to her ear and asked her to go into a deep-freeze locker and to feel very cold. She was unconscious, but she apparently did what he asked her to do. The bleeding stopped, but her skin turned a little blue. This alarmed the surgeon. Dr. Johnson quietly whispered to the patient that she could warm up now. Bleeding recommenced. Now he asked her to imagine drinking a chocolate ice cream milk shake in order to experience that local coolness in the stomach without making her entire body feel cold. Again the bleeding stopped. Her color pleased the surgeon and the operation was completed. Johnson was recognizing the ability of his patient to use familiar experiences helpfully.

What about Hypnosis as the Only Anesthetic for an Operation?

Anesthesiology is so far advanced now and those who are specialists in this field are so good that there are very few occasions when there is an adequate reason to use hypnosis alone for the operation. Twice during my professional life have I resorted to using hypnosis for this purpose.

1. A 25-year-old woman needed a breast biopsy. Her surgeon offered to use a local anesthetic but she refused. She had an unrelenting conviction that she would die if given a general anesthetic. I had used hypnosis with her during a pregnancy and knew she was a good subject. The conditioning was set up at a subconscious level for her to be wherever the subject of my reading would take her. I invited her to come with me to Africa and involve herself in the life of a little dog, "Jock of the Bushveldt," by Sir Percy Fitzpatrick.

The procedure was simple. There was no bleeding. The patient was totally relaxed. Her pulse rate climbed from about 70 to 120 when the surgeon cut into the lump after its removal. He had announced that he would do this. Her pulse rate dropped to its previous level when he said, "I'm sure this is benign." It was a benign fibroadenoma.

2. A 50-year-old osteopath who had used hypnosis in her work asked me to use hypnosis instead of an anesthetic for removal of five steel pins in her right femur. These needed to be removed before she could have a hip joint replacement in the future. I accepted her plea because she had suffered a Guillain-Barre syndrome following a dental anesthetic and was quite naturally terrified about the possibility of another similar problem. She had been totally paralyzed for a year and had to be fed by an assistant.

Comment

At the time of this revision we have substantiating reports by Dabney Ewin (1990) and others during the First International Symposium on Memory and

Awareness in Anaesthesia, held in Glasgow, Scotland (April 6–8, 1989). Although some of the papers talk about "awareness," however, it is clear that the authors, with the exception of Ewin and Henry Bennett, are referring to what an anesthetized person might consciously report when asked consciously verbalized questions.

Unfortunately, surgeons continue to be lethargic in accepting the idea that people can hear and be influenced by what they hear, or think they hear, while anesthetized. It is my hope that surgical patients in the future will advise the operating room team in advance of an operation that they will be paying attention to conversations and will be expecting their surgeon, first assistant, and anesthesiologist to be thoughtful about the subject matter of conversations while at work.

22

Psychiatric Applications of Hypnosis

All the anxiety-ridden fallacies of our day seem to congregate in the hospital delivery room, where they bring about a disaster that remains largely undetected because it works like a time bomb. None of the parties to the crime ever has to pay, for the explosion takes place in slow fusion over the years and creates such widespread and diverse havoc that few bother to trace it back to see who lit the fuse.

Joseph Chilton Pearce wrote this in his 1977 book *Magical Child*. This book, reprinted in 1992, should be required reading for every mother, daughter, teacher, patient, physician, and psychologist.

For nearly 90 years, obstetricians have centered their attention on trying to free women from pain during labor. It started with morphine and scopolamine, then chloral hydrate and paraldehyde, then groups of drugs after World War II. In the meantime the relationship between mother and newborn infant was utterly destroyed. After all, the mother is best served if she delivers in a "twilight sleep." The infant brain is incapable of thinking and remembering, said the authorities on neurophysiology.

So, my colleagues and I pulled babies out, held them by the ankles to drain, put silver nitrate in their eyes. That was it.

Depression, anxiety, phobias, and posttraumatic stress disorders all have a sequential order of development.

1. There is a primary, single, stressful experience.
2. This original trauma is empowered by later, more or less related, secondary stressful experiences.

3. Either the original or a secondary, reinforcing trauma is rehearsed many times in deep sleep cycles, where its physiological and emotional by-products accumulate because their origin cannot be recognized consciously.

The primary trauma may be at the time a mother realizes that she is pregnant. It can be reinforced during the pregnancy, at birth, and during the first three years of life. Rehearsals of imprinted traumatic early life sequences during deeper levels of sleep can occur throughout the remainder of a child's life.

All of the key experiences mentioned above will be sensed initially in the primitive brain and stored in the midbrain. They will not be registered in conscious memory and will not be accessible to orthopsychiatric methods of investigation. The nocturnal reiterations of trauma at deeper-than-dreaming levels of awareness will also not be remembered, but they will lead to both kinds of insomnia: trouble getting to sleep and trouble in getting back to sleep after awakening. Free-floating anxiety may follow many nights of disturbed sleep.

The very first sensitizing experience must be discovered and reassessed. The triggering subsequent experience must be discovered and eliminated. The patient must learn to turn on and turn off the present manifestations of the complaint.

Depression

The definition of depression as used in psychiatry is: "extreme melancholy, sadness, or dejection which, unlike grief, is unrealistic and out of proportion to any claimed cause; may be a symptom of any psychiatric disorder or the prime manifestation of a psychotic depressive reaction or of a neurosis."

I believe this definition is too narrow. How can anyone decide that the subjective feelings of melancholy, sadness, or dejection are unrealistic and out of proportion to any claimed cause? This is a measurement comparable to my saying, "Your pain is unrealistic and out of proportion to whatever you think caused it."

Michael Yapko (1988) and Israel Orbach (1988) have given excellent overviews of the incidence and importance of depression. It has been stated that one adolescent American commits suicide each 90 minutes. Each year approximately 5,840 adolescents choose to end their lives, and this number has tripled over the last 30 years (National Center for Health Statistic, Communicable Disease Center). The depressed and untreated survivors may approximate 50 percent of the population in industrialized societies.

There must be a message in this. Is it crowding in the cities? Is it related to pollution? Could it relate to intrauterine impressions and the feelings the newborn has of emptiness and silence when its mother is drugged or unconscious? Could earlier-than-birth perceptions of the fetus have something to do with this apparent increase in the incidence of serious depression that can lead to adolescent suicide?

The word *depression* can be applied as a primary diagnosis for a vast array of human problems. The incidence is growing. It is estimated that one out of four Americans will experience a major depression during a lifetime. It appears to be the major force in the collagen diseases, where immune forces are turned inward against tissues of the host instead of against invaders from the outside world.

The incidence of depression is taking on epidemic proportions. Could it relate to the population explosion now going on? Perhaps we should look at the figures:

    1850: 1 billion people on Earth
    1930: 2 billion people, doubled in 80 years
    1960: 3 billion people, up 1 billion in 30 years
    1976: 4 billion people, up 1 billion in 16 years
    1989: 5 billion people, up 1 billion in 13 years
    1992: 5.5 billion people, up 1/2 billion in 3 years!

The pharmaceutical houses have made enormous profits off depressed and anxious people who have found no relief during psychotherapy. It is increasingly apparent that psychotherapy is unsatisfactory and drugs are only used because psychiatrists have not known how to help the depressed discover where the depression began. There are ways of doing this.

1. Orient depressed patients to birth and to key moments during their mother's pregnancy with them. Attempt to reframe negative impressions and work toward a time of enthusiasm and joy in the future. Try for a commitment date for achieving that goal.

2. Use the indirect method, teaching patients to use "Christmas tree lights" and "auras" (Chapter 12), seeing themselves in a full-length mirror. See the light indicating the feeling in the head when they feel depressed. Note its color. Find out when that colored light was put there. Have them look above the image of their head and over their shoulder and tell you the colors of the aura, particularly the one closest to their body. Learn what color it should be, whether or not they believe a "good" color could be put there. If not, why not?

3. Ask if the feelings the patients have had are caused by experiences that have occurred in a previous lifetime. This may be simply allowing the patients to dissociate themselves and look at the problem of this life, but it could be a real karmic carryover. There is nothing to lose except your reputation as a scientist in case you tell the wrong people about what you learn this way. Joel Whitton (1986), a psychiatrist in Toronto, Canada, has used the subjective impressions of his hypnotized patients in an interesting way. He has asked them for reports about the intervals between lives, particularly, their beliefs about what they learned in those intervals. A number of highly regarded psychiatrists now work with the concept of karmic causes for depression. Brian Weiss (1988), a psychiatrist in Miami, Florida, is one of these. Patients have been released from their depressions by recognizing they can disconnect themselves from past lives.It does not matter if this is a means of helping patients be objective about their problem instead of suffering subjectively. The therapist does not really need to believe in reincarnation to use this modality helpfully.

4. Ask for a finger signal response to the question "Is it possible that there may be a spirit with you, the spirit of someone who was depressed at the time he or she died?" If you can raise the courage to do this, you may get a "no" or "I don't want to answer signal." Do not give up, because, as Edith Fiore (1987) has found, a spirit may be hiding and in fear because of the reason for his or her sudden death. You may get a "yes" when you ask, "Is there a spirit with you who is hiding or afraid to let us know that he or she is there?" Get her book and practice with her techniques of releasing spirits that are trapped on this Earth plane and need to move on toward another life.

We need more understanding of the perceptions and interpretations of the very young. For example, in our concern over the dangers of drugs around the house, we may have been suggesting to troubled children that they are expected to eat dangerous pills.

Subconscious understandings at any age are different from those of the conscious mind. The subconscious mind processes in favor of pessimism rather than optimism when both are considered. It makes mistakes about interpreting negative orders. It will turn a "Don't do that" command into "I expect you to do that."

For these reasons, should we wonder about the safety caps placed on bottles of drugs sold to parents of children? We should either not use those drugs at all or keep quiet about them and keep them hidden in a safe place, because the difficulty in gaining access to what is inside is a tempting challenge for depressed children.

When a child who has been imprinted with a feeling of being unwanted at birth hears parents warn against taking pills out of the bathroom cabinet, are these words interpreted as showing that the parents want the child to take those pills? We can't be too sure about the child's understandings unless we have explored its way of looking at the world.

We can get fleeting impressions about that world from adults, during an age regression to childhood, when they are asked to tell how they feel at the moment they lose consciousness being "put to sleep" with a general anesthetic for a tonsillectomy. A majority of them will be momentarily terrified and will say, "The doctors are trying to kill me." This is immediately followed by the usual euphoria experienced by all people who have been anesthetized or knocked unconscious. It is reported by those who have survived a near death experience.

The memory of this momentary terror and assumed malevolence during an anesthetic induction may be rehearsed many times during sleep and eventually lead to a pathological interest in alcohol or drugs that will recapture that sense of nirvana that came after loss of consciousness. William Hull (1986) has found that many alcoholics have been oxygen-deprived at birth and they have found alcohol creates the same euphoria they had after being comatose at birth. The problem is that they have amnesia for the euphoria and keep reverting to the alcohol in order to recapture that feeling.

Bertel Jacobson (1987, 1988, 1990) in the Department of Medical Engineering at Karolinska Institute in Sweden has been exploring the possibility that traumatic experiences at birth may unconsciously lead to the form of suicide chosen by adolescents. Physical trauma at birth evokes death in accidents; asphyxia at birth seems to lead to death by asphyxia with plastic bags, hanging, or drowning. These are speculations, and the exploration needs further information.

Again, I must reiterate, feelings of not being wanted are often misinterpretations but they are nevertheless imprinted and need to be discovered and reframed. It can be done.

An Unanswered Question: Why Did This Child Die?

A hardworking doctor and his wife had adopted a baby from an unwed mother. They left home for a weekend of much needed rest. The child, aged 2, was told to be a "good girl" (usually interpreted by the child as "they don't think I have been good") and to "mind the baby sitter" (subconscious translation: "they don't think I mind"). She was not given an explanation about the reason for her new parents excluding her from their plans. It may have reminded her subconsciously of the earlier abandonment by her real mother.

The child was dead before the horrified parents could reach home after the emergency telephone call. Their child had swallowed an entire bottle full of sweetened aspirin tablets. Was this just an accidental occurrence because the pills looked pretty?

Molestation and Depression

A psychologist, 40 years old, had married an alcoholic, divorced him, married a gambler, divorced him, and was in a tenuous relationship with a former drug user when she came to me asking for help with her swings between feeling good and feeling despondent and lethargic. Her psychiatric diagnosis was: "DSM III Bipolar Disorder, Mixed, Moderate (296.62)," for which she was taking medication.

Her complaints included symptoms that suggested possibility of childhood molestation. At night she was grinding her teeth to the point that her dentist had fitted her with a mouth guard to preserve her molar teeth. She had enough current problems that could explain the bruxism, but that symptom always requires a search for oral sexual molestation as its cause. She had frequent headaches on awakening from sleep. These had been diagnosed as an expression of temporo-mandibular syndrome (inflammation of the jaw joint). For as long as she could remember, she had been subject to frightened awakening in the early morning and inability to get back to sleep. She had never known the cause of the awakening. All of these symptoms have been associated with molestation in patients that I have treated.

During the initial history she said she was sure the depression began when she was sent away to a private, upper-class school for girls at the age of 17. The girls all came from affluent families and wore clothes that were different from her own simple clothes. She felt out of place and intensely unhappy.

When she could stand it no longer, she called her parents and abruptly came home. On arrival she was scolded by her father because she was being so selfish. He impressed her with the gravity of his financial sacrifices in order to pay for her education in a fine school. This depressed her further because she loved and respected her father. She had no comfort, no resolution to the loneliness and depression that she had felt in the school.

Her explanation about the origin of her depression sounded reasonable, but it proved to be an explosion of the time bomb, as referred to by Pearce, the time bomb whose fuse had been lighted much earlier in her life. At the first interview I limited work to teaching her to use self-hypnosis for rest periods during the day.

Finger signals were set up. She was an excellent subject. When she seemed sure of herself and comfortable with the hypnosis, I asked, "Were you ever molested when you were a child?"

Her "no" finger lifted. After a pause of about 30 seconds, she said, "While you were talking just now, I saw a little baby in a crib."

Q: Are you the little baby?

A: (The immediate response was physical. She turned her head toward her right shoulder, began to abreact with tears and moaning as she slid down in the reclining chair.)

Q: Would you, perhaps, want to see what happened then, looking at that scene from here as a grown, intelligent woman?

I did not want the obvious total age-regression to further imprint that moment of stress. I wanted to shift her to being objective in her analysis of what had happened. She is an experienced marriage, family, and child counselor, well able to reframe traumatic experiences. (The Joseph Breuer concept that repeated abreactions in total age-regression will catharse a trauma is not a viable therapeutic modality. It usually alienates patients or forces them to fabricate traumas that either are not the causal ones or have never happened.)

D.C.: Please look at that scene again. You are here with me.

A: I see a baby in a crib.

Q: Is anyone else there?

A: (finger signal) "Yes." It might be my mother's brother. No! It's my father! I see him coming in to change me. He is wearing shorts. He puts his penis in my mouth. (The patient was putting the narrative in the past tense. She was distancing herself but she again began to abreact with sobs and gasping while again turning her head sharply to her right as though trying to avoid something.)

D.C.: You know, I have been finding that children who are molested and are frightened seem telepathically to pick up the guilt that the molester is feeling. They don't need to do that. They are not guilty. The guilt belongs to him. You are just there and probably didn't know what to do to protect yourself.

Q: Is your inner mind willing to free yourself from that guilt and to recognize that this was a period of emotional illness that your father was going through? You have already told me that your Catholic mother was afraid of having more children. She may have been really shutting your father out of her life. They are still together. Things must have changed with time. As you were growing up did you love your father?

A: (finger signal) "Yes."

Q: Did he treat you respectfully as you grew older?

A: Oh yes!

Q: I wonder what would have happened if you, as a little baby with sharp little teeth, had bitten him real hard when he put his penis in your mouth? Please go over that as it might have been if you had known what power a little baby can have when she is being treated unfairly. What would happen?

A: (Laughing) He would not have been able to explain that to my mother. I think he would have been proud of me. He would have treated me with respect after that.

Q: Time had run out at this point. Have you learned anything or thought of anything today that might be helpful for you?

A: (As her "yes" finger lifted, she suddenly put her clenched fists high above her head, like a football player who has run for a touchdown.) I'm innocent! I'm innocent!

This was not the entire solution to her problems. She still had a teenaged daughter who was involved with a boy who was clearly headed for trouble with drugs and the police. Her daughter would not listen to her warnings. This patient, however, began to take action. She stopped feeling depressed. She told her useless male friend that she was not going to support him and that he should get lost. She feels that she is much more effective in her counseling work. She has been followed now for two years and is taking no antidepressant drugs.

The molestation had registered long before the origin of her consciousness. She had no chance to think about it consciously and, therefore, she had never in her therapy been able to recognize and reevaluate its influence.

Depression in young people seems treatable when the origin is discovered. By origin I mean the very first experience the patient recognizes. The therapist must not be put off the path by accepting and working with a secondary source. Depression with older people is much harder to deal with. Older people may feel they are no longer needed by loved ones. Unless they have an occupation it may be hard to keep them from feeling useless. The progressive loss of friends can have an accumulative effect. Hypnosis can be helpful if it can be used by a depressed older person to gain energy for creative writing, art work, or improving retention of information gained.

Anxiety

According to *Webster's New World Dictionary,* anxiety is defined as a state of being uneasy, apprehensive, or worried about what may happen. According to the third edition of *Gould's Medical Dictionary,* anxiety is a feeling of apprehension,, uncertainty, or tension stemming from the anticipation of an imagined or unreal threat, sometimes manifested by tachycardia, palpitation, sweating, disturbed breathing, trembling, or even paralysis.

Although not incorporated in the wording of these two definitions, it would be reasonable to conclude that the origin of anxiety would be unknown to the victim of anxiety. The troubled feeling of a person confronted by a ferocious animal or an impending crash in an automobile would be called *fear*. A decision of some sort would be made. The process would go on at a conscious level of thought integrated with the sensory input.

Anxiety is very different. There can be no direction of activity or thought. Anxiety may be experienced by anyone who has a sense of danger but does not know what the danger is, where it is, or when it may strike.

Anxiety might be a common experience for a veteran of the Viet Nam disaster, where even an innocent-looking child might be carrying a concealed knife or grenade. The anxiety while there is permanently imprinted. It is not removed by change in habitat or by constant assurance that there is no danger. It will haunt his dreams, and he will awaken without remembering his dreams. It may flash into seeming reality at any time, triggered by a special sound, a smell or a pain in an old wound.

Ordinary psychiatric treatment involving conscious communication does not remove anxiety. Continued cycles and flashes of subconsciously triggered fears will interfere with sleep and may eventually lead to a "battle fatigue" sort of depression. Variations of this pathway are occurring all the time and all over the world. Drugs only dull the reaction of anxiety; they do not cure anxiety. Anxiety and depression are twins going hand in hand, and often one precedes the other. The order varies.

The sufferer from anxiety must have access to the original danger, or what was interpreted as danger. It may turn out to be a sheep in wolf's clothing, instead of the reverse image, if the interpretation of maternal messages has been mistaken. It may have been a real danger that no longer exists.

The original danger may have created an unfortunate, maladaptive, defeatist frame of reference that has hindered positive activity when challenges have occurred. A mature look at the original impression from the viewpoint of an office conference may allow the victim of anxiety to break free of a continuing handicap and become the real therapist without further need for external help. Those who have managed to do this will have a gift that can be wonderfully helpful to friends, a spouse, children, clients, or patients if they decide to become healers.

Treatment of anxiety with hypnosis can be successful within a brief span of time if the patient is able to understand his or her feelings during important periods of intrauterine development and at birth. The reader is referred back to Chapter 14 on fetal perceptions because that formative period may set the stage for uncertainty and subsequent vulnerability.

I find the protocol that works best for me with patients suffering from anxiety is the same as that for depression and phobias. I work back from birth memories to the moment the mother realizes she is pregnant. Troubled subjective impressions are worked with before moving chrcnologically forward in time to the "first moment something is happening that you feel may have started the problem."

Patients have uncanny ability to move instantly to moments when something threatening is occurring or there is a change in body functioning. The reticular activating system monitoring all sensory input is very like a good operator of a radar screen, who watches for background details that disappear and is alerted by a new blip on the screen.

Most therapists starting with ideomotor techniques do not realize that subconscious scanning is almost instantaneous. You can ask a patient in light hypnosis to "go to the moment you are just coming out into the bright lights when you are born. When you are there, your 'yes' finger will lift." The goal will usually be reached within 10 seconds of the request unless birth has been very distressing. Facial expression and an "I don't want to answer" signal will tell you then to back off and ask for the memory to be a distant one, looking back.

Feelings of anxiety should be turned on and off as an exercise in self-hypnosis when patients are in your office and three or four times a day during the first week after working with the problem. The subconscious mind knows that a sensation purposefully turned on can be also removed.

When a Symptom Returns

Before ending successful treatment it is important to make it clear that subliminal signals from the environment or thought sequences at night may reactivate the anxiety. When this seemingly comes "out of the blue" as was the case pattern in the past, the patient should welcome it for its value as a learning process. They are to orient their subconscious horizon of time to the moment something is happening just before the feeling of anxiety commences. Their "yes" finger is to lift to mark that moment, and at that time they will know what brought about the sense of anxiety. They can ask themselves then if they really need to feel anxious now. The answer will nearly always be "no."

Phobias

The search for the triggering experience must be done with one of the techniques of Chapter 12. The beginner with ideomotor techniques should do the retrograde search and then ask if there is a sensitizing experience earlier than the one selected. The experienced therapist can move more rapidly using the time horizon of the mother recognizing that she is pregnant and moving forward in time.

After discovering what seems to be the cause, ask for an answer to the question "Now that you know this, is your inner mind willing to let you go about your life more comfortably and eventually be totally free of this phobia?"

If the answer is "yes," get the patient to project forward in time and develop the imagery of being comfortably able to do the things that previously were the source of fear. The experience first offered during an exploration is rarely the real one.

An example of a patient helped by hypnosis to overcome was a 50-year-old woman who came for help with her agoraphobia. For 20 years she has been unable to do her shopping or deposit checks in a bank. She had an inordinate fear of having her conversation recorded on an audiotape, until I assured her that the tape was being made for her. It was hard for her to maintain eye contact while she talked with me.

She had been raised in a very religious, old world European family. There did not seem to be any pre- or perinatal events of note, but she was made to feel that anything of a sexual nature was evil. She did not masturbate during her childhood. She met an attractive man who wanted very much to marry her, but she put him off because she was not in love with him. She had been convinced by her father that a man should be self-reliant and ambitious. This man was not, but he managed to get her pregnant.

She felt desperate. She could not tell her family, and she did not want to marry this man. Finally she found a kindly chiropractor who told her that the laws were changing and she should not feel troubled about terminating an unwanted pregnancy. There were no physical problems after the operation, but she was terribly troubled and guilt-ridden.

She married the man because "I felt I had to" and soon found that he was unable to hold a job. She supported him doing menial jobs and then became pregnant again. This time she unwillingly went through with it and gave birth to a daughter. The daughter has been difficult and rebellious for 22 years.

The abortion was 24 years ago. She had been well and active for 4 years, but the shame and guilt smoldered unconsciously. The onset of her agoraphobia was a crystal-clear memory. She had just learned that her husband was in love with another woman. She had a sudden feeling "as though the sky were falling in on me." Her world did, from then on, become more and more closed in.

She divorced her husband when her daughter was 10 years old. He stopped his affair and begged her to take him back, but she refused because of his lack of ambition and inability to hold jobs. She could not handle the extra responsibility and expense. A few months later he killed himself in a motorcycle accident.

In spite of her miserable fear of people and crowds, she has been able to support herself in a business with the help of a man much younger than herself. People like her and compliment her on the things she does for them, but she cannot believe them.

During the first two visits of one hour each, she was so tense and self-critical that we got very little done except to establish a sense that she trusted me. She learned how to put herself into hypnosis and conscientiously practiced with two-minute rest periods during the day.

At the third visit, while she was in an estimated medium level, I threw out this thought; "It seems to me that this problem of your agoraphobia may have started with that abortion rather than the time 20 years ago when the sky fell in. Is it possible you have been afraid that people would know that you had become pregnant and that you had gone through a criminal abortion?"

The patient instantly came out of hypnosis. "That's it! I've been afraid they would find out. Why should I think that? It's crazy!" (She was exposing unconscious emotionally stressful information to her conscious reason and was starting to free herself from the phobia without external assistance.) She went on to say, "Everybody knows that abortion is legal and lots of people have been through what I have been through."

I asked the obvious question, "Now is it possible that you could start really looking people in the eye and start opening up your life? It will be exciting for you to enjoy the freedom you will have after this 20 years of being in a sort of prison."

Her finger lifted to say "yes."

Since that third visit and the connection to what she had been suppressing as a cause of her agoraphobia, she has called to say that she has been to the bank by herself and has been able to sign important documents. Her next goal is to be able to get on an airplane and visit her mother in the old country. Being shut into an airplane has been a long-time fear, but it will be easy to teach her things to be interested in while she is flying. We will rehearse that until she is comfortable. She is strongly motivated toward making that trip because her mother is getting very old.

Posttraumatic Stress Disorder

Posttraumatic stress disorder can be a truly disabling condition. Usually the cause is consciously very well known to the patient. It can be a mugging, rape, automobile accident, coronary occlusion, or stroke, for example.

Again, I believe, it is important to see how this patient felt about himself or herself on entering the world at birth. The gravity of a life-threatening experience will be augmented if the start of that life was interpreted as being unfavorable.

Exercising in hypnosis with turning on and turning off the nervous symptoms will build self-confidence. I have found it helpful to tell patients during an interview while they are in a hypnotic state that one of the plus parts of a terribly stressful experience, such as a rape at knifepoint, is that extrasensory capabilities are enhanced. They will be alerted to situations where a similar experience could occur and will have enough warning to use their judgment and intuition in removing themselves from danger. This does, in fact, seem to occur. Most of the highly gifted psychics have had some nearly fatal experience in their early life, often at birth.

Multiple Personality Disorder

Multiple personality disorder (MPD) is a condition that is always preceded by physical and emotional abuse during childhood. It is an exaggerated form of posttraumatic stress disorder. It is often difficult to use hypnosis in a purposeful way because the victims of MPD spend a lot of their time in spontaneous, elusive states. The effort to communicate meaningfully may meet with obstruction from a rebellious or mischievous personality. The reader is referred to the writing of three national experts in the uses of hypnosis with this problem, Ralph Allison, Bennett Braun, and Richard Kluft. They talk about treatment as involving five years or more. Allison believes that many inmates of prisons are multiples. Madeleine Richport (1992) has studied various cultural attitudes about dissociative disorders and has compared the various approaches to treatment, including having the personalities break through amnesia and integrate with each other, coercively removing them, or maintaining them as useful parts of the whole personality.

The most difficult patients to work with are those who have been victims of satanic ritual abuse. They tend to continue with their compulsive, obedient imprinting on their aggressors, often their father and mother. Their genetic encoding of expecting love and nurturing from parents has been totally disrupted, and yet they continue to be attached and obedient.

An explanation that battered children invent dissociative personalities for escape from immediate trauma is reasonable, but it seems to me that children are economical in emotional moments. Why would there be 5–10–100 different personalities if one dissociative state had worked the first time?

Another consideration, taken by cultures that have believed in spirit attachment, is that a child's protective aura is shattered at the time of fear and pain. This permits an opening for a lost, earthbound spirit to get back into a living body when it could not get back into its own body at the time of sudden death. The belief is that such spirits have not had time to learn that they could move on toward another incarnation. With repetitive beatings there would be frequent openings for new spirits to come in.

Viewed from this standpoint, there is not as much confusion. Speaking through the voice of a hypnotized subject, "spirits" give their name, birth date, age at death, and the reason for that death. Often when regressed to the scene of death, they are greatly distressed until offered a chance to move into the light toward a new life with a healthy body. These do not sound like the accounts one would expect from a beaten child who had split off a part of himself or herself to escape pain.

Thoughtful experts with whom I have discussed this matter have suggested that there are two forms of dissociative states. I have seen only the ones relating to multiple spirits because I am prejudiced about splits in the original personality; therefore I am not consulted by patients with the purely dissociative process. Both sides of the issue deserve careful thought and exploration. Dissociative states are fascinating and very difficult to treat. Many people with this condition have been treated as schizophrenic.

Psychotic Patients

Are psychotic patients highly sensitive and psychically endowed people who have become battle-fatigued because of the emotional overload under which they have been living? For many years, psychiatrists have warned that hypnosis should not be used with psychotic patients. Joan Scagnelli (1980, 1981), later writing as Joan Murray-Jobsis (1988), is a psychologist who has shown the value of hypnosis with schizophrenic patients. In her writings she has outlined the techniques she uses.

Comment

This chapter is offered in the hope of stimulating the reader to investigate possibilities that have been suggested by my patients. I believe we will know much more about psychiatry as we extend our explorations to permit access to previously unrecognized sources of maladaptive behavior and permit our patients to reframe unfavorable patterned behavior.

23

Hypnosis with Children

RAYMOND L. LASCOLA, M.D.

Of all age groups, children are undoubtedly the best hypnotic subjects. Many children apparently spend much time in a spontaneous form of hypnotic state.

Because of their capacity for visual imagery, it is possible to use fantasy situations and illustrations in a therapeutic way that the adult patient many times is unable to grasp. The child will slip into hypnosis so very rapidly and with such ease that the inexperienced operator may not feel that the patient has achieved the hypnotic state.

One marked difference in child and adult subjects that should be pointed out is the behavior of children while in any stage of trance. Children may squirm, twist, scratch, pick their noses, and so on and remain quite deeply hypnotized, while these same actions in an adult subject are considered signs of resistance.

It is often asked at which age children are the best subjects. Most experienced therapists feel that the 8–10 age group responds best. However, in my experience, children seem to respond equally well at any age; and the response is primarily dependent upon the rapport the operator is able to establish with the child. A few minutes spent visiting, talking about the child's interests, family situation, and the like will quickly establish a feeling of camaraderie that is invaluable for a later therapeutic situation.

The first session with a child is without doubt the most important. We should approach the children on their level, using their language, while avoiding any attitude that might be interpreted as talking down to their level.

An initial induction can be very rapid, quite unlike the common types of slow relaxation inductions used with adults. I will simply say, "Now, as you close your eyes, you can let your whole body just go limp, just the way a wet towel does when you drop it on the floor." Or, "When I snap my fingers, your whole body will become as limp as cooked spaghetti."

A simple deepening technique is to suggest walking down a stair as I count down from ten, "taking a step and going more relaxed with each count." Deepening techniques are rarely necessary because children will go as deep as needed during the interview if they feels comfortable with your attitude.

When I use the word "sleep," I say it is a "kind of sleep and you will hear everything I say." "Drowsy" is a good word to use rather than "going to sleep" because children often object to parental orders about sleep.

Depending on their age, little patients may be asked, "Do you like to watch television?" I follow this with, "What is your favorite program?" I might mention that I have a "magic TV set over here." If they seem interested, I will call on their ability to fantasize with, "Why don't you just turn it on and let's look at a rerun of one of your favorite programs? Just close your eyes and watch it in your mind. Nod when you can see it." They will have slipped right into hypnosis by the time their head nods to indicate that they are hallucinating the picture.

Some children are so quickly able to go into hypnosis that I can say, "If you like, you might be able to open your eyes and see the rest of the picture over there where I am putting the magic TV against the wall. We can turn it on and there come the wavy lines and the sound. First there's a commercial. You can see it and hear it now. And now the program is starting. There it begins. Just watch it now."

It is surprising how easily most children can hallucinate in this way. To do so, they will enter a deep trance state. It is also very easy to distort time during the hallucination of a TV program. We can speed it up to a remarkable degree. I can say, "I am going to count to ten. That is all the time it takes to see a half-hour show. I'm going to start—one, two, and so on." Some children can do this very easily and can fill in a lot of details when asked about the program later.

This method is particularly effective to use with either frightened children or ones who are obstreperous and hard to handle. Almost all children are interested in magic and enjoy television. They would much rather watch a program than have some unpleasant treatment from a physician or a dentist. They may not even notice an injection being given. Dentists who use hypnosis find this an excellent way of dealing with children while their teeth are being worked on. All their attention is on the TV program.

Asthma in Children

The child asthmatic responds most dramatically to the hypnotic approach, and the cure is so gratifying that it seems incredible for any other method of treatment ever to be considered. When first dealing with asthmatic children, the author spent much time bringing out all, or as many of the underlying causal factors as possible. Later, however, very little time was devoted to uncovering these factors, and the children did just as well. In the adult, just the opposite seems to be the case.

To illustrate the technique in detail, first the children are induced by any methods appropriate to their age. The following approach might be used:

"Not many people understand what asthma is. Most people think that you wheeze and can't breathe because you can't get the air into the lungs, but you and I know differently. We know it's just the opposite. When you're having an attack, you can't get the air out of the lungs to let fresh air in." The child asthmatic will usually show agreement by a smile or a nod of the head.

There should then be a simple explanation of the mechanics and the anatomy of the lungs. Particular attention is given to the small muscles that encircle the smaller bronchi. The patients are given as vivid an image as possible of how the muscles tighten, like a purse string, keeping the air in the airspaces at the end of the bronchial tubules.

The description has little resemblance to the way *Gray's Anatomy* puts it, but this oversimplification permits patients to see their problem as mechanical in nature. I continue with, "So, you see, all a person has to do to be able to breathe comfortably is just let all of these little muscles relax." The meaning of "let all of these muscles relax" is that there is no effort in doing so. This is different from saying, "Make these muscles relax."

Other illustrations are added to show as vividly as possible the effect of contracting or relaxing musculature. Children enjoy blunt, often crude, humor, especially if it is aimed at an adult. Their vivid imagery and sense of the ridiculous make it possible to put these illustrations on a fun or joke basis.

As soon as the concept of relaxing the muscles is clearly understood, an example is given as follows: "If you were holding a hot potato in your hand and it was burning you—too hot to hold—what would you do to get rid of it? Would you tighten all of your hand muscles? Of course not. That would be stupid. You'd just relax the muscles and let the potato roll out." The child will usually nod and smile at the use of the word "stupid," the implication being that only stupid people tighten muscles when they are supposed to relax them.

Another illustration used is, "Suppose you lit a match and were holding it as it burned. Pretty soon the fire would get closer and closer to your fingers. Would you tighten all of your hand muscles to hold the match tighter?" I wait for a head movement response before saying, "Of course not! Only a fool would do a dumb thing like that. All you'd need to do is to relax the muscles and you could drop the match before it burned your finger."

By now I have established a friendly camaraderie with the children. I have implied that we both know what to do if there is a problem that can be solved by simple muscle relaxation. We have agreed that "other people" who are not able to solve such a simple problem are stupid, dumb or fools.

We then very casually return to the problem of asthma. If children are having an attack or having any wheezing at all, the following suggestions are given:

"Now we both know that asthma is a condition in which a person without realizing it tightens all of the little muscles around the air sacs of the lung and holds the old air in so that there is no room for fresh air. This simply means that he is holding these muscles so tight that he can't breathe out. Right?"

Wait for them to acknowledge this before continuing with, "Now, notice that you're wheezing. Don't you feel kind of silly?" Children will usually smile at this point. I continue in this simple, casual manner. "Of course this isn't your fault. No one ever explained asthma to you before. So now that you know, let me see you relax those tiny muscles that are holding the air in and get all of this wheezing stopped."

Invariably the children will lean slightly forward, and lower the chin, and in a few seconds the respirations become much slower and the asthmatic noises begin to subside. Keep in mind that children's ability to do this is in direct proportion to their conviction that they *can* do it. It is, therefore, vital that this conviction be reinforced as much and in as many ways as possible. One excellent way of doing this is to take out a stethoscope and listen to their chest *after* there has been a noticeable improvement and find an area where there are still some rales. Then say, "There are a few whistles here. Let's clear them up next." Notice particularly that the approach is one of positive conviction by the way I am talking. I don't say something like, "Let's see *if* you can clear these up." A word like "if" suggests a doubt that they can do it; this will bring failure. Frightened children are amazingly able to perform miracles when we show respect for their ability.

When the chest sounds are entirely clear, some complimentary comment is called for, such as, "Now it's as clear as a bell. That's fine!" This is positive reinforcement.

In order to get children free of a dependence on drugs and to give them a feeling of "Now that I know, I can handle this," the following is interjected: "Now, I'm sure in the past when you've had an attack of asthma and couldn't breathe, somebody gave you a *shot* of adrenalin or aminophylline, or some other *shot*. They gave the shot just to do what you now know how to do all by yourself. If you had known then what the problem was, you wouldn't have needed any of those shots, would you?" Wait for a nod of agreement.

My tone of voice in saying all this is to make fun of those who are archaic and "not in the know" as we are. "Suppose you woke up in the middle of the night with an attack of asthma. Naturally you'd realize that you must have had a bad dream that brought it on. So what would you do? Act like a gooney bird and stay awake all night and wheeze? Of course not. You'd simply relax those little muscles and go right back to sleep, wouldn't you?"

It is now established in the children's mind that asthma is a matter of choice. "Since you now know how to stop an attack of asthma, you naturally have already figured out how to start one, so let's see you start a real bad attack. I want you to tighten all of those little muscles so much that you'll sound like a leaky steam engine. Make your face turn blue."

Asking for the most severe attack possible reinforces the fact to the children that they can clear any attack, no matter how severe, and that I know they can do this. In a surprisingly short time the children will have produced a severe, genuine attack of asthma. It will not be quite as bad as usual because they already know they have some control. Now I compliment them with, "Wonderful! It's more fun to clear these bad ones up than it is those little simple ones."

When they are really wheezing and looking a bit uncomfortable, I say, "Now I'm going to time you with my watch. I want to see how fast you can get it completely turned off." If time permits, I will ask them to do it once or twice again while they are with me and know I will help if needed. Every skill improves with repetition and practice. When I know that they know they are in control of the situation I will say, "Now, do you think you ever need to have another attack of asthma again?" Wait for a shake of the head. "If you ever wake up in the middle of the night after a bad dream and you are wheezing, do you think you will remember what to do?" Wait for a nod. "Well, I guess that's all there is to it. Do you feel that you're cured of asthma?" Wait for a nod. Each response is strengthening the mental set for success. "Do you think you'll ever have another attack? Don't you wish somebody had explained this to you sooner? Isn't asthma kind of a dumb thing to have, now that you know all about it?" Wait for another nod. "So that's all there is to it."

When the above is finished, I usually take the children on an imaginary scuba-diving trip or on some other excursion where respiration is controlled or restricted. Much play and fantasy about finding treasure are used to prolong the "trip." This all tends to reinforce further the children's new feeling that they are no longer a slave to the caprice of contracting musculature.

In developing this imagined scuba-diving expedition, I bring out details, describing the trip to the ocean and donning all of the scuba-diving gear. This includes a nose stopper, mouth-breathing bit connected to tanks worn on the back, and so on. Putting on all this respiratory-inhibiting equipment is treated quite casually as though I am absolutely sure there will be no difficulties for them.

The fantasied descent into the water is described with all of the pleasurable associations possible. While in the depths of this fantasy, sea fish are sighted, a sunken pirate ship or a sea cave is explored for treasure, being sure to "find" a chest containing coins or jewels.

When the fantasy trip is finished and the hypnosis terminated, I ask, "How did you like that trip?" The children are usually very enthusiastic. "But you forgot your coins (or jewels)." The children usually smile on recognizing that this has been a fantasy. Now, I say, "Well, I thought you might forget, so I brought them up for you." This always produces a hearty laugh as I pull out a few coins or a dime-store necklace from my pocket.

In cases involving real or supposed allergy to various foods (wheat, eggs, chocolate, etc.), the children are asked at the end of the session, after they have learned how to control their symptoms, "Do you think you can eat (mentioning the specific allergen) and be completely free of symptoms?" They usually will say "yes" as they flash a look at Mom. "Then," I say "How would you like to come with me to the restaurant across the street and have a chocolate malt with an egg in it and a piece of cake?" This is greeted with enthusiasm. The accompanying parent usually turns pale at the thought, having been thoroughly indoctrinated with the limitations of food allergy. (I have told the parent privately before the session that he or she is not to comment or interfere with anything I say.) The excursion to the restaurant is made, and what was previously considered pure poison is eaten with relish and without any ill effect whatsoever.

It is wise to point out to the children that they may never have another attack of asthma, but there is always the possibility that one will sneak up on them. I tell them, "The big difference now is that it won't matter because you know how to turn it off."

A point to be emphasized is the fact that attacks can occur during the night, precipitated by a dream. I say, "Suppose you awoke in the middle of the night and were having an attack. What would you do?" The child may be puzzled and unable to respond. I say, "Why, you'd turn it off just like you would if one started in the daytime, wouldn't you?"

I find it wise to have a consultation with parents to explain their role in supporting their children in their new-found freedom to control the asthmatic attacks. Any display of skepticism, doubt, or apprehension on the parents' part may completely negate the positive results obtained with me. The feelings and beliefs of relatives will take priority over any doctor-patient relationship.

It has been our experience also that allergists tend to disbelieve quick improvements, especially when hypnosis is used. This is not their fault. The discipline in which they specialized has always been to consider allergies as organic and unmodifiable. It is important to point out to the parents that they should expect their doctor to be upset if children refuse to take the usual medications and emergency treatments of the past. It is up to the parents to evaluate the evidence and to support their children in what they are doing.

It might be wise to avoid confrontation and bitterness, if they went along with medical treatments for a time and gradually gave them up. Freedom from dependency and freedom from fear of illness returning are goals that seem justifiable. I remind the parents that the children will only be able to succeed in reaching this goal if they are convinced in their own mind that they can do it.

One child with chronic asthma was seen by me in one of our Hypnosis Symposiums at the request of his pediatrician. He came up to the platform wheezing audibly. He turned it off. A doctor found no rales when he listened to the boy's chest. They were back and easily heard by the participants around the room when I asked the child to turn on the asthma again.

Several weeks later, his mother wrote a glowingly grateful letter telling how pleased she was that her 9-year-old son had been completely free of his asthma for the first time in six years. I called her several months later to check on the boy's condition. She said her son had been seen in a Navy medical clinic for a routine visit. The officer who had referred him to me was no longer there. In his place was a resident who proceeded to tell her son how certain he was that the attacks would return, that hypnosis could not replace the vasodilators. He persuaded the mother to continue the old regimen. She then had made appointments to resume desensitization shots "just as soon as he had his next attack." The boy had begun wheezing on the way home and had a severe attack that night just as had been suggested. Hypnosis can work both ways. Unfortunately, the knowledge about what hypnosis can do does not go unchallenged by our medical colleagues.

Thumb Sucking

Persistent thumb sucking by a 2- or 3-year-old child is often an annoying problem for parents. Parents often make the mistake of using forceful measures to stop the habit, and these can lead to other behavioral disorders. The following approach has been effective most of the time in my experience.

One of the techniques of inducing hypnosis is used after assuring the children of my sympathetic understanding of what they have been going through. I will say, "I understand that your parents feel you should stop sucking your thumb. Now I don't see anything wrong with thumb sucking, do you?" The children, after some hesitation, will agree. "There's nothing wrong with it as long as you play fair." The children will seem puzzled by the last statement. I continue to explain. "By that, I mean since you have ten fingers, each one of them should be entitled to the same amount of attention. That sounds fair, doesn't it?" Wait for agreement.

"Now, I can tell you haven't thought of it this way, because I can see that you've given all of the attention to one thumb. Is that so?" The children will usually nod in agreement. "Well, now that you realize that you haven't been playing fair with the other fingers, would you be willing to be a good sport and play fair with all of them?"

When presented this way, agreement is the only choice. I go on to explain what playing fair entails. "Now that you understand about being fair to all of the fingers, you can still suck your thumb, but whenever you do, you'll suck each of the other fingers just as long as you did the thumb—one after the other. In this way you'll be giving each of them the same amount of attention."

I say this in a matter-of-fact way, stressing the word "fair" as often as possible. It seems quite reasonable. Rehearsing the procedure in hypnosis will further reinforce the suggestion. "Now, let's go over this one time. I'm going to count to ten, and when I start counting, you can begin with the thumb. With each number, change to the next finger." After going over all ten fingers, the last suggestion can be, "Now, that's fine. All of your fingers have had the same amount of attention. You can suck them any time you like, but remember always to do it this way."

For the first time, the children have been treated as equals, and fair ones at that. They will leave with a feeling of triumph. They have not been told that they can't suck their thumb anymore. An appointment is made for two weeks later to hear how things are going. In most instances the second appointment is canceled. After being a "good sport" and "playing fair" for a few days at home, the whole procedure of thumb and finger sucking becomes dull and boring, and the habit is usually given up. If at any time it is resumed, I tell the parents to give a gentle reminder of what the children promised the doctor about playing fair with the rest of the fingers.

Pain Control

It is much easier to teach children the control of pain than to teach it to adults. The techniques of glove anesthesia commonly used with adults can be used here. There is another, simpler method taught in our courses, and children seem to enjoy the visual imagery involved.

After hypnosis has been induced, I ask the children to visualize a long row of light switches as though they were in their head. Above each switch they are to see a colored light bulb. All are turned on and each one is a different color or shade of color. I then tell them how this system is like their nervous system. The description is tailored to each child's age and level of understanding.

I tell them that by turning off any one of these switches, they can make a particular part of their body numb. It is specified that a certain switch, with its light, controls a hand. Turning it off and seeing the light go out means that the nerve current is turned off and the hand will be numb, like a piece of wood. I might tell young children that the hand will seem as though it had "gone to sleep." I always choose the hand that is farther away from the place I want to have numb for the work I will be doing.

I then test the hand after they have turned off the switch. I explain that they will feel touch and pressure but will not feel any hurt or "owie." The word "pain" is carefully avoided. When they recognize how well they have done with the unimportant hand, I ask them to go back and turn the switch on again to get all the feeling back. They test themselves to make sure their hand is normally sensitive again. The next step is for them to turn off the switch that goes to the place they will want to make "sleepy" before I treat it to make it well.

I routinely teach my pediatric patients how to do this turning off of switches as a sort of game during ordinary visits. Then they know all about it at a later time of need. Simple lacerations can be repaired, and it can be very effective if any injections are given. It is possible, and should be tried, I have found, for setting a fracture before resorting to a general anesthetic.

Another method of suggestion for anesthesia that works well with young children involves a form of fantasy based on an initial fact. There are a number of variations on this method. I use a cotton swab saturated with rubbing alcohol. The skin that is moistened with the alcohol will feel cool as the alcohol evaporates. As I wipe the area where the needle will go in, I say "I want you to close your eyes, and when I rub this cotton on your arm, it is going to feel like I'm using an ice cube. The colder you can let it feel, the better. I am going to give you the injection right here, so make that place feel frozen. Nod your head when you're beginning to feel it get cold. Nod again when you know you won't even feel a pin prick when I give you this medicine. Remember that every time we give you an injection it will be given to keep you from getting sick some day.

"Is the ice cube making it real cold so that it is beginning to get numb? Good!" I wait a few seconds and then add, "Is it numb enough now for the injection? The needle will feel as though I am pressing with my finger on the place. OK, now, notice how easy it is."

Until you have confidence that this will work, I suggest that you pinch the skin a few inches away from the injection site to attract their awareness just as you give the injection.

For injections in the buttock you don't need to use hypnosis or fantasy, just a little distraction. You can hold the syringe in the palm of your hand so that the needle will be extending about 3/4 of an inch from the little finger side of your hand. Tell the children that you are going to gently hit their buttock with the side of your hand just before you give the injection. The side of your hand covers a much wider area than the diameter of a needle. The injection will be finished while they are waiting for the needle injection to be done *after* you have hit them.

Bedwetting

Enuresis is undoubtedly one of the most difficult pediatric problems to treat medically. Various child therapists I have consulted have agreed that the usual approach is of questionable value unless a long-term analytical therapy is used. This involves looking at bedwetting as a part of a symptom complex. This is time consuming and expensive treatment that will add to the children's belief that they are not like other kids.

A hypnotherapeutic process goes directly to the problem, is much less costly, much less time-consuming and offers the children some skills in addition to curing their problem.

An understanding, sympathetic approach is used. After inducing hypnosis I say to the children, "From now on we are going to ignore the 'wet' bed. We are only interested in the 'dry' bed. So are you willing to go along with me and start thinking how good it's going to feel to wake up every day in a nice, clean, 'dry bed?'" This usually gets a nod and a smile because they have associated failure and guilt with the words "wet bed." This is a new concept.

"Now, of course we all know why people wet their beds. It's because they urinate while they are asleep. Well, as far as you are concerned, this will never happen again. Let's find out if the inner part of your mind is willing to make it impossible for you ever to urinate again unless you are wide awake."

The ideomotor questioning method with finger signals is used here to get unconscious answers. If the "no" finger lifts, it means there are probable emotional reasons that will have to be searched out and removed with further ideomotor questioning. There may be some reasons for resentment and/or rebellion relating to a parent or a sibling. These usually are quite transparent and easily removed when compared with the miserable feelings they have had in the past after wetting the bed and being ridiculed for it. The usual response is "yes" to the question about their inner mind being willing to make it impossible ever to urinate again unless they are wide awake.

I repeat the idea of always awakening before urinating. I stress it many times while the children are in a hypnotic state. I talk about keeping track of the number of "dry beds" and ignoring the old nuisance, wet, messy bed. I add, "Now, of course, you must remember that anyone can have an accident at some time. I mean that if you do wet your bed ever again, just think of it as an accident, because now you are no longer a 'bed wetter.'"

This suggestion can be reinforced by further ideomotor questions such as, "Let's see what you inner mind has to say to this question, ' Will it be OK for me to have lots of dry beds from now on?'" The answer is usually "yes." If so, I will say, "Your right arm will begin lifting all by itself when your inner mind *knows* that you will instantly wake up and go to the real bathroom any time after this when you feel that your bladder is full." I will go on quietly talking to them about how smart they are and how much fun it will be to wake up every morning with a dry bed, until the arm lifts after about three minutes.

I add that the kidneys will save their work for the daytime then, because the children will not be afraid of "accidents" any more. Their bladder will not get full anymore at night and they will not have to wake up to go to the real bathroom. Healthy kidneys secrete during the daytime and pretty much shut down during sleep in young people. Anxiety about bedwetting disturbs this normal cycle.

The children should be seen weekly. Each time the number of dry beds is noted, the wet ones not mentioned. The same suggestions are repeated during the brief hypnosis periods. I like to inform the children who are totally cured that they now have a skill that their friends will not have known about. I ask them to keep the secret to themselves and not show their friends how to do what they know they can do. I say it this way because I have learned that if you tell children not to hypnotize their friends, this will be interpreted as your expectation that they will do just that.

General Pediatric Principles

I have discussed three of the most common pediatric problems. Others can be handled in much the same way, keeping in mind the principles involved:

1. Keep an understanding and nonjudgmental, sympathetic form for your communications.

2. Respect the intelligence and the information your little patients can offer when given the chance by you. Parents tend to dictate and to override the offerings of their children. Your role is as an older friend and is not to be confused with a parental role.
3. Keep in mind that you rarely need to use a formal way of helping a child get into hypnosis. Hypnosis will occur spontaneously as you work with the problem at hand.
4. Children's head movements are as trustworthy as finger signals and occur more rapidly than finger signals up to about 6 years of age, when they have started school and have lost a lot of their joyful, wonderful spontaneity. Older children and adults do better with finger signals, and if the answer with a head movement differs from the finger answer, the finger is to be trusted. It reflects a deeper zone of thinking.

Comment

I want to say here that Raymond LaScola is a specialist in pediatrics as well as a master of subliminal communication. His gestures, facial expressions, and voice intonations are only the tip of the iceburg that can be recognized by ordinary adults. Every idea he conveys is couched in terms of absolute certainty that the idea is understood and will be implemented by the child he works with. There are no "ifs," "maybes," or "trys" in his pediatric vocabulary.

His demonstrations are so facile and the children look so natural in his presence that the uninitiated frequently assume that the kids are just trying to please him. LeCron, if he were living, would agree with me that what Dr LaScola accomplished during one contact with a severely asthmatic and disabled child in one of our Symposiums was no humbug. More often he was just demonstrating what normal children can do in learning to use self-hypnosis and developing localized analgesia.

24

Pain: Its Meaning
and Treatment

*I have been increasingly impressed with the
dynamic characteristics of pain, its urgency and
its remarkable ability to find a new route when the
customary channels have been blocked. Sometimes, when
one thing after another that I do to relieve pain has failed, there seems to be a malicious insistency about it. I
feel almost that it acquires a personality, like a
spoiled and stubborn child which fiercely resents
interference and punishment, and deliberately
goes ahead seeking means to break over restraint.*
—W. K. LIVINGSTON, Pain Mechanisms (1943)

Consciously Perceived and Subconscious Pain

By definition, pain must be a consciously perceived, uncomfortable
awareness. There is no word to describe subconscious perception of inflammation or any of the defense mechanisms initiated by trauma, infection,
or antigens. The expression "subconscious pain" will be used here to refer
to the very large area of discomfort that is not noticed at conscious levels
of awareness.

We can understand that all learned processes of adaptation may be
shifted from consciousness into subconscious levels of awareness. Beginners have to concentrate with effort on each step of driving a car. A few

months later they can talk and look at scenery while letting their unconscious mind make appropriate decisions about acceleration, applying brakes and turning the steering wheel.

We know that consciously perceived, unpleasant experiences may be suppressed or pushed out of conscious awareness. They are not eliminated by this mechanism. They are pushed into unconscious horizons of thought where they can dictate unreasonable reactions to real or imagined threats in the future.

We are learning that ideation during natural sleep may be injurious to the dreamer (see Chapter 16), but the experiences are too disturbing for conscious recognition on awakening. They are repressed at a subconscious level and may continue their harmful effect on subsequent nights of sleep or even on successive cycles of sleep during the same night.

The minds of experimental animals and of humans may not only repress a particularly unpleasant experience but also go on to repress conscious knowledge of events preceding the moment of trauma (retrograde amnesia), as though trying to forget everything leading up to the experience as well. We have for years assumed that this phenomenon is caused by actual brain damage. Now we know how to break this form of amnesia with repetitive subconscious review. We are learning that retrograde amnesia is merely suppressed or repressed memory. It is not obliterated memory.

It seems naive to exclude all the possible ramifications of consciously unrecognized discomfort and limit our thoughts about pain to the zone dictated by definition. This is comparable to considering only the part of an iceberg that is above water. If we so restrict our thoughts on pain, we miss the whole phylogenetic meaning of pain. Our patients suffering from sterile fractures, bruises and surgical incisions are therefore forced to recover as best they can with methods originally designed to make animals survive dirty and infected wounds. Uninfected wounds have the same muscle spasm, the same stasis of circulation, the same deposition of collagen, exudation of fluid and mass migrations of inflammatory cells.

We must be very rigid in our thinking to believe that a central nervous system is going to ignore messages from traumatized or infected tissue just because conscious attention is absorbed in fighting off another animal or in looking for a safe place to hide during recovery. We find the same gross and microscopic changes occurring in liver, brain, and skin abscesses, yet those in liver and brain are often "painless."

When we question people suffering from rheumatoid arthritis, we find that several joints are consciously painful and some with visible pathologic changes are not painful. There may be muscle guarding and limitation of motion in the nonpainful joints. Now, set up ideomotor symbol responses to questions and ask the patients about pain. They may shake their head and answer "no" verbally while their finger is lifting to say "yes, there is pain" in the joints that they thought were comfortable. If we go a step further and evoke an unconscious signal that all "subconscious pain, soreness or discomfort" has been removed, we will begin to observe relaxation of the neighboring muscles. With relief from subconscious pain protracted over a period of 24 hours, there will be increasing mobility and a decrease in local edema.

Blisters

Blisters fluid contains painful enzymes. Ask a person with a three-day-old blister if the blister is painful as you press on its surface. She will probably say, "No." Ask this question: "Is there any *subconscious* soreness, tightness or pain as I touch this blister?" Her "yes" finger will lift. Get permission to show her how to make that blister "numb." Some people punish themselves for getting the burn. Show her how to prolong the analgesia for four hours. At the end of that time the fluid will be resorbed and the second-degree burn will heal faster than expected.

Ankle Sprain

A sprained ankle will heal more rapidly when subconscious pain is removed. Response in a simple sprain of the ankle, without fracture, is dramatic when both conscious and unconscious components of pain have been removed with ideomotor questioning and hypnosis. But here we must move carefully again, because another factor in pain and tissue reaction must be considered. We are not always at liberty to order freedom from pain. Injured people have a tendency to feel either stupid or guilty about the factors leading to the injury and we must clear their attitudes first because they may subconsciously think they need to punish themselves.

Sequence of Events with Blockage of Subconscious Pain

1. An ideomotor signal will indicate that pain has been blocked subconsciously.
2. Facial expression will change to reflect spread of subconscious relief to preconscious recognition. The interval of time between the signal and moment of realization that pain is gone will vary from one to ten minutes, depending upon how severe the pain has been and how long it has been there.
3. The regional muscles will begin relaxing in the previously painful area. The interval will be approximately two minutes after the change in facial expression.

4. Conscious movements of regional muscles will be made about two minutes after relaxing the regional muscles as the patient verifies the reality of feeling comfortable.
5. A verbal acknowledgement will follow a few minutes later.
6. There will be diminishing signs of inflammation visible after two or more hours from the ideomotor signal of step 1 (subconscious signal of turning off pain subconsciously).

Hypnosis, Inflammation, and Healing

As stated in earlier chapters, Esdaile discovered that repetitive lulling mesmeric passes not only permitted patients to undergo painless surgery but diminished the signs of inflammation, reduced surgical hemorrhage, and lowered surgical mortality. Why did hypnosis decrease surgical mortality and increase resistance to infection in the days before surgeons washed their hands and sterilized their instruments? There may be some answers to this question.

Delboeuf, in 1877, studied thermal second-degree burns and noted that they healed without blister formation on an arm rendered painless with hypnotic suggestion. He concluded that pain made the victim think about his burn and that thinking rendered the burn more severe. This speculation has been substantiated by Ewin's research regarding the progression of a second degree burn to a full thickness, third-degree burn. Ewin (1986) stated that concern of attendants and the pain caused by debriding and repeated dressing augments the anxiety and increases the victim's attentiveness to the burn area. Ewin showed that hypnosis can prevent this progression and will speed healing.

Sixty-two years after Delboeuf's observations, Duthie and Chain (1939) in England reported presence of pain producing polypeptide enzyme activity causing acute inflammation. Armstrong and colleagues (1957) at Cornell found pain-producing substances in blister fluid. These were polypeptide, proteolytic enzymes. Ostfield and his co-workers (1957) at Cornell in New York found similar enzymes released in pericranial transudates of patients during attacks of migraine headache. In 1959, Chapman, Goodell, and Wolff in the same laboratories were studying the effect of painful stimuli on release of these inflammatory polypeptide enzymes. They repeated the experiments of Hilton and Fox (1958) with "bradykinin," using their methods of collecting subcutaneous fluid and concentrating the enzymes. They found that anything interrupting the continuity of messages from an injured site to the brain and back would diminish the output of these enzymes. It could be a local anesthetic in either the afferent or efferent nerve pathways. They added a test with the use of hypnosis to block pain. There was moderate diminution of "neurokinins" (the name substituted for bradykinin secretion because it seemed transmitted by nerve fibers) on the suggested numb side as compared with the normal sensitive side. The difference became accentuated when they added an element of alarmed expectancy by telling hypnotized subjects that something really disturbing would happen to the normal arm. This was a contribution to our understanding of what happens during surgery, particularly with surgery involving personal risk or possibility of finding cancer.

Harold Wolff, Professor of Neurology at Cornell University Medical School in New York, initiated the biochemical research on pain. After his untimely death from a massive cerebral hemorrhage in February of 1962, Stewart Wolf and Helen Goodell (1968) edited and revised Harold Wolff's classic *Stress and Disease*, published in 1953. From his guidance came many famous research workers, including L. E. Hinkle, Adrian Ostfield, Thomas Holmes, H. S. Ripley, Ian Stevenson and Stewart Wolf.

It seemed clear to Harold Wolff that the significance of the seeming paradoxical reaction of the central nervous system to noxious stimuli, that is, sending back inflammatory enzymes, had survival value for animals whose wounds would be expected to be infected.

A wounded animal's chance for survival depends on photophobia to get away from the light. This diminishes risk of exposure to predators when movement might be difficult. A painful wound leads to decreased renal filtration to preserve fluid and electrolytes. A wounded animal in hiding cannot get to water. It can survive for a long time without food, but survival time without water would be measured in hours. Spasm of regional muscles diminishes circulation to the affected area. This diminishes the chance for bacteria to enter the general circulation. Leakage of plasma-containing lymphocytes and polymorphic leukocytes through capillary walls allows a favorable combat with bacteria localized in the wound. A wounded mammal licks its wound. Its saliva contains antibacterial substances.

George Crile and "Anoci-Association"

George Crile, Sr. in the first decade of this century believed that apprehension was the major factor in surgical mortality with toxic goiter. Death during or shortly after surgery for removal of hyperactive thyroid tissue was secondary to what was termed a "thyroid crisis." All the signs of explosive panic would occur prior to death.

Crile lowered the mortality from his thyroidectomies to less than 5 percent from the very high previous level in the days when surgery offered the only hope for this illness. He "stole" thyroid tissue after a graduated series of daily "breathing exercises" that helped his patient get used to losing consciousness with nitrous oxide and oxygen. She would awaken each day in her room with the usual feeling of euphoria and relaxation produced by this anesthetic agent. Breakfast was withheld on the unannounced day of surgery. The patient was anesthetized in her room, her pupils were dilated with eye drops and her ears packed with wet cotton to diminish awareness of sights and sounds on the way to the operating room. Crile had known that anesthetized people hear and can react to things they hear, as he revealed in his autobiography (1947).

His plan was very successful until one frightened young woman unexpectedly died on the table with the dreaded thyroid crisis. Investigation revealed that a friend had told this patient that the difference between a day of exercise and the day of operation would be that breakfast would be withheld on the day of surgery!

With this and other observations on the role of fear, Crile and the internist William Lower developed the principles of "anoci-association' in surgery. This included careful handling of tissues, and regional anesthesia as well as inhalation anesthesia with nitrous oxide which they felt was less damaging to the nervous system than ether. He insisted on careful avoidance of scrubroom conversations and the clashing of instruments.

Psychological Methods of Alleviating or Blocking Pain Perception

Methods That Do Not Seem to Alter Tissue Reactions

1. Misdirection of attention.
2. Recognition of more important threat (an assailant)
3. Dissociation in time or place (Erickson)
4. Guided imagery suggestions of relaxation, i.e., confusing the mind's programming for injury or stress
5. Altering the subjective meaning of pain (Beecher: the wounded soldier realizing freedom now from danger)
6. Manipulating duration and intensity of pain (Erickson)
7. Direct hypnotic suggestion of pain relief and comfort without reaching acceptance at a physiological level of perception.

Methods Permitting Decreased Tissue Reaction

1. Mesmeric passes continued to end-point of trance and subconscious analgesia (Esdaile)

2. Combined analysis of the meaning of pain with permissive directions for subconscious pain relief for continued periods of time (conditioned stimuli must be removed, resistances must be cleared, and the patient must be protected from "this-is-too-good-to-last phenomenon ["slip-back"] and the iatrogenic misunderstanding caused by "you'll just have to live with this pain."

Discussion

In the first group, only #6 and #7 might be considered truly related to hyp-nosis. The others can be achieved with patients who do not seem to be hyp-notized and may not show commonly recognized signs of hypnosis. Number 1 (misdirection) had been taught us by children who use their first name in reporting injury: "Mary fell down and skinned her knee," instead of "I fell down and skinned my knee." It seems to hurt less when the injury hap-pens to self in the third person. The pain tolerance is elevated by recognized danger. Pain has no phylogenetic value for the endangered animal because it might deflect attention from the enemy. The boxer feels no pain until the fight has ended. This is the essence of the #2 item regarding a more impor-tant stimulus.

Milton Erickson has extended the use of the misdirection used by children who have, without influence from elders, often used associations with pleasant experiences to soften a present pain. A small son of my secretary told me that he went down to the store in his mind and ate an ice cream cone to ease the pain when he fell on his knee. Erickson would shift the orientation of an uncomfortable patient to another period of life when pain was not part of the experience. By drawing attention to scenery and various happy sensory stimuli, he diluted the capacity of the mind to pay attention to the incongruous painful messages. He might ask a patient in labor to come out of her body and sit across the room watching her body over there on the bed giving birth to her baby. The patient's thinking mind is, therefore, free from her feeling body.

Reactions of the Body to Perceived Danger

The nervous system reacts to danger and pain by accelerating heart and respiratory rates, decreasing circulation to the vegetative organs and increas-ing blood supply to skeletal muscles. At the same time, the tonicity of these muscles is increased by the hyperventilation. The reverse of these reactions occurs when the environment is peaceful. Purposeful relaxation of muscles seems to evoke the reactions of peace and freedom from pain, even in the presence of danger and injury. The patient must cooperate and, therefore, should recognize reasons for using suggestions of this sort when they seem ridiculously out of tune with the situation. There are many times, however, when patients seem willing to accept such suggestions as a sort of mental escape from pain.

Using a Pleasant Memory to Recall Helpful Physiological Action

A man suffering anginal pain can readily understand that slowing his heart rate will allow better filling of his coronary arteries. These vessels get their oxygen and nutrition in the interval between contractions of the heart. It makes sense then for him to hallucinate a peaceful setting and his reaction to the situation of having a lazy vacation, stretched out on a sunny beach. He can be asked to signal with an ideomotor response when he is there, give another signal when he knows his heart is getting better circulation, and another signal when the subconscious element of the pain is totally gone. This is an intelligent way of reprogramming mental activity during an emergency. It uses conditioned responses, and the process of attention given to the act will also diminish awareness of the pain.

Henry Beecher has pointed out the significance of motivation in tolerance of pain. He witnessed severely wounded soldiers during World War II at Anzio lying quietly, free of pain and without need for narcotics. Their tolerance for pain was high, he believed, because they realized that they would be removed to safety by virtue of being honorably wounded. Another view, however, would be that severely injured people automatically enter a medium to deep hypnotic state in which pain disappears.

Pain Tolerance Relating to Guilt and Self-Punishment

In contrast to this example of improved pain tolerance was the experience of a woman who fractured her thigh in a motorcycle accident under circumstances that made her ashamed of having gone with the cyclist. For eight months she had been in the hospital, separated from her 2-year-old daughter. Efforts to connect the ends of the bone with steel plates had been made three times. Her pain was so constant and intense that the local inflammatory enzymes had weakened the connection of the screws to the bone. The spasm of her thigh muscles had twice pulled the distal bone so as to overlap the proximal part of the shaft. This had happened twice and was threatening to do so again when I saw her for the first time.

It took five hours of failed efforts to relieve her pain and to permit healing before I finally awakened to the possibility of motivating her to accept suggestions in order to get out of the hospital and be with her little daughter. She was subconsciously willing to stop the self-punishment and accept hypnotic efforts to eliminate her pain for her daughter's sake. She was consciously unaware of this powerful source of resistance until the last interview. She left the hospital a few weeks after recognizing her right to get well.

Manipulation of Pain

Erickson (1967) has described uses of time-distortion and diminution of pain in increments when circumstances do not permit complete removal of pain. He has struck bargains with patients who need their pain but are willing to suffer in some unimportant part of the body or who will compress a long period of mild pain into a few moments of excruciating pain. He found it possible for patients to substitute night pain during sleep for disabling daytime pain. He has arranged for episodic pain of long duration to seem like pain of a few seconds' duration and has exercised patients in forgetting various aspects of their pain. These methods are interesting. Their general goal is to permit time for the patient to recognize that the pain is really not essential for constructive living and that pain can eventually be eliminated if it can be manipulated. Erickson was constantly searching for ways to help troubled people discover their resources when interfering factors could be removed.

Hypnotic Suggestions for Pain Relief

Direct suggestion of pain relief may work dramatically or it may fail miserably and force the therapist into a position of diminished prestige. It has a place in dentistry and during acute emergencies when patients show spontaneous trance-like behavior. Indirect methods are more successful at all other times, I believe.

Mesmeric Passes

Habituation is the name given the phenomenon of reduced response to a repeated nonmeaningful stimulus. As Hernandez-Peon, Scherrer, and Jouvet (1956) showed in their work with cats, the evoked electrical response to an evenly spaced sound as registered on EEG tracings would diminish with time. A new interval between sounds would reestablish the full response. In nature this type of alertness to unusual stimuli is essential for survival.

It seems logical that the effect of repeated mesmeric passes must be comparable. Research by Becker and Seldon (1985), however, suggests that mesmeric anesthesia may be an electrical phenomenon. Possibly the repetitive movement of hands with their electrical field polarity, opposite to the polarity of the central axis of the nervous system alters susceptibility to pain by reversing the polarity of the electromagnetic fields of the body.

An anesthetic agent reverses the polarity; it returns to the original polarity as the anesthetic wears off.

The classic studies of Harold Saxton Burr and Northrup at Yale University and the contributions of one of Burr's students, Leonard Ravitz, are worth the attention of the reader interested in the phenomena of tissue and organ electromagnetic fields.

Working with Pain Control

The general principles of working with pain states are essentially the same as are used with combined hypnosis and ideomotor techniques with any psychosomatic problem:

1. Discover the first moment pain seemed important.
2. Ask if there might be an earlier sensitizing event.
3. Learn what circumstances made pain personally important.
4. Knowing these things, does your inner mind feel willing to let me help you get well?
5. If the answer is positive, attempt to obtain a commitment on an hallucinated cure date.
6. Is there anything else we need to know before working toward that goal?
7. Teach the patient how to use self-hypnosis and how to alter sensation awareness in an unimportant part of the body.
8. Ask permission to turn down the volume of painful awareness in the involved location. Work with fractions of total elimination.
9. Having reduced the subconscious perception of pain to zero, bring sensation back to previous level and then double the amount of pain after assuring the patient about the instant way of removing the pain.
10. Teach the patient how to review thoughts and dreams during the night (Chapter 16). The reason for this is that daytime problems may have been removed, but deep subconscious patterns of thought may keep interfering with total relief. Teach the patient how to check each morning: "Was my sleep last night and this morning pleasant and comfortable?" The wording of this question avoids suggestion that sleep could have been otherwise.
11. Advise the patient that there will be subliminal signals in the future that might cause a flashback to experiencing pain again. This is a chance to learn more about the pain; it is not a sign of failure.

In the years since 1985 I have started all sessions involving maladaptive behavior with a quick check of subjective impressions about:

1. Birth: Feeling accepted. Feeling free of guilt. Was mother able to feed patient at her breast?
2. Get subjective impressions of father's impact on patient. Was he present at the birth? How did he react when mother told him of the pregnancy?
3. Maternal reaction, as understood by the embryo, on being told she was pregnant. Attempt to reframe impression if it was negative (Chapter 20).
4. Move forward then from horizon of birth to the first moment pain was a personal experience. Remember that head pain and a mother's pain in labor can be conditioning factors for subsequent pain of any sort when the patient is emotionally distressed.

25

Emergency Uses
of Hypnosis

Frightened and unconscious people are overly suggestible and may be treated as though already in a hypnotic state. Whether conscious or unconscious, their thinking processes are literal, direct and somewhat paranoid. They move slowly when able to move. They tend to hold new positions even though these would seem to be uncomfortable. This is catalepsy and indicates the hypnoid character of their condition.

Facial expression is "ironed out." If the eyes are open, they seem not to focus on objects; if closed, they may move about slowly and apparently without convergence. If the eyes are open, the lids will flutter several times as they blink. Speech tends to be slow and without inflection. These are all signs of hypnosis. Remember that even though appearing unconscious or dead, they are acutely aware and attentive to the meaning of your touch and the meaning of your words.

Use of their spontaneous trance behavior can diminish dangers of hemorrhage and shock or even stop hemorrhage and reverse the physiological reactions of shock. There is no need for ordinary induction methods. Merely assume that the victim is going to behave as though in hypnosis and you are going to use his or her resources helpfully.

Keep suggestions simple and optimistic. Avoid negative statements and words like "if," "perhaps," and "maybe." These always imply unfavorable possibilities and may act as damaging suggestions. You can never harm a frightened person by offering a positive, hopeful target to aim for or by detailing hopeful steps along the way towards recovery of good health.

Frightened people are peculiarly sensitive to touch. Avoid touching an unconscious person if you are worried or pessimistic about his or her state as you approach. Take a few moments to size up the situation and catch your breath. Your voice will sound more confident when you are directing someone to do something you know about, such as "Stand back," "Go to that house and call 911." If you are sure of yourself from the start, put your hand on the victim's shoulder or head before speaking. This makes the connection between you as a person and your voice.

Seemingly unconscious people need to be informed of each thing you will do before you do it. Sudden, unheralded movements may throw the unconscious injured person into cardiac arrhythmia or may produce massive intravascular coagulation and the picture of shock—absent pulse and cold moist skin that looks like marble.

Before you start cardiopulmonary resuscitation (CPR) with an unconscious person who is not breathing, say something like, "You are really relaxed. Now take a deep breath. I am going to help you breathe. If you have trouble doing that, I will be pushing on your chest." It takes seconds only to do this and you might find it unnecessary to do CPR. Speak firmly into the victim's ear. You do not need to shout.

Pain is diminished when thoughts are shifted from the source of pain and the events of the moment. Draw attention to some other part of the body by your questioning or by direct suggestion—"Relax your left leg, frown, smile." Attention can next be shifted to some external object or to some prior experience associated with peacefulness and calm.

During a state of fear and pain, the victim is often wasting energy in unnecessary muscle action, increasing the need for oxygen and increasing the load on the heart. These handicaps are reversed when a victim is recalling memories of times when his or her body was relaxed and comfortable. Do not be concerned about whether you think the victim is conscious or unconscious. The mind of the victim is less able to react to painful stimuli if it is concerned with purposefully relaxing facial muscles and the muscles of the shoulder girdle. These are the muscles we tighten when frightened or in pain.

An Example of Communicating with a Moribund, Hostile Person

Grace, a 30 year-old obstetrical patient who had a 2-year-old child came to my office in the last part of her pregnancy. She wanted me to deliver her second child with hypnosis. She had been insistent that I be her doctor and, unlike most of my patients, had paid me in advance. I was planning to teach her to use hypnosis but planned to do this during the last weeks because she was apparently healthy and free of complaints.

As things turned out, she misinterpreted some communication of mine because she failed to keep the last two of her weekly visits. She called me at 6 o'clock on Friday morning to say she had a cold and wanted some medication for her cough. She sounded friendly at that time. I did not detect any respiratory difficulty during our conversation. I called in a prescription for the cough when the pharmacy opened.

At 10 o'clock I received a call from a family doctor stating that he had just delivered Grace at another hospital. It had been an emergency call. She had delivered precipitately on a carriage in the hallway of the emergency room. She had gone into shock immediately after delivering a flaccid, unresponsive, term-size male baby. The intern had said in the woman's presence that the baby "might not make it." In addition the baby was found to have an imperforate anus and would be operated upon "if it survived." Dr. "F" said that the mother apparently had pneumonia and was being treated by an internist at the hospital in the critical care unit.

This was a surprise. Grace had not called again after the first telephone call. I was not on the staff of this hospital because it was in a part of San Francisco that was out of my usual range of action. The doctor seemed to explain the situation when he said that the delivery had been very fast. Still, it did not seem reasonable that she or her husband had not called. In addition, there was a hospital much closer to her home and she could have been there within minutes. Ethically my hands were tied. I waited to hear more.

Twenty-four hours after delivery, her husband called to ask if I would come to the hospital to see his wife. He wondered if I might be able to help, because the attending obstetrician and internist had both told him that Grace would not survive. They had done a tracheotomy in the emergency room. A portable x-ray had shown massive pneumonia. This clearly fitted the picture of an amniotic fluid embolism: a precipitate delivery followed by shock and respiratory failure. Her status was critical and her prognosis poor.

The husband obtained permission from her internist for me to see Grace in consultation. I called the internist when I arrived at the hospital. He corroborated the husband's statement. He added that he hoped hypnosis might help her but he did not think she was going to survive.

I met the husband in the hallway. He said Grace was comatose but the baby boy was now doing well after his surgery to open the imperforate anus. He said that Grace had been hostile toward him ever since she learned of her unplanned and unwanted pregnancy. (This pregnancy was long before abortion was legalized in California.) Grace had insisted on his being sterilized before the baby would be born. He did this for her. What had been worrying him the most was that just before she lapsed into coma, Grace had said, "I don't want to live."

The husband and I walked to the door of her room. I went in alone and introduced myself to the nurse, who was adjusting the tracheostomy tube and checking the flow of oxygen from a tank. Grace was unconscious and motionless except for her gasping, irregular respiration at the rate of 50 per minute. Her pulse was thready at 116 per minute. I was reassured slightly by seeing that she was still putting out clear urine in spite of her low systolic blood pressure ranging from 60 to 80 millimeters of mercury. Her diastolic pressure was unobtainable.

I leaned over the metal restraints on the bed and said, "Hello, Grace. I'm Doctor Cheek. I'm sorry to have missed your delivery, but you chose the wrong hospital. Your baby is doing very well now. You wouldn't want him to grow up feeling he had made you very sick, would you?"

There was no change in expression; no responsive movement of her eyes or head to indicate that she had heard me. I continued, "You are relaxing very well right now. Take advantage of this rest and go a little deeper to sleep for the next two hours. This is the kind of rest that can be valuable to you after you are home with your baby. I'll show you how to put yourself into hypnosis and come out after brief rest periods before you go home. Take a couple of deep breaths now, Grace."

She took two quick superficial breaths but showed no other signs of recognition or reaction. I continued with, "In two hours you'll feel like awakening, and during that time I would like to have you begin to feel really hungry because you have not had anything to eat for 24 hours. You need nourishment to speed up your recovery from this pneumonia that you had. That tube in your throat gives you the maximum amount of oxygen, and it will be removed in a few hours because you are already recovering from your pneumonia."

Three hours later, the same suggestions were given when I made another hospital visit. Her color was good this time. Her respiration more regular, but her blood pressure was still too low to measure. Her doctor had just been in to see her. I paged him to learn what he thought now. He said that he felt her chances were poor unless she could be motivated to live for the sake of her family. I went back into her room. The bottle under her bed still showed good output of urine. She was motionless and unresponsive. After making my presence known to her I gently moved her left ankle. She immediately put it back in place. I tried to get some ideomotor signal but nothing happened. I lifted her eyelid to look at her pupil. She shut it tightly against my effort. I felt these were encouraging signs, even though they were not friendly. Clearly, a part of her mind knew I was there and was not happy about it.

I returned at the same time the next day and walked into her room. She was sitting up, sipping water through a straw. The tracheostomy tube had been removed. She did not turn to look at me. Instead she put her index finger on the tracheostomy opening in her throat in order to speak. I heard the word "bed pan" which meant that I was to remove myself from the room.

About five minutes later the nurse came out to talk to me. She said, Grace says she does not want to see you. That was the end of my contact with her.

Grace's husband said that he and her sister felt that my intervention had been helpful. Neither could understand Grace's anger with me. I do not know if it was a generalization of hostility toward her husband that included me. Perhaps she truly was suicidal and blamed me for her recovery. At any rate, I learned subsequently that she had divorced her husband. Her baby was developing normally.

This was an interesting example of a deep drive toward survival that permitted a very sick woman to hold on to her life and to accept suggestions from a person she resented. Her husband refused the refund of her money.

During the nearly 50 years that I have had contact with surgical, obstetrical, and occasional accident emergencies it has been impressive how wonderfully people can react in a crisis as long as someone takes charge and treats them with respect for their ability to regain so-called homeostasis after being in shock, after hemorrhaging profusely.

Too often I have witnessed serious complications of relatively simple coagulation problems that could have been very easily handled with calmness and with positive suggestions. The hypnosis that has appeared spontaneously at that time seems to have been the secret. Conversely, however, the overly suggestible state of the injured or hemorrhaging patient takes seriously the verbal or implied worries of inexperienced doctors and nurses. The condition deteriorates and can even end fatally.

Pyramiding Fears in a Time of Crisis

We can see evidence of what I call "pyramiding fears" under a number of circumstances. Most frequent, I believe, are those that can occur in a hospital center where a patient begins to have a complaint that is not expected by the nurses and medical staff. With each sign of activity, with each diagnostic effort, the patient's alarm grows more intense. The negative implication of each process takes priority over the reason the action is taken. Coagulation mechanisms can be thrown out of balance. People have died, not from an initial problem but from the building of apprehension that occurs during the medical reactions to the problem.

Hemorrhaging Near Death

I obtained this history during a hypnotic age-regression more than 20 years after the fact but I feel sure that the details are accurate. Similar near-tragedies are occurring to this day in hospitals throughout the United States and Canada.

I saw this 62-year-old catholic woman in my office. She has had multiple complaints since nearly dying of hemorrhage 20 years ago following the birth of her fourth baby in 6 years. It was an unplanned pregnancy. She was worried about being unable to be a good mother for such a large family. Her doctor became concerned about her rising blood pressure and admitted her for induction of labor. His diagnosis was preeclampsia.

These are the complaints she has had since that hospital admission: chronic fatigue, right shoulder and arm discomfort, chronic tachycardia (her pulse rate after hypnosis and at rest was 100 per minute). She experiences intermittent bloating of her abdomen and a sense of churning of her intestines, accompanied by sharp pains that occur at night as well as during the day. All of these complaints started during the recovery period from her disastrous delivery.

A search of her sleep patterns at the first interview revealed that she has been chronically reliving the hours after starting to hemorrhage about an hour after an apparently normal delivery. As is often the case with conscientious people, she had long ago unconsciously accepted the idea that God must have been punishing her for her unmotherly resentment about this unwanted pregnancy.

Crescendo of Experiences

The patient was returned to her room in satisfactory condition. Her husband and the obstetrician went home in good spirits, thinking that the problem of her mild preeclampsia was finished now.

Bleeding started and became progressively worse while the nurses were trying to stimulate her uterus into contracting. The doctor was called back to the hospital. A transfusion was given, followed by another while the operating room was being prepared. A preliminary diagnosis of a uterine rupture or a laceration of the broad ligament was the reason for an abdominal exploration, but neither condition was found. The surgeon elected to do a subtotal hysterectomy in the hope this would control the hemorrhage, which was becoming progressively worse.

Bleeding continued. She went into shock. The priest was called to give her last rites as she was being prepared for a second abdominal operation. This time, the surgeon tied off the internal iliac artery on one side. Theoretically this procedure drops the pulse pressure in the uterine arteries to about 30 percent of the original force and allows coagulation to occur in the bleeding sites. Her condition continued to deteriorate after her abdomen was closed. The priest was called back. Her husband was told that she would probably not survive. After she had received a total of 18 units of blood, her bleeding gradually stopped. She eventually recovered enough to leave the hospital with her healthy fourth baby.

Comment

It will be possible to stop those recurring dreams and help release her unconscious guilt feelings, but physical and emotional recovery from 20 years of unconscious rehearsal of this nightmare is going to take much effort on her part.

During two hours of work she learned how to put herself into hypnosis and awaken after two minutes of relaxation. This exercise was to be done four times a day. She was able to experience the churning and pain attributed to her irritable bowel and was able to feel comfortable again. Pressure between the thumb and index finger on her left hand was her signal for recalling the symptoms and pressure with the other hand turned them off.

Because of her near death experience in the hospital I did a quick check for spirit attachment. Her ideomotor response was "no" to the question "Could there be a frightened spirit that is afraid to be recognized?"

Finger signals established that she is not using her illness to punish her husband for the pregnancy or her surgical team for her complications. An organic problem remains with residual liver damage from a hepatitis "B" viral infection. This was caused by one of the units of blood she received. Her doctor believes this is not the source of her complaints.

I find myself wondering, though, what might have happened if a doctor had inquired into her subconscious knowledge of the dreams and thought sequences that preceded the stress phenomena we label "preeclampsia." If her blood pressure and edema had disappeared, as it will do, she would have gone into labor on her own and might have escaped the entire disastrous scenario.

Patients who discover the reasons for repetitive, troubled, deep sleep sequences can terminate the progression from mild preeclampsia to eclampsia and fatal disseminated intravascular coagulation.

This woman's preeclampsia was the original emergency, which would have been easily treatable and would have been less threatening than the subsequent ones. It should have been addressed without admitting her to the hospital.

The so-called "toxemia of pregnancy" that is not preceded by kidney disease is psychosomatic in origin and can be successfully treated when patients are kept at home rather than being admitted to the potentially alarming environment of drug sedation, repeated blood pressure measurements, blood and urine evaluations, and questions about symptoms the nurses and interns hope will not occur.

Emergencies Seen in an Office

Some emergencies that are first seen in an office will call for use of hypnosis in dramatic ways, as was twice witnessed by Ernest Werbel (1965), a surgeon in San Luis Obispo, California. These were both instances of incarcerated inguinal hernias that could not be reduced and were causing exquisite pain. Emergency surgery is indicated in such cases because a loop of small intestine is locked in the hernia sac and has its blood supply cut off.

His first case was a man referred to him by a colleague and seen for the first time in Dr. Werbel's office. The man's pain, the size of the protruding mass, and the impossibility of pushing the bowel back through the inguinal canal all called for immediate surgery. The hospital was called and the man told to get dressed. Werbel spent a few minutes hypnotizing the man to relax him, relieve his pain if possible, and prepare him for a comfortable postoperative recuperation before sending him to the hospital emergency room.

Dr. Werbel writes:

About one and one-half hours later, I saw this patient on the operating table, but the swelling of his incarcerated hernia had disappeared completely. I asked the scrub nurse if the hernia had disappeared during induction of anesthesia, and she advised me that when the patient was brought into the operating room, no incarcerated hernia was evident. I next called the male nurse, who had shaved this patient, and asked him about the incarcerated hernia. The male nurse said that there was no incarcerated hernia when the patient arrived at the hospital, and he confessed that he wondered why I was making an emergency surgical procedure out of a simple hernia case so late in the afternoon.

Werbel was naturally embarrassed about what had happened with his "emergency." He asked the patient about his miracle the next day. The man said that his pain had immediately disappeared while Werbel was hypnotizing him. Evidently the muscles that had been rigidly in spasm began to relax. This would have allowed trapped fluid and congested blood vessels to drain back into the abdomen.

A few weeks later a frantic husband brought his moaning wife into the office. She had an incarcerated inguinal hernia that Werbel could not reduce. This time he was prepared and aware of what hypnosis would do. While the patient was still undressed on his examining table, he hypnotized her and gave suggestions for turning off the local pain. The hernia reduced itself without any help from him. He was able to repair the hernia as an interval operation with a well-prepared patient instead of having to operate as an emergency.

Emergency Treatment of Burns

There are some principles of action that are generally useful in emergency situations. We may be dealing with burns, for example. Until an ambulance team arrives, we can tell the victim to close his eyes and listen carefully to what you say. This is a time when you need to be authoritative. Tell the victim that help will be arriving, but for the moment you want him to focus attention on relaxing the muscles of his face, neck, and shoulders and to let the relaxation be progressive with each breath as he lets it out. Ask him after a few seconds to shift his memory to some time when he was swimming in cool water. Explain that the sensation of coolness prevents inflammation from damaging the burned areas and starts the healing process, that it can begin right now.

Next, tell him that one of his fingers will lift when he gets that memory of coolness clearly in his mind at a subconscious level. Tell him that within two minutes of feeling the finger lift, he will begin feeling consciously cool. His "no" finger is to lift when his inner mind "knows" it can keep the coolness for the next four hours. Continue the suggestions of relaxation and coolness.

As reported in an earlier chapter, Dabney Ewin (1986), a surgeon and clinical professor of psychiatry at Tulane Medical School, has documented interesting examples of what hypnosis will do with second- and third-degree burns. He has shown that blocking subconscious pain immediately after a burn will prevent a second-degree burn from progressing to a full-thickness, or third-degree burn.

There is an initial lack of conscious pain because of the shock associated with the total experience, but there is always a flood of subconsciously perceived painful messages going to the primitive brainstem area that sets up the return flow of inflammatory responses. This circuit of incoming painful stimuli and outgoing inflammatory responses can be turned off with suggestions, a matter of greatest importance as was shown by Esdaile 150 years ago in India.

26

Enhancing Inner Resources in Serious Illness

There are several books that can be very helpful for patients who are seriously ill. These books by Chopra, Cousins, Dossey, LeShan, Pelletier, Rossi, Siegel and Simonton are identified in the references cited in this chapter. They should be read by everyone, but especially by people with serious illnesses because they give hope to sick and discouraged people who too often have been told, "I'm sorry, there is no more that we can offer you."

The authors of these books give assurance that seemingly hopeless illnesses can be turned around without the need to search out possible early life causal factors for the problem although emotional considerations are paramount. All of them present hope-giving evidence of amelioration or cure of serious illness. This evidence can open the mind of patients who might have been uninformed about psycho-neuro-immunological possibilities for help.

I believe, however, that there is a need to go further. The information in these books needs reinforcement from friends, colleagues, and physicians who also believe in the resources of people to overcome "impossible odds." People with serious illness need to meet with support groups composed of others who have been victims and are now well. There is a power imparted to the individual in such groups. This fact that was known more than 2,000 years ago in the sleep temples of Egypt and the Aesculapian temples of the Roman Empire during its occupation of Greece and what is now Turkey. It was known to Emile Coué at the turn of the nineteenth century when he was teaching groups of troubled people to use "autosuggestion." There is tremendous energy created by groups of motivated people in the presence of one or more gifted healers such as the late Katherine Kulhman (Spraggett 1967).

Physicians and psychologists need to be advised that sick people can put up a facade of appearing motivated toward recovery while at the same time being locked into a conviction that their condition is hopeless and that they should accept their lot. Some patients can look you in the eye, begging for help with their conscious words while at the same time subconsciously shutting out any form of therapeutic hope—chemical, physical, or psychological.

The roots of serious illness and the resistances "difficult" patients put in our way can often be found long before the origin of conscious memory. The negative information is just not available to conscious recall. Physicians working with patients can have their work made lighter by learning the ways in which early life trauma and misconception can form a basis for dis-ease. They now have tools to remove the obstructions that can be most frustrating for those of us providing health care.

Suggested Psychological Strategy for Exploration

Start with discussion of case examples where people have overcome odds with cancer, infection, or disabling injury. You could tell about the businessman in Seattle, diagnosed as having bilateral and inoperable lung cancer, who got well and showed no evidence of cancer at a five-year evaluation. He had seen friends who could not eat and who lost weight before they died. After being told his diagnosis and his expected few months before dying, he forced himself to eat frequently and almost continuously. Only the Creator would know how he did it, but the fact that he did it is evidence for the usually untapped resources of sick people who refuse to die.

Another example was the Irish woman with far advanced leukemia in the days before the advent of chemotherapy, who went home to die among her people in Ireland and returned to New York five years later to confound the hematologists who could find no trace of leukemia.

My parents hired a Chinese cook in Singapore in 1922, before there were chemicals available to treat tuberculosis. This cook came down with a chest cold that did not clear up. His cough grew worse during the next six months. X-rays were taken that showed extensive tuberculosis with cavities in both lungs.

The doctors told my father that "Cookie" could not live more than a few months. My father felt, instinctively, that this feeble man should go home to be with his own people in Canton. He bought a steamship ticket for the dying man. To his surprise, Cookie returned 13 years later to Singapore and repaid my father! This time he was plump, had rosy cheeks, and was already working after being examined by the doctors and diagnos-ed as an arrested case.

Tilden Everson and Warren Cole (1966) surveyed the world literature about spontaneous disappearance of cancer and added cases of their own. Unfortunately, the title of their book carefully substituted *Regression* in place of *Cure* in order to avoid being considered "unscientific." The authors re-mained objective throughout the book. They were careful to omit considera-tion of the inner world of the cancer patients. They gave no credit to the miraculous survivors.

Physicians are generally hesitant about using the word "cure" in their communications with patients. They do not want to promise a cure. There are legal risks in doing so. This attitude of personal fear of being wrong tends to generate pessimistic attitudes in their patients. It may guarantee the negative result the doctors fear.

There is little danger when you ask questions about the readiness for "cure." You have a right to search when a patient does not believe cure is possible. I use the word in order to discover whether or not a patient can accept the possibility of cure. There is so much indoctrination about "con-troling" or perhaps getting a "remission" of a serious illness that patients can passively accept their illness and fail to put up the necessary fight.

Informative Questions to Ask After Setting Up Ideomotor Signals

Ask first, "Does your inner mind know you can get well and stay well?" If the answer is "no," "Is there some past event that has convinced you that you could not be well?" The answer is usually "yes" and can be traced to a doctor or an authoritative, pessimistic friend or relative.

After a retrograde search, be sure to ask if something earlier set the stage for letting the reported negative event become important. If the key mo-ment is determined, I ask, "Before that happened, did your inner mind know that you could get well and stay well?" (You are lucky if the answer is "yes". That gives you an opening to say, "The discouraging information came from the outside and had no right to trouble you. Now that you know this, can we work together to really get you well?") If the answer is "no" or "I don't want to answer," we have to continue the search for sources of resistance (Chapter 27).

If there are no remaining negative emotional factors as revealed by finger signals, we can move on to the task of helping the patient build self-confidence in altering physiological behavior such as turning symptoms on and off, becoming hungry or thirsty, remembering what diarrhea feels like, turning off the sensation, observing that tissue reaction to scratches depends on whether or not the scratch is painful and eventually selecting a target date for reaching the goal of "cure."

(Those who are new to uses of ideomotor level questioning will, by this time, be thinking "How controling, coercive, and unscientifically leading!" It certainly is all of the above but the answers, I have found, cannot be forced if unconscious negative beliefs persist. Any successful method of positive coercion appears to be worth trying in life and death situations in medicine.)

Now comes a chronological search for negative expectations, as described in Chapter 14. I feel it is important to search the patient's feelings at the time his or her mother learns she is pregnant. Moving forward during the pregnancy, does the mother feel good about her pregnancy? Does the fetus feel it is all right to be there at the beginning of labor? Is the mother comfortable during the labor? Is she awake and able to greet her baby in the delivery room? Does she nurse the patient in a caring way? Is the father happy with the baby?

It is important to find out how an older sibling reacts toward the patient. Does the patient, as a child, feel troubled at the arrival of a younger sibling? The sense of not being as loved or cared for as the younger sibling can register unconsciously before your patient is old enough to remember the sense of being a second-class member of the family.

There are many possibilities for a newborn infant to feel unwanted and for this feeling to be continued into adult life. The sense of being unwanted can make a child too anxious to please everyone. Such children are frequently the targets for molestation because of their overt friendliness and inner needs for acceptance and love.

An instructive question to ask is "Have you any trouble accepting compliments from people?" An adult who has felt unwanted as an infant will usually have considerable difficulty in graciously accepting compliments.

If all responses seem optimum, it may be time to assess the readiness of a patient to move toward a goal of complete cure. Start this attempt at helping a patient make a commitment by saying that there is no such thing as linear time. Time of the past and time of the future are constantly around us. We can know, for example, when we will reach a desired goal. You can say, "Please let your subconscious, clairvoyant mind go forward to the moment you know you are well and will stay well for the sake of all the people who love you and relate to you. When you are there, your 'yes' finger will lift. As it lifts, you will see the date written up there on a chalkboard. Read it off when you see it."

If a date is seen it must be complete—month, day, year. Failure to see a date or one of the components of the date tells you there is resistance at work. Resistance needs to be discovered and removed.

Of course, there will be patients whose disease is so far advanced that their resources for healing will be gone and they will die. My feeling, however, is that asking for and failing to get a "cure date" projects your belief that cure is attainable. It can do no harm and it may have a powerful positive influence on them.

Therapy After Eliminating Resistances

Induce hypnosis in a way that feels right to you. When the patients appear to be deep enough to get an arm levitation, suggest that their subconscious mind knows which cells are diseased and which are healthy. Ask for a "yes" finger to lift unconsciously when their inner mind will allow the x-ray or radium to destroy only the abnormal cells. Their cleaned-up macrophages can then go eat the injured cancer cells.

Suggest that the surrounding, normal cells will avoid injury by feeling cool, "like the feeling in your mouth when you suck on a peppermint and then breathe in." No matter how you phrase your suggestions, the main issue is to impart your faith that your patients' subconscious mind will work out a way to get the job done.

Add the suggestion that every time your patients put themselves into hypnosis for a few minutes, they will be adding to the process of eliminating harmful cells and preserving the normal ones. Make it clear that self-hypnosis is to be used at least four times a day.

Helping to Implement Beneficial Effects of Irradiation and Chemotherapy

When irradiation or chemotherapy or both of these Western medical modalities are being used with cancer patients, we have a duty to help the patient preserve immune capabilities while targeting the limited area of presumed remaining cancer cells. Irradiation injures adjacent tissues around cancer growth.

Chemotherapy has damaging influences on appetite, food assimilation, liver and kidney function, blood-forming tissues of the body, and the epithelium of hair follicles. Loss of hair is not a big problem, but the other systems are working against the positive cancer-killing effects of chemotherapeutic agents.

Probably the greatest help you can give will be to assure the patient of remaining free of the nausea. All oncologists warn patients about this unpleasant side effect of treatment. The idea is embellished as a negative suggestion by the leaflets that are given to each patient before treatment is started.

You can help counteract this type of unpleasant expectation by teaching patients to remember some time when they felt *really nauseated*. In hypnosis, ask for a "yes" finger to lift when the feeling is starting subconsciously. Ask for a verbal acknowledgement that the sensation is now a conscious one. Point out that our gut is very suggestible. It can feel nauseated when we see someone vomiting in the street.

By the same token, we can remember hunger that will override the sensation of nausea. Tell the patients that our subconscious mind knows it can reverse anything that it is able to produce. This is the reason for starting the learning process with a review of the feelings of nausea.

When this has been accomplished, ask the patients to recall subconsciously some time when they experienced a feeling of great hunger, "as though you had not had anything to eat for a couple of days." The "yes" finger is to lift at that accomplishment again. Ask for the finger to lift again when the feeling of hunger has been doubled.

Patients facing chemotherapy with all its negative associations are really motivated to work on this project of nausea that is replaced by great hunger. Now move on to training them to use the same left index finger and thumb pressure for turning on nausea and the right side for replacing the nausea with hunger. Ask your patients to practice with these feelings after going home.

The next step is to suggest that circulation carrying the treatment chemicals wants to be greatest whereever there are cancer cells. The brain knows where they are. Circulation is increased when there is a feeling of warmth. The patient is to concentrate on experiencing the warmth in the subconsciously recognized target areas while the medicine is going into the vein. It is not necessary for the warmth to be experienced consciously because many of the tissues deep within the body have had no experience feeling that sensation. The brain will control the "blushing" of the cancer cells so that they get a maximum amount of poison during about two hours.

At the end of that time the warmth is to be replaced by an unconscious sense of coldness, as though the blood vessels leading away from cancer cells are clamped down to hold the chemical agent in so it can do the best amount of work.

I hope the scientifically trained reader will understand my use of this type of imagery based on hopeful trust in the resources of a patient to find a way to implement what cannot be as yet proven in the laboratory. There is, however, much evidence that nausea and loss of appetite need not be accompaniments of chemotherapy.

By focusing the idea of concentrating the chemical in the tissue you will be tacitly teaching patients that there will be diminished amount of the chemical affecting the scalp, the kidneys, and the liver.

27

Resistance: Recognition and Removal

Primary Resistance

Resistance to therapy can be primary in relation to hypnosis itself. Patients may have come to you thinking that hypnosis would be helpful in correcting a problem and be disturbed as you start talking about how you will use hypnosis. They may have accepted a referral to you from someone you have treated with hypnotic techniques and can not only fail to understand what you are talking about but may give unconscious signals of hostility toward you. This will always come as a shock to you unless you are aware of the state dependent nature of hypnosis. You may be subliminally reminding these patients of someone who treated them badly at a time when they were spontaneously in a trance.

People showing this sort of paradoxical behavior are usually unconsciously flashing back to another time in their life when they went into hypnosis spontaneously and were unhappy about the reason for the hypnosis occurring (Cheek 1960c). It can be a molestation during the night when a patient was an infant in a crib. It can be a frightening molestation during which the molester threatened the child with grave consequences if he or she told anyone. Often such molestation is followed by the command to "forget" the experience or "don't tell anyone about this."

The spontaneous "hypnoid" experience can occur during the struggle of losing consciousness for a childhood tonsillectomy. It can be at the moment of impact on falling out of a tree. There may never have been a conscious memory for the cause.

Be alert for signs of distress when you begin talking about the use of hypnosis. Be alert for signs if you are carrying out a formal induction of hypnosis. Watch for an increase in respiration and an increase in the rate of neck pulsations if they are visible. Particularly look for a frown or tightening of the muscles around your patient's eyes. Back off a little if you see signs of alarm.

Example: Doctor Who Rejected Hypnosis Because of Flashback

A physician in his sixties had to leave the conference room several times during the first day of a symposium in Salt Lake City. During an intermission, he came forward to tell us that he had been forced to leave each time we had given a demonstration of an induction method because he had felt short of breath and could not control the pounding of his heart and the strong feeling of apprehension. He added that his feeling had been responsible for his giving up the study of hypnosis 30 years earlier. He had read everything he could find about the subject and was convinced hypnosis could be of great service to him in his practice of medicine until he tried it on his first patient. The terrifying reaction in himself during this experience had led him to believe that hypnosis was not for him.

Finger signal replies to questions revealed that he had once experienced something like what he felt while watching demonstrations. Other questions brought out that it was a tonsillectomy performed in a doctor's office. His parents had not told him he would have the operation. His mother had said to get dressed because the family was going shopping in the city. When he found himself in a doctor's office, he felt betrayed. He fought the ether and went to sleep thinking they wanted to kill him.

This review permitted the doctor to reframe the original experience. His finger indicated he could go into hypnosis comfortably without having to relive that tonsillectomy. He enjoyed the experience and had no further flashback sensations.

Comment

Space has been given to this flashback mechanism for intrinsic resistance to hypnosis because it affects results with patients directly by making them afraid to go into hypnosis. It also may influence them indirectly by making them resist possible constructive hypnotherapy.

What to Do with the Unconsciously Alarmed Patient

Use your Chevreul pendulum with people who show these signs of alarm or are able to recognize a sense of tension or discomfort at the beginning of your introducing hypnosis to them. Ask for a pendulum response to the question "Has there ever been an earlier time in your life when you have felt the way you were feeling just now?" In my experience the answer has always either been an "I-don't-want-to-answer" or a "yes." Both responses mean "yes." Then find the origin with retrograde questioning in time brackets. A stressful event will be uncovered and reassessed.

At this point ask, "Now that you know what it was, would you be willing to use hypnosis in a nice friendly way and not be reminded of that frightening experience?" You will get a "yes" response to that question and can then proceed comfortably.

Losing Control

There can be resistance that shows up only after you attempt a formal induction of hypnosis. It rarely appears when you start off an interview with the setting up of ideomotor finger signals and are advancing toward the source of trouble without any effort to induce a hypnotic state. I prefer this indirect method of obtaining hypnotic level behavior without an induction. I am dealing only with ideomotor responses as a means of accessing information that cannot otherwise be reached.

Fear of losing control or thinking that being in hypnosis is tantamount to losing control is very common among highly self-critical professional people such as physicians, attorneys, accountants, actors, and editors.

Usually this fear will be relinquished after an explanation and a demonstration of how self-suggestions of weight on one arm will bring about a lowering of that arm. It seems to help when I point out that it is my job to show my patients the ways in which they can gain control over their healing potentials. I am a teacher as opposed to being a hypnotist.

Another way of getting patients over their fear of hypnosis is to get them into a light level and then order them to come out of it. I do this several times. This technique was invented by Oscar Vogt many years ago in Europe. With repetition of going in and coming out, patients are recognizing their part in control but are also recognizing an increasing comfort with the going in as contrasted with the effort to awaken at the direction of the hypnotist.

This "fractionation" method is comparable to what children do before jumping into a swimming pool. They put a hand in, a foot in, and then, perhaps, a leg in before they jump.

Secondary Sources of Resistance

Assumed Guilt

Resistance occurs with patients who have somehow believed they deserve to suffer. Their belief may stem from childhood imprinting of poor self-image caused by tyrannical parents. Children may have assumed that they were responsible for maternal pain in labor, for illness suffered by their mother at the time of delivery, or for difficulties during the first few years of their life. Guilt seems to be an inborn trait for children. I once believed that only Jewish and Catholic babies were born feeling guilty, but I have learned that the trait is much more general.

First-born Girls and Second Boy or Second Girl

Cultural belief that a first child should be a male has been responsible for shrunken self-esteem in female first-born Chinese, Japanese, Greek, German, Arabic, Persian, and Turkish women that I have had as patients. We should keep this factor in mind during history taking.

The second girl or second boy may have entered the world feeling she or he should have been a different sex. The onus diminishes when we as therapists point out that these imprints occur before their parents know them as individuals. Their parent or parents have simply been thinking about a gender for the next baby so there will be a variety of the sexes.

Often it is the father who creates maternal conflict over the expected sex for his child. The fetus picks this up telepathically. You can ask for an ideomotor answer to this question: "Does your father ever show that he loves you because you are a girl, because you are his daughter?" The answer is usually "yes." Then ask, "Could he have shown you this appreciation more than once? More than a few times?" Negative imprints can sometimes be removed when they are matched against numerous positive messages.

Resistance from Progress Too Soon Achieved

When we move too quickly with a good hypnotic subject, we may evoke an alarm reaction that usually shows itself at the second or third office visit. This patient will have filled you with optimism about the future. He or she is an excellent hypnotic subject, is unconsciously willing to let you help, is confident of being able to get well, and is successful in producing various phenomena in the process of learning about his or her body.

At the second visit you notice a strange difference in behavior. Your patient did not listen to the tape you made and has not practiced with self-hypnosis. It may be hard to get ideomotor responses this time, but if they are available, it is important to ask several questions:

1. "Is there some unconscious fear that something worse will occur if you are free from your problem?"
2. "Has any important person been troubled by your using hypnosis?" (Recovery from an illness may threaten the relationship between a husband and wife. There are various aspects of this problem that will become clear as you pursue this area.)
3. "Has any doctor told you that you would have to live with this problem?" (The unconscious literal understanding of this is that "I will not be alive if I have no problem.")
4. "This may sound weird, but I would like to ask your inner mind if the difficulty appearing today could come from the influence of some past life experience of yours?"
5. If the ideomotor answer is "no" to question 4, I will ask, "Does your inner mind feel that there could be some energy or some entity that wants to keep you feeling as you have felt?" (This question may bring out the influence of spirit involvement and may require careful investigation and a special treatment process, as will be discussed. (See Fiore 1987.)

Case Example: Resistance Caused by Past Life Memory

A 37-year-old woman had struggled with a weight problem since her teen years. She was attractive and had no trouble making friends. She had not been molested or rendered insecure in childhood. She seemed to have none of the contributing factors that make people have trouble with an overweight problem. All my efforts to change her attitude toward food—to absorb less, to relax in hypnosis for brief period before and after eating—had failed to solve her problem.

After seven consultations I finally asked if there might be some karmic carryover of a reason for her weight problem and our difficulty to work successfully. Her "yes" finger lifted. She described herself as shabbily dressed, a middle-aged woman, alone in a war-torn part of the world. Her family had been killed. She eventually died after several weeks of starvation. There was no place to turn, no one to care for her. Her estimated time for this life was about 1500.

Her "yes" finger lifted when I asked, "Since time is a continuum and past lives are still around us, would you be willing to cut the connections to that life and allow your body to lose weight gradually until you reach the weight that feels the best and looks the best for you?"

A change in attitude toward food took place. A month later she reported that she no longer thought a lot about food. She said that she had stopped dreaming about food as had been her previous obsession. When I saw her again two years later, she was approaching the goal she had set, but she was still spending too much valuable effort on watching her diet and attending meetings of groups concerned with weight control.

In her case, however, she believed that letting go of that starvation imagery in a past life was a valuable step. Overweight and tobacco addiction are two of the hardest problems for people to fight.

Case Example of Resistance Caused by a Hungry Spirit

A bright, outgoing young woman came to me for help with her weight problem. She was about 15 pounds overweight. She was a good hypnotic subject and had followed all my efforts to help her diminish her unconscious yearning for food. She had succeeded in feeling less craving for nibbling between meals. She was highly motivated to lose weight, but there was no loss of weight. Dieting had never been successful.

All the usual childhood possibilities had been explored and found to be unimportant factors. Several times she had mentioned the feeling that there was an unconscious force that insisted on her maintaining her overweight status. During five wasted consultations she struggled along with my efforts. I had failed to pick up on this revelation about an unconscious force, but finally I thought it would be worthwhile to explore the possibility.

I asked first if there might be some past life experience that could be responsible for this impasse. Her finger indicated "no." Her "inner mind" agreed with this. When I asked, "Could it be possible that there is some entity or some spirit with you that really likes to eat," her "yes" finger lifted immediately.

I had not discussed spirits with her before this. I explained that I had heard about spirits in Brazil where the Spiritist Centers believe that many chronic illnesses stem from the patient's energy being drained by spirits of people who die suddenly. They believe that these spirits do not know they can move on toward another incarnation so they will attach themselves to a person whose aura of protection is damaged by sickness, anesthesia, or injury. They believe that people who die slowly in an illness move on into a bright light, but those who die suddenly seem not to "know" they can do this.

My patient (I will call her "R") seemed to understand what I was saying, was not shocked, and showed genuine interest in the subject. I felt comfortable continuing to look for this as a last possible reason for the resistance she was unconsciously displaying. I addressed R with my questions.

Q: Spirit, will you let us know who you are? (There was a long pause. Then R's "yes" finger lifted. Nothing was said. Please tell me your first name. You can speak through R's voice.

A: (After a pause of 30 seconds a rather boisterous voice with a distinctly Italian accent came forth.) I am Maria!

Q: Maria, what happened? How did you die?

A: I was too fat. I *love* to eat. I could not see my feet going down those stairs. I fell—broke my neck.

Q: When is this, Maria?

A: Eighteen-twelve.

Q: Where are you when you die?

A: A little town near Florence.

Q: That was a long time ago, Maria. Did you go to anyone else before you came here to R ?

A: Yes. Several. . . . They all died.

Q: So, you see, when R dies you will have to move on to someone else. It has been a long time now. You have been stuck on this Earth plane. You have a right to move on to the other side. You could have a new life. You have a right to be slender and pretty. Maria, please move on into that bright, white light. Do you see it out there? Go with our blessing. Will you do that, Maria.?

A: Oh, yes, I will go. I don't get enough food here. She is always just eating little bits.

Q: Thank you, Maria. When you have gone, R's yes finger will lift to let us know. (The "yes" finger lifted about 15 seconds later.

At this point, R, who had been sitting back in a deep trance, came out of hypnosis laughing. She said, "That is wild, but I felt she left from about here in my body." (She pointed to her epigastric area.) "I could see her going up and to the right. She seemed happy."

The patient called me two weeks later to say that she felt a lot lighter. She was sure she had lost weight, but the scale said she was just the same. A month later she had lost five pounds and felt much more relaxed about the former problem. She "knew" she could go on gradually losing weight.

This type of revelation is always surprising as well as interesting. I cannot say it is valid and not a symbolic fabrication. I would give more credence to the reports if I could find just one that I could verify for time and place of death as reported by the "spirit."

In May of 1990 a woman who had been operated upon in a local hospital a year earlier gave a "yes" finger answer to my question about the possibility of a spirit joining her in the hospital. Here it was just a matter of curiosity during a casual conversation. We had been talking in a study group about the possibility of spirit attachment.

This participant went into a deep trance almost instantly. She spoke for a 22-year-old man who described his death. He had been on his motorcycle at night near the center of town. It had been raining and the street was slippery. He gave us the date of his death. His front wheel hit a rock on the street. His motorcycle went out of control and he broke his neck. At first he was sure he was not dead because he saw the ambulance pick his body up and transport him to the emergency room of the hospital. He could not get back into his body, so he joined this woman who was recovering from her anesthetic. He had not known where he could go.

An explanation of his right to move on and not to be trapped in a woman's body was given, and he was willing to move into the bright light on his way to a new life with a healthy body.

I was excited about this report. Here might be a chance to see how valid these spirits can be. It was a recent event. I could go to the library and look at the newspaper for that day and the next day. Surely I would now have my evidence. There was no report of a motorcycle accident on that night. A young man with a different name had been injured two days earlier when he left the freeway at an excessive speed and lost control on the curved offramp. He had been admitted to the same hospital with a possible broken neck. He did not die, however, and I am still searching for a confirmation of what I have to consider metaphor until further evidence appears.

Comment

Ideomotor questioning methods offer a valuable means of discovering sources of resistance that have been outlined here. They can be discovered very early in the course of psychotherapy, even at the first visit if the investigator is careful to ask such questions as "Does your inner mind feel willing to let me help you get well?" or "Does your inner mind know you can get well and stay well?"

When things seem to be moving well and both you and your patient are optimistic, there still may be a problem that will make itself known when you ask for a commitment on a date when the patient will be totally "cured" and "unafraid of the problem returning."

The experienced hypnotherapist will look for these sources of resistance and improve therapeutic results by exposing resistance factors to the conscious reasoning faculties of the patient. Do not ever pull down the curtain on hope. If you are frustrated and disappointed, please take the blame and offer a glimmer of hope with a referral to a colleague who can start with a fresh outlook on the problem.

A frequently asked question relates to hypnotized subjects speaking in ordinary language for a spirit of another nationality who might not know English. The answer, I believe, is the same here as it would be to explain how adults can use adult language in describing their subjective impressions at birth. If they had taped a lecture in Chinese and later studied Chinese, they could translate the original lecture. Age-regressed adults are still in contact with their adult knowledge and their adult world.

I could only guess about Maria's talking through Rs language. This is perhaps a telepathic sort of communication, similar to that of children communicating with children whose language is different. They seem to understand each other very well.

There have been reports of age-regressed people talking in a different language when reporting speech in another lifetime. I have not had this experience so far.

28

Forensic Uses of Ideomotor Techniques

Hypnosis can be helpful in law enforcement and insurance work to help victims recall details of an assault or an accident. It is also helpful for witnesses whose conscious memory has faded because of the emotion involved in the experience. Hypnosis, however, is not an infallible source of information, for reasons I wish to stress.

Before doing so, I want to explain that what I call a "talking level" of memory resides somewhere in the cerebral hemispheres, the most recently acquired part of the nervous system. Physiological memory that is accessed with the help of unconscious gestures, or ideomotor responses, resides within the more primitive mid- and hindbrain centers.

The directions of stage hypnosis affect the recent, talking level of awareness. It is highly responsive to authoritative commands and is the part that is dangerously unreliable when we are interested in verifiable facts. I believe it is very malleable because this immediate and trusting responsiveness has survival value for young birds and mammals, as I have pointed out in Chapters 13 and 14. There must be no "Why, Mommie?" when a mother bird or mammal telepathically commands them at a time of danger.

We do not need verifiable facts when we are dealing simply with psychological and other health problems. Whatever the patient comes up with as a subjective statement is accepted at full face value and may be valuable in therapy. With victims and witnesses we are greatly concerned with the validity and accuracy of reporting. Similarly, I felt it was very important for me to know whether an anesthetized person really heard the surgeon say, "This looks malignant." Could the patient just be trying to please me with some fabrication gleaned from reading or viewing a television show about surgeons?

I learned that I could trust the information and that I could verify the reports, although they were not always absolutely accurate. Anesthetized patients can understand conversation in a different way from what they would know if they were conscious. "This damn thing doesn't work!" leveled at an imperfect instrument might be understood as an abusive personal statement by the patient on the table.

I could be sure of the source of a memory when there was a sequence in the process of its elevation from a physiological horizon of awareness toward the conscious one where it could be reported verbally. This was the sequence:

1. First there would be a change in respiration or heart rate.
2. This was followed in a few seconds by an ideomotor response indicating that something stressful was encountered during a the operation. This ideomotor response usually was accompanied by another ideomotor response, a frown or a grimace. If I interrupted by asking "What is happening," there would be silence or the subject would say, "Nothing!"
3. The verbal report might not be given until fingers moves indicating the beginning and ending of the operation had been repeated ten or more times. The number would reflect the degree of distress that the conversation in the operating room had caused, that is, how suppressed was the impact.

These criteria apply also to my investigations with witnesses to crime.

Another Method of Testing Validity

Since subjects in medium to deep levels of hypnosis are capable of very real positive and negative hallucinations, I wanted to know if we might do a test to see if there could be some level of awareness that would have a realistic and down-to-earth integrity, a level that could not be modified by suggestion.

A simple test can be made with good subjects who are capable of remaining in a medium trance while opening their eyes. We can ask for a designated finger to lift unconsciously when the subjects know they are able to open their eyes and stay at the same level of hypnosis. This may take four or five minutes.

Finger signals have been set up for "yes" and "no." With the usual authoritative tone used by a stage hypnotist, I say to the subject, "Oh! Can you see that cute little dog that has just come in over there in the corner?"

The subject will usually smile, nod, and say something about the dog and may even call out a greeting while at the same time his "no" finger is lifting to say there is no dog there.

In terms of animal survival, it is a logical deduction, that animals cannot afford to hallucinate a tiger that is not there. It would be bad for the animal's nerves. Even worse would be the negative hallucination of a blank space in the forest when there is, in fact, a fierce, hungry tiger in that space.

An additional means of checking for validity of reporting stemming from this test has been often repeated, with the same results. Sometimes while interviewing a witness or a victim, I ask, "Does the inner part of your mind agree with what you have just told us?"

When Do We Use Hypnosis with Victims of Assault or Witnesses?

First, when do we *avoid* using hypnosis? We do not use forensic hypnosis with alcoholics, drug addicts or suspected criminals. Their evidence cannot be trusted. Hypnosis should not be used with a suspected criminal who claims amnesia from a "blackout" at the scene of a crime. Hypnosis for this purpose is justifiable, however, on appeal after a conviction if there might be a possibility that the wrong person has been convicted. Criminals, alcoholics and drug addicts can avoid the truth in hypnosis just as well as they can under the influence of "truth serum" (sodium amytal or thiopental).

We use hypnosis with victims and witnesses who volunteer to use hypnosis to help retrieve forgotten information. They must feel comfortable when they are in hypnosis and have been freed from possible flashback experiences to traumatic early life moments like a frightening tonsillectomy. Recent traumatic events can be contaminated by residual traumatic early life experiences.

Fallibility of Eyewitness Testimony

It is well recognized by law enforcement authorities and defense lawyers that the testimony of eyewitnesses to crime is fallible and may be very damaging to innocent suspects. Munsterberg (1908) was one of the first to write about mistakes that can be made by full acceptance of eyewitness testimony. Elizabeth Loftus (1979) has reported her carefully researched findings on the ways in which the memory of eyewitnesses can be twisted by chance or intent. She discusses the Sacco-Vanzetti case in Boston on April 15, 1920, as one of the most alarming examples of conviction and then execution of two men based on very questionable testimony that became fixed and unshakable during cross-examination in court.

Spontaneous Hypnosis as a Factor with Eyewitnesses

It is quite probable that eyewitness observations are trustworthy and accurate to begin with, but because of the highly suggestible state the witness is in at the time of the stressful episode, this memory can become confused and twisted by "talking-level" communications from bystanders who did not see the event.

Milton Erickson observed many years ago that people enter a hypnotic-like state when they are recalling sequences of activity. Hypnosis can occur spontaneously during police interrogation at the scene, with conversation while trying to tell the family about sequences that night at home, and again during interrogation and cross-examination if a case comes to trial. After several repetitions, the scrambled details can become fixed in the mind of a witness and may be defended with a conviction that grows when contradicted in the courtroom.It takes thought and training to become expert in the art of obtaining untainted information from witnesses.

Victims of Assault and Witnesses to Crime Are Forgetful

Conscious amnesia can be caused by the mechanism of repression that blocks out recall of memory for experiences too painful to remember. The biological reason for this, as outlined in Chapter 13, seems to be caused by the adrenalin (epinephrine) released by the adrenal glands of people who feel threatened or experience shocking and unexpected events like a physical assault, an accident, earthquake, fire, or a tornado.

Repressed information of this sort possibly could be remembered if we recreated the scene and injected the witnesses with some adrenalin. This would be using the mechanism of state-dependent learning (Overton 1978). A more available and less rigorous method would be to relax victims or witnesses with hypnosis and help them review, in their mind, the sequences involved from the time they got up that morning until the end of the action. This is the preliminary method we use in combining hypnosis with the interview technique.

Elizabeth Loftus has found that memory is more accurate but with fewer details when people give an uninterrupted narrative about what they saw in a film or a staged crime. There will be more but less accurate details when the narrative is interrupted by questions. Interruption with a question requires a conscious process in remembering and putting thoughts into speech, whereas the spontaneously occurring light hypnotic state developing during a narrative allows access to clearer and more accurate information.

Experience with Forensic Hypnosis

My experience with forensic hypnosis started in 1976 and continued with the San Francisco Police Department until the *Shirley* decision of the California Supreme Court of 1982 ruled that witnesses who had been hypnotized could not testify in court. Occasionally after that I was asked to interview what were called "throwaway witnesses" when there were several witness to the same crime who could qualify to testify in court.

The Federal Bureau of Investigation is not affected by California law. I have been a consultant on cases in California, Guam, and Hawaii since 1980. I have worked in each case with Special Agent Robert K. Goldman, an expert in interrogation who is also highly trained and knowledgeable in uses of hypnosis.

FBI Protocol for Examining Witnesses

1. The witness must be a volunteer without being coerced.
2. He or she has good vision and is not colorblind.
3. The use of hypnosis for investigation is explained by the agent and questions are answered by both of us.
4. The reason that video- and audiotaping is being done is explained. It is needed if the case goes to trial and defense attorneys want to review the information.
5. The original protocol excludes everyone from the room except the special agent conducting the interview and the hypnosis specialist. We have included case agents, who are introduced on the videotape. They are helpful when detailed questioning is needed later during the interview. A police artist may also be present when a picture of a suspect may be helpful.
6. The witness is asked to give a narrative of as much as he can remember from some time before the target experience until the action has ended.
7. The consultant then hypnotizes the witness and deepens the trance state until he feels that a second, uninterrupted narrative can be obtained.
8. Questioning and specific periods of time are then rehearsed in order to obtain more data.
9. The usual interview time period runs from an hour to two hours. It is ended by the consultant suggesting that further information may come to the witness and that the department will welcome a telephone call at any time. Suggestions are then given that the witness will feel relaxed and comfortable on coming out of hypnosis.

Modification of Protocol in Using Ideomotor Signaling

It was my experience in retrieving verifiable information with surgical patients who had been unconscious under general anesthesia that details are lost in the process of translating information into speech but can be recalled if the patient repeatedly reviews the operation from start to finish at an unconscious level of awareness. This unconscious review method has proven valuable with witnesses.

I have reserved the verbalized narrative after induction of hypnosis until it is clear that the witness is comfortable being in that state and has had practice reviewing relatively unimportant periods of time such as the night before the interview, a birthday, or some vacation trip.

Interviews with witnesses are very different from exploration of a surgical experience with patients. Witnesses are coming into an unfamiliar environment. They come in usually without having had previous experience with hypnosis and with doubts about whether or not they can be hypnotized. They may have a considerable amount of muscular and emotional tension building in them as they come to the place of the investigation. All of the witnesses I have worked with have been concerned about the possibility that their memory may point to the wrong person or give misleading data. A few have been afraid that a criminal may have seen them and might endanger them or their relatives.

For these reasons, I do not induce hypnosis and go directly to asking for a verbalized narrative to compare with the narrative given before the hypnosis. I want the witnesses to be relaxed and entirely confident of their ability to recall unimportant things before returning to the day of the event that concerns us.

Forensic hypnosis is a special field that does not interest everyone but those who are interested or plan to get into this field are urged to read the handbook by Martin Reiser (1980), a pioneer in this field and a gifted teacher. The books by Hibard and Worring (1981), Loftus (1979), and Yarney (1979) are valuable also. There is also a discussion by Rossi (1988) on the subject.

29

Habit Problems

Some of the problems we commonly associate with "habit" may more correctly be given the label of "addiction." These would include smoking, some eating disorders (bolemia, anorexia), drug use (alcohol, amphetamines, sedatives, marijuana, narcotics), and gambling. With each of these there often is an underlying depression that becomes more tolerable because of the habit.

Some habits may be the result of identification with a meaningful other person. Smoking and some eating disorders fall into that category. Patients need to know they are a separate entity from the other person and that they have the right to be themselves.

The LeCron Seven Keys are very helpful when starting to work with a habit disorder. Here the patient has a chance to work with you as a colleague in sorting out factors that have been working without conscious recognition.

Some habits are clearly state-dependent. These include habitual abortion (three or more early losses of pregnancy without ability to carry a pregnancy to term), bedwetting, sleepwalking, smoking, excessive need for sexual release, premature ejaculation, impotence, inability to ejaculate during intercourse, vaginismus, dysorgasmia, and anorgasmia. The list could go on and on.

I believe that the logical approach to treating a person who comes to us because of what he or she considers to be a recurring habit problem is the same as for any of the other maladjustment pattern of behavior. An underlying depression may be revealed in the course of taking a careful history. This should, I believe, be addressed first and would include helping the patient during the hypnosis to understand his or her impressions during intrauterine life, at birth, and during the months of existence before the dawning of conscious memory (Chapter 14).

Some hypnotherapists feel that all habits can be treated directly, by discovery of triggering experiences, by rehearsing the feeling of accomplishment in avoiding the patterned response, and by capitalizing on the resulting improved self-image. Symptom removal has seemed to be the easy pathway to success with hypnotherapy, but time has shown this to be pretty much an illusion. Coupling a habit with suggestions of nausea, vomiting, or dizziness has worked temporarily with smoking and drinking. LeCron found that this idea could backfire, however. A doctor thought his great distaste for castor oil would help him quit smoking if he associated that taste with each cigarette. When he returned for another Hypnosis Symposium he reported sadly that he had really learned to like the taste of castor oil and was still smoking three packs a day. Such measures are inadequate. The underlying primal factors will find a new means of causing distress when the old habit has been removed in an artificial way.

Exploration and the reframing of negative early life attitudes can be quickly carried out during the first interview. The steps have been outlined throughout this book. Successful treatment of any habit, however, is time consuming and will need extensive follow-up efforts by the therapist. Two points are important, I believe. Any behavior that has started with a sense of pleasure and gratification after experiencing unhappiness in some form will be difficult to change. Thumb sucking, use of alcohol, amphetamines, tranquilizers, and narcotics come under this classification.

Conversely, those that cause physical or emotional distress will tend to respond more readily to appropriate treatment. These would include bedwetting followed by parental punishment and compulsive gambling where losses are greater than gains. A habit that has been painful, such as vaginismus and premature ejaculation, will also be relatively easy to treat successfully.

Sexual forces and those related to eating are powerful. They will overpower simple, logical thinking. The energy connected with them is comparable to the behavior stemming from recognized danger or physical injury. This is right-hemisphere oriented and basically relates to survival. In this category are smoking, alcohol use, drug use, and compulsive eating.

I believe it is important to help patients in either category to remove sources of guilt, feelings of rejection, and passive acceptance of distress before directly addressing the habit disorder.

Habits often are state-dependent. They may relate to a certain time of day, to mood swings, to occupational stress, to what people are doing. It is important to recognize and document in the patient's chart the factors that are consciously recognized by the patient as relating to the habit. They may not be the real triggers, as you will discover during hypnosis interview.

Anorexia nervosa and bulimia occurring in young women are serious problems that should be handled by a psychiatrist in conjunction with an expert in internal medicine. There can be very rapid changes that can necessitate immediate hospitalization and nutritional replacement. Failure to recognize a dangerous endpoint can be fatal. It is an illness rather than a simple habit. The true anoretic woman carries a self-image of being overweight in spite of being skin and bones. She may be unconsciously suicidal.

Cigarette Smoking Habit, a Flow Sheet of Steps

Prehypnosis Search.

1. Explore personal motivations for stopping. Are they honest?
2. What would be the values of stopping: for self, for loved ones?
3. Did the habit start with identification: relatives, friends, stage personalities?
4. Has television, radio, or advertising played a triggering role?
5. Does smoking equate in any way with self-punishment?
6. Family history: Is the marriage of parents happy? What is remembered about feelings in infancy and early years? Where does the patient come in the order of siblings? Do others in the family smoke?
7. Was the patient breast-fed during infancy?
8. Health history: illnesses, allergies, operations.

Hypnosis Work

1. Set up ideomotor responses with finger signals.
2. Teach patient a quick way of getting into hypnosis. Have the self-hypnosis rehearsed in your presence. Suggest that any time self-hypnosis is used there will be an associated immediate and prolonged feeling of good health and satisfaction.
3. Demonstrate difficulty in "trying" to do something as opposed to letting imagery overcome the challenge involved with trying. The idea of one arm being very heavy is reiterated until it moves downward. Follow with suggestion to *try* to lift the arm. Then show the ease of getting the arm to levitate with the imagery of big balloons pulling it up.
4. Get permission (ideomotor response) to explore the patient's birth impressions. Is mother able to speak? Does he or she feel welcome at birth?
5. Check for maternal attitude when she is told she is pregnant. Move chronologically to the moment the father is told about the pregnancy. Sense his reaction. Attempt to soften the effect of feeling rejected by asking if the mother had an unconscious desire to be pregnant when she conceived. Ask if there were times during intrauterine development when the patient recognized maternal and paternal acceptance.

6. Follow this with a second review of the birth "as it would have been" with good obstetrical preparation for labor (see Chapter 20). Ask patient to hallucinate feeling of being nursed at mother's breast (this is built-in, chromosomal knowledge).

7. Continue the chronological, forward shift to the first moment the habit behavior becomes apparent. Check the timing with the question "Could there have been an earlier experience that set the stage for the behavior?" With the first cigarette, there often is a feeling of nausea and burning of mouth and eyes. It is very helpful to have the patient vividly remember these negative feelings that were ignored because of desire to be like other kids. Constant advertising tactics of the tobacco industry have added to this toleration. Try to recapture the "honest" feelings, before the hypnosis effect of the tobacco industry advertising distorted the smoker's reality. Have this take effect whenever the smoker thinks about reaching for a cigarette.

8. "With knowledge, so far understood, can you now be able to let go of the habit?" (If the answer is "no," ask, "Does your inner mind recognize now that you can be free of this habit at some future time?")

9. If the answers have been favorable, ask for an orientation forward to the time this will have been accomplished.

10. If the first cigarette was a pleasant experience, this can be the time to introduce the idea that an unpleasant sensation will immediately occur any time the smoker even thinks about repeating the habit behavior. Let the patient name the best negative sensation to be used.

11. Get the patient to rehearse this negative feeling as he or she starts to repeat past behavior.

12. Follow this with suggestions of well-being and pride on avoiding the old behavior once triggered by a thought, by the time of day, etcetera.

Comment

In no way should the therapist project the idea that removal of a troublesome habit is going to be easy. Most habit-ridden patients are hoping for a quick fix with you at the controls and you being tolerant of slip-back phenomena along the way. Regular appointments should be set up over a period of weeks after establishing an initial rapport. There should be monthly, brief appointments for reinforcing new life patterns.

Most therapists have learned that it is useless to treat for drug dependency when the habit evolved because of chronic or recurring pain. The patient has to be motivated to stop use of the drug prior to treatment. On the other hand, the drug dependency may abruptly cease if hypnosis can be successfully used in controling or removing the pain state (Chapter 24).

Motivation is the ruling force. It has to be there and it needs constant reinforcement during therapy. We need to remember, however, that hopelessness, unconscious guilt feelings, and passive acceptance of bad luck and illness may create an outward semblance of poor motivation. Ideomotor questioning can be very helpful in sorting out causes of resistance or failure to continue treatment (see Chapter 27). Look for unconscious resistance if there has been initial responsiveness followed by return of the problem.

30

Notes on Hypnosis in Office Practice

Thirty-five years have passed since publication of *Clinical Hypnotherapy*. Hypnosis is widely used in many fields of professional work. I want to offer some suggestions for those of you who are ready to add hypnosis to what you have already been doing. Concerns often expressed in our workshops relate to the following matters:

- How will I introduce the idea of using hypnosis?
- Will hypnosis take too much time?
- Will medical insurance pay for hypnotherapy?
- Am I at risk for malpractice litigation if I use hypnosis?
- Should I charge separately for using hypnosis or include hypnosis as just part of my practice?

Introducing the Subject of Hypnosis

To attempt to answer these questions, I must report as accurately as possible what I did 46 years ago as I began my practice of gynecology and obstetrics. This was in a small community in northern California. Hypnosis was considered in the category of alchemy, as kind of weird. I limited myself to using only postural suggestion as a means of showing a patient that she could pay attention to the imagined heaviness of a large book hanging on one arm. It surprised the patient to find that the "book" arm did, in fact, feel heavy and did move downward while the other arm was relatively ignored. "Trying" to lift the heavy arm was difficult, but putting in a new thought, such as replacing the book with big balloons tied to the arm, resulted in the arm feeling light and moving unconsciously upward. The patient could understand how thoughts could influence muscles.

I used my normal voice with these suggestions. There was no mention of hypnosis. This test proved to be very helpful in showing patients that muscles can move or can be unconsciously tight and uncomfortable when we are under stress of some sort.

Since I was just starting in practice, I was afraid to do something that my colleagues might criticize. Now, circumstances are very different. Hypnosis is recognized by the American Medical Association as a valuable means of treating pain and for relieving stress. Physicians are given continuing education credits by the AMA when they attend the carefully monitored workshops offered by the American Society of Clinical Hypnosis and the International Society of Clinical and Experimental Hypnosis.

The addition of ideomotor questioning techniques was very helpful in allowing patients to recognize that forgotten experiences could have a lot to do with a present difficulty. I could explain to a patient that we are constantly reflecting our thoughts with muscle actions like nodding or shaking our head. A pendulum can react to very minute body movements that will be slightly different for a "no" answer after we have seen the response to a repeated thought, "yes," "yes," "yes." Our brain is like a computer. It knows the difference between a "yes" and a "no." The question "Is there some past event that might have been responsible for your first headache?" (Chapter 11) can interest and impress patients with their hidden knowledge.

Time Requirements of Hypnosis

Many professional people are afraid to get started. They fear that the patient will not go into hypnosis and this could be embarrassing. The matter of how much time hypnosis takes will only be a consideration before you have confidence in the ability of your patients to understand ideas and to use their imagination. Avoid projecting your doubts to them. Treat your patients as though you are absolutely sure they can do remarkable things. The only handicap they might have would be their skepticism and their being analytical about whether or not they are following directions.

LeCron and I felt that a beginner should set aside a special time for hypnosis treatments. Explain during the ordinary office visit what hypnosis can do, and then, if the patient seems interested, set up an appointment. Let the working time be 30 minutes to begin with and be limited to relaxation suggestions and the development of arm numbness. Teach the patient to use self-hypnosis (Chapter 8).

If you work with hypnosis, please remember that your hypnotized subject will be greatly irritated if your communications are interrupted by telephone calls or communications from your secretary. If an emergency arises, apologize in advance and again on returning to your patient.

Don't try to introduce the idea of hypnosis when you are pushed for time. Your explanation will not get across well. Don't try to use hypnosis if you are not well or are very tired.

Insurance Payments for Medical Hypnosis

Insurance companies should pay, but most of them do not when the bill stipulates "Hypnotherapy." Most of the time I have to make a diagnosis for which I can give a number. I then charge for an office visit. Perhaps there will be changes in the future and we will have more freedom to use hypnosis and be paid adequately for our time. There is no doubt that results with hypnosis are better, more rapid, and more lasting than anything we do without hypnosis. It is cost efficient.

Malpractice Dangers

The danger of malpractice litigation will always be there if we are rude, careless, or incompetent. Most professionals in the healing arts have found that the relationship during hypnotherapy is friendly and nonthreatening as long as we explain what we are doing, ask permission for each part of the process, and are careful about making sure the patient is normally alert and out of hypnosis before leaving our office. I have been sued for gynecological and obstetrical work a few times, as have most of my colleagues, but I have never been threatened in any way by a patient with whom I have used hypnosis.

I have discussed the matter of unfriendly flashback in Chapter 9. It is easily recognized, and you can remove it as a possible problem with a few simple questions.

Charges for Hypnosis

The answer to these questions will become apparent as you become expert in your work. Hypnosis, for example in preparation of obstetrical patients and surgical patients, is highly valuable and takes so little time that I have not charged extra for its use. It has saved me from complications that could take much more time and effort.

It is important to set aside time and charge for the time when there is a problem requiring an assessment of background sources of trauma. The needed length of time will vary but I have not been able to do this kind of work in less than an hour. I have charged what a psychiatrist would charge for that length of time.

Many doctors set aside time at the end of the day for hypnotherapy. At first they may assign part of their day off for this, either in the early morning or toward the end of the afternoon.

Figure what your time available will cost you in terms of rent, secretary's salary, and so forth. It is impossible at the present time to give helpful figures on what you should charge. Fortunately, you usually will have colleagues who can help you with this matter. Fees are no problem for psychiatrists and psychologists. The value of their work when using hypnosis will soon become apparent. It is different for doctors who would only use hypnosis sparingly at first.

When I was in an active practice in San Francisco, I might take a few minutes to offer a nonthreatening entree to hypnosis by saying, "There are a lot of factors that can have a bearing on the trouble you have been having. Some of them have started long before you can remember. We can use gestures to learn about these things, very much like having your head go up and down unconsciously when you agree with someone." Usually the patient will recognize that she has been nodding while I am talking. I add that very light hypnosis coupled with unconscious finger movements can allow me to ask questions and get nonverbal answers that can be very helpful in the treatment of what has been bothering her.

Comment

We cannot be sure about the future. I can strongly urge my colleagues who want to use hypnosis in their practice to spend an increasing amount of time taking workshops as a preparation for shifting from regular practice into work that can be useful and economically valuable when you are considering retirement.

It is a well-recognized fact that we grow old when we lose the joy of living. Continuing with hypnotherapy can offer a valuable nest egg as well as a continuing source of interest and enthusiasm for the "mature" doctor.

References

Arms, S. (1975). *Immaculate Deception*. Boston: Houghton Mifflin.

Armstrong, D., Jepson, J. B., Keele, C. A., and Stewart, J. W. (1957) Pain-producing substances in human inflammatory exudates and plasma. *Journal of Physiology, 135,* 350.

Aserinsky, E., and Kleitman, N.(1953). Regularly occurring periods of eye motility and concomitant phenomena during sleep. *Science, 118,* 273–274.

Aserinsky, E., and Kleitman, N. (1955). Two types of ocular motility occurring in sleep. *Journal of Applied Physiology, 8,* 1–10.

Barber, T. X. (1969). *Hypnosis a Scientific Approach.* New York: Van Nostrand Reinhold. (Republished New York: Psychological Dimensions, 1976.)

Baudouin, C. (1920). *Suggestion and Autosuggestion. A Psychological and Pedagogical Study Based upon the Investigations Made by the New Nancy School.* London: Allen and Unwin.

Becker, R. O., & Seldon, G. (1985). *The Body Electric.* New York: Morrow.

Becker, R. O. (1990). *Cross Currents.* Los Angeles: Jeremy P. Tarcher, Inc.

Beecher, H. K. (1950). Perception of pain and some factors that modify it. Problems of Consciousness. First Conference, New York, Josiah Macy Jr. Foundation, 89–120.

Berger, G., Goldstein, M. and Fuerst, M. (1989). *A Couples Guide to Fertility,* New York, Doubleday.

Bernheim, H. (1895). *Suggestive Therapeutics.* New York: Putnam.

Bonke, B., Fitch, W. and Millar, K., (Ed.) (1990). *Memory and Awareness in Anaesthesia.* Amsterdam, Swets & Zeitlinger.

Bower, T. G. R. (1974). *Development in Infancy.* San Francisco: Freeman.

Braid, J. (1843, 1899). *Neurypnology, or the Rationale of Nervous Sleep.* London: Redway.

Bramwell, J. M. (1930). *Hypnotism, its history, practice & theory.* London: Rider & Co.

Braun, B. G. (1983). Psychophysiologic phenomena in multiple personality and hynposis. *American Journal of Clinical Hypnosis, 26,* 124–137.

Braun, B. G. (1984). Uses of hypnosis with multiple personality. *Psychiatric Annals, 14,* 34–40

Brazelton, T. B. (1961). Psychophysiological reactions in the neonate. *Pediatrics, 58,* 508–512.

Breuer, J. (1957). In Breuer and Freud, (Eds.), *Studies on Hysteria.* New York: Basic Books.

Brooks, C. H. (1922). *The Practice of Autosuggestion by the Method of Emile Coue.* Albuquerque, NM: Sun.

Brunn, J. T. (1968). Retrograde amnesia in a murder suspect. *American Journal of Clinical Hypnosis, 10,* 209–213.

Burnet, M. (1968). *Changing Patterns, an atypical autobiography.* Melbourne-London: Heinemann.

Burr, H. S. (1972). *The Fields of Life.* (formerly titled *Blueprint for Immortality.*) New York: Ballantine Books.

Chamberlain, D. B. (1990a) *Babies Remember Birth.* New York: Ballantine Books.

Chamberlain, D. B. (1990b). The expanding boundaries of memory. *Pre- and Perinatal Psychology Journal, 4*(3), 171–190.

Chapman, L. F., Goodell, H., and Wolff, H. G. (1959a). Augmentation of the inflammatory reaction by activity of the central nervous system. *Archives of Neurology, 1,* 557–572.

Chapman, L. F., Goodell, H., and Wolff, H. G. (1959b). Changes in tissue vulnerability induced during hypnotic suggestion. *Journal of Psychosomatic Research, 4,* 99–105.

Cheek, D. B. (1957). Effectiveness of incentive in clinical hypnosis: 3 examples, obstetrical patients. *Obstetrics & Gynecology 9,* 720–724.

Cheek, D. B. (1958). Hypnosis, an additional tool in human reorientation to stress. *Northwest Medicine 57,* 177–182.

Cheek, D. B. (1959a). Unconscious perception of meaningful sounds during surgical anesthesia as revealed under hypnosis. *American Journal of Clinical Hypnosis, 1,* 101–113.

Cheek, D. B. (1959b). Use of rebellion against coercion as a mechanism for hypnotic trance deepening. *Journal of Clinical and Experimental Hypnosis, 7,* 223–227.

Cheek, D. B. (1960a). What does the surgically anesthetized patient hear? *Rocky Mountain Medical Journal, 57,* 49–53.

Cheek, D. B. (1960b). Use of preoperative hypnosis to protect patients from careless conversation (during anesthesia). *American Journal of Clinical Hypnosis, 3,* 101–102.

Cheek, D. B. (1960c). Removal of subconscious resistance to hypnosis using ideomotor questioning techniques (recognize the flash-back phenomenon). *American Journal of Clinical Hypnosis, 3,* 103–107.

Cheek, D. B. (1961a). Possible uses of hypnosis in dermatology. *Medical Times, 89,* 76–82.

Cheek, D. B. (1961b). LeCron technique of prenatal sex determination for uncovering subconscious fear in obstetrical patients. (Patients who do not think they know the sex of their baby are indicating unconscious fear). *International Journal of Clinical and Experimental Hypnosis 9,* 249–258.

Cheek, D.B. (1961c). Unconscious reactions and surgical risk. Editorial by invitation of the Editor, Robert Rutherford, M.D., *Western Journal of Surgery, Obstetrics & Gynecology, 69,* 325–328.

Cheek, D. B. (1962a). Hypnosis without fear. *Northwest Medicine, 61,* 174–176.

Cheek, D. B. (1962b). Importance of recognizing that surgical patients behave as though hypnotized. *American Journal of Clinical Hypnosis, 4,* 227-236.

Cheek, D. B. (1962c). Areas of research into psychosomatic aspects of surgical tragedies now open through use of hypnosis and ideomotor questioning. *Western Journal Surgery, Obstetrics & Gynecology, 70,* 137-142.

Cheek, D. B. (1962d). Ideomotor questioning for investigation of subconscious "pain" and target organ vulnerability. *American Journal of Clinical Hypnosis, 5,* 30-41.

Cheek, D. B. (1962e). Some applications of hypnosis and ideomotor questioning methods for analysis and therapy in medicine. *American Journal of Clinical Hypnosis 5,* 92-104.

Cheek, D. B. (1962f). The anesthetized patient can hear and remember. (Paper offered by invitation of the Editor, *American Journal of Proctology, 13,* 287-290.

Cheek, D. B. (1963). Physiological impact of fear in dreams: Postoperative hemorrhage. (Case report of hemorrhage 8 days after cold cone excision of precancerous cervical dysplasia). *American Journal of Clinical Hypnosis, 5,* 206-2089.

Cheek, D. B. (1964b). Surgical memory and reaction to careless conversation. *American Journal of Clinical Hypnosis, 6,* 237-240.

Cheek, D. B. (1965a). Can surgical patients react to what they hear under anesthesia? Paper presented at Western Nurse Anesthetists' Convention, San Francisco. *Journal American Association Nurse Anesthetists 33,* 30-38.

Cheek, D. B. (1965b). Emotional factors in persistent pain states. *American Journal of Clinical Hypnosis 8,* 100-110.

Cheek, D. B. (1965c). Some newer understandings of dreams in relation to threatened abortion and premature labor. *Pacific Medicine and Surgery, 73,* 379-384.

Cheek, D. B. (1966a). The meaning of continued hearing sense under general anesthesia. *American Journal of Clinical Hypnosis 8,* 275-280.

Cheek, D. B. (1966b). Therapy of persistent pain states, Part I: Neck and shoulder pain of five years' duration. *American Journal of Clinical Hypnosis, 8,* 281-286.

Cheek, D. B., and LeCron, L. M. (1968). *Clinical Hypnotherapy.* New York: Grune & Stratton.

Cheek, D. B. (1969a). Significance of dreams in initiating premature labor. *American Journal of Clinical Hypnosis, 12,* 5-15.

Cheek, D. B. (1969b). Communication with the critically ill. *American Journal of Clinical Hypnosis, 12,* 75-85.

Cheek, D. B. (1974). Sequential head and shoulder movements appearing with age regression in hypnosis to birth. *American Journal of Clinical Hypnosis, 16,* 261-266.

Cheek, D. B. (1975). Maladjustment patterns apparently related to imprinting at birth. *American Journal of Clinical Hypnosis 18,* 75-82.

Cheek, D. B. (1976a). Hypnothrapy for secondary frigidity after radical surgery for gynecological cancer: Two cases. *American Journal of Clinical Hypnosis, 19,* 13-19.

Cheek, D. B. (1976b). Short term hypnotherapy for frigidity using exploration of early life attitudes. *American Journal of Clinical Hypnosis, 19,* 20-27.

Cheek, D. B. (1978). Were you originally left-handed? Presented at the first European Congress on Hypnosis, Psychiatry and Psychosomatic Medicine, Malmo, Sweden. *"Hypnos," Swedish Journal of Clinical & Experimental Hypnosis.* September 17-25.

Cheek, D. B. (1979). Consideration of LeCron's ideomotor questioning methods. *"Hypnos," Swedish Journal of Clinical and Experimental Hypnosis,* August, 44-51

Cheek, D. B. (1980a). Ideomotor questioning revealing an apparently valid traumatic experience prior to birth: A clinical note. *Australian Journal of Clinical & Experimental Hypnosis, 8,* 65–70.

Cheek, D. B. (1980a). Two approaches to causal events in disease using ideomotor responses and light hypnosis. *"Hypnos," Swedish Journal of Clinical and Experimental Hypnosis,* August, 80–86.

Cheek, D. B. (1981). Awareness of meaningful sounds under general anesthesia: Considerations and a review of the literature. In Wain, H. J., *Theoretical and Clinical Aspects of Hypnosis.* Miami: Symposia Specialists Inc.

Cheek, D. B. (1982). Considerations relative to Doctor Bernard L. Diamond's opinions on the use of hypnosis as a forensic tool. *International Journal of Investigative and Forensic Hypnosis, 5*(2), 22–30.

Cheek, D. B. (1986). Prenatal and perinatal imprints: Apparent prenatal consciousness as revealed by hypnosis. *Pre- and Perinatal Psychology Journal, 1*(2), 97–110.

Cheek, D. B. (1989). An indirect method of discovering primary traumatic experiences (Use of hallucinated "Christmas tree" lights and auras): Two case examples. *American Journal of Clinical Hypnosis, 32*(1), 38–37.

Cheek, D. B. (1990). Feto-maternal telepathic communication and its significance. Paper presented at 5th European Congress of Hypnosis, Psychiatry and Psycho-Somatic Medicine, Konstanz, Germany. *"Hypnos," Swedish Journal of Clinical and Experimental Hypnosis, 17*(2), 71–82.

Cheek, D. B. (1992). Are telepathy, clairvoyance and "hearing" possible in utero? Suggestive evidence as revealed during hypnotic age-regression studies of prenatal memory. *Pre- and Perinatal Psychology Journal, 7*(2), 125–137.

Cheek, D. B., and Davis, J. E. (1946). Pathologic findings in genital bleeding two or more years after spontaneous cessation of menstruation. *American Journal of Obstetrics & Gynecology, 52,* 756–764.

Chopra, D. (1990). *Quantum Healing.* New York: Harmony Books.

Cousins, N. (1989). *Head First, the Biology of Hope.* New York: Dutton.

Crile, G. W., and Lower, W. E. (1914). *Anoci-Association.* Philadelphia and London: Saunders.

Crile, G. W. (1947). *An Autobiography* (G. Crile, Ed.) (Vol. 1 & 2). Philadelphia: Lippincott.

Darwin, C. (1965). *The Expression of the Emotions in Man and Animals.* Chicago: The University of Chicago Press.

Davis, L. W., and Husband, R. W. (1931). A study of hypnotic susceptibility in relation to personality traits. *Journal of Abnormal and Social Psychology, 26,* 175–182.

DeCasper, A., and Fifer, A. W. (1980). Of human bonding: Newborns prefer their mothers' voices. *Science, 208,* 1174–1176.

Delboeuf, M. (1877). Origin of the curative effects of hypnotism. Bulletin of the Royal Academy of Belgium. Reference in Burnheim, H. (1895) *Suggestive Therapeutics,* p.411. New York: Putnam.

Dement, W., and Kleitman, N. (1957). The relation of eye movements during sleep to dream activity: An objective method for the study of dreaming. *Journal of Experimental Psychology, 53,* 339–346.

Dement, W., and Wolpert, E. A. (1958). The relation of eye movements and body motility and external stimuli to dream content. *Journal of Experimental Psychology 55,* 543–553.

Diamond, B. M. (1980). Inherent problems in the admission of pretrial hypnosis on a pretrial witness. *California Law Review*, March, 68–314.

Dossey, L. (1982). *Space, Time & Medicine*. Boulder and London: Shambhala.

Dunbar, H. F. (1954). *Emotions and Bodily Changes*. New York: Columbia University Press. (Chapter 12, pp. 488–451, 965–971 contain reviews of pertinent papers on this subject.)

Duthie, E. S., and Chain, E. (1939). A polypeptide responsible for some of the phenomena of acute inflammations. *British Journal of Experimental Pathology, 20,* 417.

Erickson, M. H. (1937). Development of an apparent unconsciousness during a hypnotic reliving of a traumatic experience. *Archives of Neurology and Psychiatry, 38,* 1282–1286.

Erickson, M. H., and Erickson, E. M. (1941). Concerning the nature and character of posthypnotic behavior. Reprinted in Rossi, E. (Ed.) *The collected papers of Milton H. Erickson on hypnosis.* (pp. 381–411) New York, Irvington.

Erickson, M. H. (1960). Breast development possibly influenced by hypnosis: Two instances and the psychotherapeutic results. *2*(3), 157–159.

Erickson, M. H. (1961). Historical note on the hand levitation and other ideomotor techniques. *American Journal of Clinical Hypnosis, 3,* 196–199.

Erickson, M. H., and Erickson, E. M. (1958). Further considerations of time distortion: Subjective time condensation as distinct from time expansion. *American Journal of Clinical Hypnosis, 1*(2), 83–88.

Esdaile, J. (1851/1902). *Mesmerism in India. Chicago and London: Psychic Research Company. Reprinted as Hypnosis in Medicine and Surgery.* New York: Julian Press, 1957.

Estabrooks, G. H. (1948). *Hypnotism.* New York: Dutton.

Everson, T. C., and Cole, W. H. (1966). *Spontaneous Regression of Cancer.* Philadelphia and London: Saunders.

Ewin, D. M. (1986). The effect of hypnosis and mental set on major surgery and burns. *Psychiatric Annals, 16*(2), 115–118.

Ewin, D. M. (1990). Hypnotic technique for recall of sounds heard under general anesthesia. In Bonke et al. (Eds.), *Memory and Awareness in Anesthesia* (pp. 226–232).

Ferenczi, S. (1926). Further contributions to the theory and technique of psychoanalysis. London, Hogarth Press.

Fiore, E. (1987). *The Unquiet Dead.* (Discussion of spirit attachment and the ways of using hypnosis to release them with ideomotor techniques.) New York: Doubleday.

Fodor, N. (1949). *Search for the Beloved.* New York: Hermitage Press.

Forel, A. (1907). *Hypnotism, Suggestion, Psychotherapy.* New York: Rebman Company. (Reprinted 1927, 1949), New York: Allied Publications.

Foulkes, D. (1966). *The Psychology of Sleep.* New York: Scribner.

Fox, R. H., and Hilton, S. M. (1958). Bradykinin formation in human skin as a factor in heat vasodilatation. *Journal of Physiology, 142,* 219.

Freud, S. (1957). Five lectures on psychoanalysis. In J. Strachey (Ed. and Trans.), *The Standard Edition of the Complete Psychological Works of Sigmund Freud* (vol. 11). New York: Norton.

Gaskin, I. M. (1977). *Spiritual Midwifery.* Printed on the Farm, Summertown, TN: The Book Publishing Company.

Greenberg, I. A. (1977). *Group Hypnotherapy and Hypnodrama.* Chicago: Nelson-Hall.

Grof, S. (1985). *Beyond the Brain*. New York: State University of New York Press.

Haley, J. (Ed.), (1967). *Advanced Techniques of Hypnosis and Therapy. Selected Papers of Milton H. Erickson*. New York: Grune & Stratton.

Hardaway, R. M., and McKay, D. G. (1959). Disseminated intravascular coagularion: A cause of shock. *Annals of Surgery, 149*, 462–470. (This is a classic paper.)

Hensch, P. S. (1954). The discriminative use of the cortisones and corticotropins in general medicine with special reference to collagen diseases. Third International Congress Internal Medicine, Stockholm, September 15–18.

Hernandez-Peon, R., Scherrer, H., and Jouvet, M. (1956). Modification of electrical activity in the cochlear nucleus during "attention" in unanesthetized cats. *Science, 123*, 331–332.

Hess, E. H. (1958). Imprinting in animals. *Science, 130*, 133–141.

Heyer, G. (1929/1954). *References in Dunbar: Emotions and Bodily Changes*. (Heyer is one of the pioneer observers of psychological causes of heart disease and digestive and gynecological disorders.)

Hibard, W. S., and Worring, R. W. (1981). *Forensic Hypnosis*. Springfield, IL: Thomas.

Hilgard, E. R. (1965). *Hypnotic Susceptibility*. New York: Harcourt Brace Jovanovich.

Hilgard, E. R., and Hilgard J. R. (1975). *Hypnosis in the Relief of Pain*. Los Altos, CA: Kaufmann.

Hudson, T. J. (1923). *The Law of Psychic Phenomena* (Original printing 1893). Chicago: McClurg.

Hull, W. F. (1986). Psychological treatment of birth trauma with age regression and its relationship to chemical dependency. *Pre- and Perinatal Psychology Journal, 1*(2), 111–134.

Hunter, J. (1794, 1835). Treatise on the blood. In *Works (J. F. Palmer, Ed.)*. London: Longman.

Jacobs, D. T. (1991). *Patient Communication for First Responders*. Englewood Cliffs, NJ: Prentice-Hall, Brady Division.

Jacobson, B. (1987). Perinatal origin of adult self-destructive behavior. *Acta Psychiatr Scand, 76*, 364–371.

Jacobson, B. (1988). Obstetric pain medication and eventual adult amphetamine addiction in offspring. *Acta Obstet Gynec Scand, 67*, 677–682.

Jacobson, B. (1990). Opiate addiction in adult offspring through possible imprinting after obstetric treatment. *British Medical Journal, 301*, 1067–1070.

James, W. (1902). *The Varieties of Religious Experience (On Saintliness), in Lectures, Edinburgh, 1901–2)*. London: Longmans, Greene and Company.

James W. (1950). *Principles of Psychology. Authorized Edition, Two Volumes Bound as One*. Dover Publications, II, 522. (*Originally Published in 1890 by Henry Holt & Company*).

Jung, C. J. (1975). *Critique of Psychoanalysis. Response to letter from Dr. Loy, January 12, 1913. In The Collected Works of C. G. Jung*. (vol. 4 & 18). Princeton, NJ: Princeton University Press, Bollington Series.

Kehrer, E. (1929/1954). *References in Dunbar: Emotions and Bodily Changes*.

Klaus, M. H., and Kennell, J. H. (1976). *Maternal-Infant Bonding*. St. Louis, MO: Mosby.

Klaus, M. H., and Kennell, J. H. (1982). *Parent-Infant Bonding* (2nd ed.). St. Louis, MO: Mosby.

Klaus, M. H., and Klaus, P. H. (1986). *The Amazaing Newborn*. Reading, MA: Addison-Wesley.

Kleitman, N. (1960). *The Nature of Dreaming*. In G. E. W. Wolstenholme and M. O'Connor (Eds), *The Nature of Sleep* (p. 350). Boston: Little, Brown.

Kleitman, N. (1965). *Sleep and Wakefulness* (Rev. ed.). Chicago: University of Chicago Press.

Kluft, R. P. (1982). Varieties of hypnotic interventions in the treatment of multiple personality. *American Journal of Clinical Hypnosis, 24*(4), 230–239.

Kluft, R. P. (1984). The treatment of multiple personality: Results in 33 cases. *Psychiatric Clinics of North America, 7*, 9–29.

Kluft, R. P. (Ed.)(1985a).*Childhood Antecedents of Multiple Personality*. Washington, DC: American Psychiatric Press.

Kluft, R. P. (1985b). Hypnotherapy of childhood multiple personality disorder. *American Journal of Clinical Hypnosis, 27*(4), 201–210.

Kroger, W. S., and Freed, S. C. (1951). *Psychomatic Gynecology*. Philadelphia and London: Saunders.

Kroger, W. S. (Ed.) (1962). *Psychosomatic Obstetrics, Gynecology and Endocrinology*. Springfield, IL: Thomas.

Ladd, G. T. (1892). Mind, 1, 299. Reference in Wolstenholme (Ed) page: 350. (First to observe eye movements during sleep.)

Lagemann, J. K. (1957). What the groundhog really tells us. *Coronet Magazine*, February.

Lashley, K. S. (1929). *Brain Mechanisms and Intelligence*. Chicago: Chicago University Press.

LeCron, L. M., and Bordeaux, J. (1949). *Hypnotism Today*. New York: Grune and Stratton.

LeCron, L. M. (Ed.) (1952a). *Experimental Hypnosis: A Symposium of Articles on Research*. New York: Macmillan.

LeCron, L. M. (1952b). The loss during hypnotic age-regression of an established conditioned reflex. *Psychiatric Quarterly*, October.

LeCron, L. M. (1954). A hypnotic technique for uncovering unconscious material. *Journal of Clinical Experimental Hypnosis, 2*, 76–79.

LeCron, L. M. (1964). *Self Hypnotism, the Technique and its Use in Daily Living*. Englewood Cliffs, NJ: Prentice-Hall.

LeCron, L. M. (1967). *Better Health Through Self-Hypnosis*. New York: Delacorte.

LeShan, L. (1976). *You Can Fight for your Life*. New York: Evans.

Liebeault, A. A. (1892). Concerning Sleep and Related States (written in French). Vienna, Austria, Duetricke.

Livingstone, D. (1858). *Missionary Travels and Research in South Africa*. New York: Harper & Row.

Loftus, E. F. (1979). *Eyewitness Testimony*. Cambridge, MA and London: Harvard University Press.

Lorenz, K. (1935). Imprinting. *Journal of Ornithology, 83*, 137. (Lorenz coined the term "Praegung"—as stamping a coin, translated into "imprinting", a short-term learning that does not fade with time.)

Luce, G. G., and Segal, J. (1966). *Sleep*. New York: Coward-McCann.

Macfarlane, R. G. and Biggs, R. (1946). Observations on fibrinolysis, spontaneous activity associated with surgical operation trauma, Lancet, 862–864.

Macfarlane, R. G. (1961). The reaction of the blood to injury. In R. G. Macfarlane and A. H. T. Robb-Smith. *Functions of the Blood.* New York and London: The Academic Press.

Magoun, H. F. (1950). Caudal and cephalic influences of the brain stem reticular formation. *Physiological Review. 30,* 459–474.

Magoun, H. F. (1963). *The Waking Brain.* Springfield, IL: Thomas.

Markee, J. E. (1940). Menstruation in intraocular endometrial transplants in Rhesus monkey. *Contributions in Embryology, 177,* 219–224. (A unique study.)

McGaugh, J. L. (1984). In G. Lynch, J. L. McGaugh, and M. Weinberger. *Neurobiology of Learning and Memory.* New York and London: Guilford Press.

McGaugh, J. L., Liang, K. C., Bennett, C., and Sternberg, D. B. (1984). Adrenergic influences on memory storage. In G. Lynch, J. McGaugh, and M. Weinberger (Eds.), Neurobiology of Learning and Memory. New York: Guilford Press.

McKay, D. (1965). *Disseminated Intravascular Coagulation.* New York: Hoeber.

Meares, A. (1960). *A System of Medical Hypnosis.* Philadelphia: Saunders.

Mehl, L. (1980). Turning breech presentation with relaxation and guided imagery. In L. Feher, *The Psychology of Birth.* London: Souvenir Press.

Melichnin, A. (1962). The Pavlovian syndrome: A trance state developing in starvation victims. *American Journal of Clinical Hypnosis, 4,* 162–168.

Melichnin, A. (1967). *Hypnosis.* (tr. Galena Solevey). Bristol: Wright.

Moebius, P.J. (1957). In Breuer and Freud. *Studies on Hysteria.* New York: Basic Books.

Monroe, R. (1971). *Journeys out of the Body.* New York: Doubleday.

Montagu, A. (1962). *Prenatal Influences.* Springfield, IL: Thomas.

Montagu, A. (1971). *Touching.* New York: Columbia University Press.

Moreno, J. L., and Enneis, J. M. (1950). *Hypnodrama and Psychodrama.* New York: Beacon House.

Moody, R. (1975). *Life After Life.* Atlanta: Mockingbird Books.

Moss, A. A. (1952). *Hypnodontics.* Brooklyn, NY: Brooklyn Publishing Company.

Muhl, A. (1952). Automatic writing and hypnosis. In L. M. LeCron (Ed.), *Experimental Hypnosis.* New York: Macmillan.

Munsterberg, H. (1908). *On the Witness Stand.* New York: Doubleday.

Murray-Jobsis, J. (1988). Hypnosis as a function of adaptive regression and of transference: An integrated theoretical model. *American Journal of Clinical Hypnosis, 30*(4), 241–147.

Noble, E. (1980–1991). *Having Twins.* Boston: Houghton Mifflin.

Noble, E. (1992). *Inside Experiences.* New York: Simon & Schuster.

Orbach, I. (1988). *Children Who Don't Want to Live.* San Francisco: Jossey-Bass.

Orne, M. (1979). The use and misuse of hypnosis in court. *International Journal of Clinical & Experimental Hypnosis. 27,* 311–341.

Ostfield, A. M., Chapman, L. F., Goodell, H., and Wolff, H. G. (1957). Studies in headache: a summary of evidence concerning a noxious agent active locally during migraine headache. *Psychosomatic Medicine, 19,* 199.

Overton, D. (1978). Major theories of state-dependent learning. In Ho, Richards, and Chute (Eds.), *Drug Discrimination and State-dependent Learning* (pp. 283–318). New York: Academic Press.

Pauerstein, C. J. (1987). *Clinical Obstetrics.* New York: Wiley.

Pavlov, I. (1928). *Lectures on Conditioned Reflexes.* New York: Liveright.

Pearce, J. C. (1977). *Magical Child*. New York: Dutton. (Reprinted in paperback, Penguin Books, 1992.).

Pelletier, K. R. (1977). *Mind as Healer, Mind as Slayer*. New York: Dell.

Pert, C. (1981). Type 1 and Type 2 opiate receptor distribution in brain—what does it tell us? In J.Martin, S. Reichlin, and K. Bick (Eds.), *Neurosecretion and Brain Peptides. Advances in biochemical psychopharmacology* (vol. 28) (pp. 117-131). New York: Raven Press.

Pert, C. (1985). Neuropeptides, receptors, and emotions. *Cybernetics, 1*(4), 33-34.

Pert, C., Ruff, M., Weber, R., and Herkenham, M. (1985). Neuropeptides and their receptors: A psychosomatic network. *Journal of Immunology, 135*(2), 820-826.

Pribram, K. (1971). *Languages of the Brain*. New York: Brandon House.

Quackenbos, J. D.(1909). *Hypnotic Therapeutics*. New York: Harper & Row.

Raikov, V. L. (1980). Age regression to infancy by adult subjects in deep hypnosis. *American Journal of Clinical Hypnosis, 22*(3), 156-163.

Rank, O. (1929). *The Trauma of Birth*. New York: Harcourt Brace Jovanovich.

Ravitz, L. (1950). Electrometric correlates of the hypnotic state. *Science, 112*, 341-342.

Ravitz, L. J. (1959). Application of the electrodynamic field theory in biology psychiatry, medicine and hypnosis. General survey. *American Journal of Clinical Hypnosis, 1*, 135-150.

Rechtschaffen, A., Verdone, P., and Wheaton, J. (1963). Reports of mental activity during sleep. *Canadian Psychiatric Journal, 8*(6), 409-414.

Reiser, M. (1980). *Handbook of Investigative Hypnosis*. Los Angeles: LEHI.

Richport, M. M. (1992). The interface between multiple personality, spirit mediumship, and hypnosis. *American Journal of Clinical Hypnosis, 34*(3), 168-177. (A very interesting and thoughtful consideration of many view points. Dr. Richport is at the University of Miami.)

Ring, K. (1982). Life at Death, a Scientific Investigation of the Near-Death Experience. New York: Quill.

Ring, K., and Franklin, S. (1981-82). Do suicide survivors report near-death experiences? *12*, 191-208.

Ritchie, G. (1978). *Return from Tomorrow*. Waco, TX: Chosen Books.

Rossi, E. L. (1986). *The Psychobiology of Mind-Body Healing*. New York: Norton.

Rossi, E. L., and Cheek, D. B. (1988). *Mind Body Therapy*, New York: Norton.

Salter, A. (1944). *What Is Hypnosis, Studies in Conditioning Including Three Techniques of Autohypnosis*. New York: Farrar, Straus and Company.

Sarbin, T. R. (1950). Contribution to role taking theory. *Psychology Review. 5*, 255.

Scagnelli, J. (1980). Hypnotherapy with psychotic and borderline patients: The use of trance by patient and therapist. *American Journal of Clinical Hypnosis, 22*(3), 164-169.

Scagnelli-Jobsis, J. (1982). Hypnosis with psychotic patients; A review of the literature and prsentation of a thoretical framework. *American Journal of Clinical Hypnosis, 25*, 33-45.

Schiff, S. K., Bunney, W.E., and Freedman, D. X. (1961). A study of ocular movements in hypnotically induced dreams. *Journal of Nervous and Mental Disease, 133*, 59-68.

Schneck, J. M. (1959). *Hypnosis in Modern Medicine*. Springfield, IL: Charles Thomas.

Scott, D. (1974). *Modern Hospital Hypnosis*. Chicago: Year Book Medical Publishers.

Sheehan, H. L. (1939). Simmond's disease due to postpartum necrosis of the anterior pituitary. *Quarterly Journal of Medicine, 8,* 277–285.

Shor, R. E., and Orne, E. C. (1962). *Harvard Group Scale of Hypnotic Susceptibility.* Palo Alto: Consulting Psychologists Press.

Siegel, B. (1986). *Love, Medicine and Miracles.* New York: Harper & Row.

Simon, A., Herbert, C. C., and Straus, R. (1961). *The Physiology of Emotions.* Report of the Third Annual Symposium of the Kaiser Foundation Hospitals in Northern California, San Francisco. Springfield, IL: Thomas.

Simonton, C., and Creighton, J. L. (1978). *Getting Well Again.* Toronto, New York, London, Sydney; Bantam Books.

Sluckin, W. (1965). *Imprinting and Early Learning.* London: Methuen.

Solovey, G., and Milechnin, A. (1958). Some points regarding hypnosis in dentistry. *American Journal of Clinical Hypnosis, 1*(2), 59–78.

Sontag, L. (1961). Effect of maternal emotions on fetal development. In J. Steinberg. (Ed.), *Childbirth with Hypnosis.* New York: Doubleday.

Spiegel, H. (1960). Hypnosis and the therapeutic process. *Comparative Psychiatry, 1,* 174–185.

Spiegel, H. (1972). An eye-roll test for hypnotic susceptibility. American Journal of Clinical Hypnosis, 15, 25–28.

Spraggett, A. (1967). *The Unexplained.* New York: New American Library.

St. Clair, D. (1974). *Psychic Healers.* New York: Doubleday.

Stein, I. (1945). Bilateral polycystic ovaries. American Journal *Obstetrics and Gynecology, 50,* 385–398.

Stevenson, I. (1966). *Twenty Cases Suggestive of Reincarnation.* New York: American Society for Psychical Research.

Suomalainen, P. (1960). *Hibernation and Sleep.* Ciba Foundation Symposium on The Nature of Sleep. Boston: Little, Brown.

Taylor, H. C., Jr. (1949). Vascular congestion and hyperemia. *American Journal of Obstetrics & Gynecology, 57,* 637–668.

Van de Carr, F. R., and Lehrer, M. (1988). Prenatal University; Commitment to fetal-family bonding and the strengthening of the family unit as an educational institution. *Pre- and Peri-Natal Psychology, 3*(2), 87–102 .

Verny, T., and Kelly, J. (1981). *The Secret Life of the Unborn Child.* New York: Summit Books.

Volgyesi, F. A. (1966). *Hypnosis in Man and Animals* (2nd ed.). London: Tindall & Cassell.

Wallach, C. (1989). Fetal telepathy. Personal communication.

Watkins, J. G. 1987). *Hypnotherapeutic Techniques.* New York: Irvington.

Weinberger, N. M., Gold, P. E., Sternberg, D. B. (1984). Epinephrine enables Pavlovian fear conditioning under anesthesia. *Science, 223,* 605–607.

Weiss, B. L. (1988). *Many Lives Many Masters.* New York: Fireside Books, Simon & Schuster.

Weitzenhoffer, A., and Hilgard, E. R. (1959). *Stanford Hypnotic Susceptibility Forms A and B.* Palo Alto: Consulting Psychologists Press.

Weitzenhoffer, A., and Hilgard, E. R. (1962). *Stanford Hypnotic Susceptibility Form C.* Palo ALto: Consulting Psychologists Press.

Werbel, E. (1965). *One Surgeon's Experience with Hypnosis.* New York: Pageant Press.

Wetterstrand, O. (1897). *Hypnosis and Its Application in Practical Medicine.* New York: Putnam.

White, R. W. (1941). An analysis of motivation in hypnosis. *Journal of general Psychology, 24,* 145–157.

Whitton, J. L. (1986). *Life Between Life.* Garden City, NY: Doubleday.

Wolff, H. G. (1953). *Stress and Disease.* Publication No. 166, American Lecture Series. Springfield, IL: Thomas.

Wolff, H. G. (1968). *Stress and Disease* (2nd ed.), (revised and edited by S. Wolf and H. Goodell). Springfield, IL: Thomas.

Wolstenholme, D. E. W., and O'Connor, M. (Eds.) (1960). *The Nature of Sleep, A Ciba Foundation Symposium on Sleep.* Boston, Little, Brown.

Yapko, M. (1988). *When Living Hurts.* New York: Bruner/Mazel.

Yarney, A. D. (1979). *The Psychology of Eyewitness Testimony.* New York: Free Press.

Yudine, S. (1935). Use of cadaver blood after sudden death. *Lancet, 2,* 360–366.

Index